BROADCAST NEWS HANDBOOK

WRITING, REPORTING, AND PRODUCING

C.A. Tuggle

University of North Carolina at Chapel Hill

Forrest Carr

KGUN9-TV

Suzanne Huffman

Texas Christian University

Boston   Burr Ridge, IL   Dubuque, IA   Madison, WI
New York   San Francisco   St. Louis
Bangkok   Bogotá   Caracas   Lisbon   London   Madrid   Mexico City
Milan   New Delhi   Seoul   Singapore   Sydney   Taipei   Toronto

McGraw-Hill Higher Education

A Division of The McGraw-Hill Companies

BROADCAST NEWS HANDBOOK: WRITING, REPORTING, AND PRODUCING
Published by McGraw-Hill, an imprint of The McGraw-Hill Companies, Inc. 1221
Avenue of the Americas, New York, NY, 10020.

Some ancillaries, including electronic and print components, may not be available to customers outside the United States.

This book is printed on acid-free paper.

1 2 3 4 5 6 7 8 9 0 DOC/DOC 0 9 8 7 6 5 4 3 2 1 0

ISBN 0072396822

Editorial director: *Phillip A. Butcher*
Senior sponsoring editor: *Valerie Raymond*
Editorial assistant: *Amy Shaffer*
Marketing manager: *Kelly M. May*
Project manager: *Laura M. Healy*
Production supervisor: *Michael McCormick*
Coordinator freelance design: *Mary Christianson*
New media: *Kimberly Stark*
Freelance cover designer: *Tin Box Studio*
Cover photograph: © Jim Arbogast/*SuperStock*
Compositor: *Lachina Publishing Services*
Typeface: *10/12 Palatino*
Printer: *R. R. Donnelley & Sons Company*

Library of Congress Cataloging-in-Publication Data

Tuggle, C. A.
   Broadcast news handbook : writing, reporting, and producing / C.A. Tuggle, Forrest Carr, Suzanne Huffman.
     p. cm. -- (The McGraw-Hill series in mass communication)
   Includes index.
   ISBN 0-7239-6822- (pbk. : acid-free paper)
   1. Television broadcasting of news--Handbooks, manuals, etc. I. Carr, Forrest. II. Huffman, Suzanne. III. Title. IV. Series.

PN4784.T4 T76 2001
070.1'95--dc21   00-031027

www.mhhe.com

DEDICATIONS

From C.A. Tuggle
To my wife Tracey and children Brynne, Bethany and Jenny; and to the memory of my father, T.B. Tuggle, my inspiration to always do my best.

From Forrest Carr
To the memory of Bruce Breslow, a good friend and the finest photo-journalist I have ever known.

From Suzanne Huffman
To my husband August F. Schilling III and to my parents, Carrol Statton Huffman and Margaret Anne Byrd Huffman.

Dr. C.A. Tuggle began teaching at the university level in 1994 after a 16-year broadcasting career in local television news and media relations. He spent the majority of his career at WFLA-TV, the NBC affiliate in Tampa. He has held numerous newsroom positions, but spent the bulk of his career reporting and producing. He covered both news and sports, including six Super Bowls. Tuggle earned undergraduate and masters degrees from the University of Florida in Gainesville, and his Ph.D. at the University of Alabama in Tuscaloosa. He is currently teaching electronic communication at the University of North Carolina at Chapel Hill. His research has appeared in nearly a dozen scholarly journals and trade publications, and centers on television news practices and procedures. He regularly conducts writing workshops for local stations, professional and academic groups, and high school journalists. He has overseen student newscasts at three universities and helped to develop more than 50 interns during his professional career.

Forrest Carr celebrated his 20th year in the news business in January 2000. He joined KGUN9-TV, the ABC affiliate in Tucson, Arizona, as news director in September of 1997. During his tenure, KGUN9 has made waves locally and nationally with its innovations in viewer service and community-responsive journalism. KGUN9 solicited viewer input for a statement of principles, the only television station in the United States ever to have done that, and it appointed one of only three viewer ombudsmen in the country. Carr began his career as a radio reporter but quickly switched to television, serving at various times as a copy writer, reporter, newscast producer, managing editor, and assistant news director in the Memphis, San Antonio, and Tampa markets before going to Tucson as news director. Carr has contributed to numerous scholarly and trade publications, and has won or shared credit in four dozen professional awards, including a regional Emmy for investigative reporting. He is a graduate of the University of Memphis.

Dr. Suzanne Huffman is Associate Professor of Journalism and Broadcast Journalism Sequence Head at Texas Christian University in Fort Worth, Texas. She earned a B.A. from Texas Christian University. She earned an M.A. at the University of Iowa, and a Ph.D. at the University of Missouri–Columbia. Huffman has reported, anchored and produced news at commercial television stations in Cedar Rapids, Iowa; Santa Maria, California; and Tampa, Florida. She taught at three other universities before joining the TCU faculty, and her former students occupy newsroom positions throughout the South and Southwest. Her research centers on the practice of broadcast journalism. It includes television station and newsroom workplace issues, such as the current proliferation of live reporting, the use of mission statements, coverage of women's sports, the history of broadcast journalism in Texas, and broadcast news writing practices and style.

Her research has been presented at both regional and national symposia and has been published in numerous scholarly journals.

FOREWORD

Bob Dotson

Senior Correspondent
"NBC Nightly News" with Tom Brokaw

My grandmother always worried about my life's work. The first time she got a chance to see one of my stories on "NBC Nightly News," I called to see what she thought.

"Did you like my story on Tom's show tonight?" I asked.

There was a long pause on the other end of the line. Then she said, "Bobby, I think you should learn a trade."

"A trade?"

"Yes, they're not going to keep paying you for two minutes of work a day."

Well, they have. For 37 years I've been traveling the world on someone else's nickel. I've been in more motel rooms than the Gideon Bible.

And it's been a wonderful life.

The ticket to that life begins on the pages that follow. They contain the nuts and bolts of our business—the basics that hold us all together. This book will help you master our complex and challenging profession. It will also refresh your memory in the years ahead, so keep it handy.

I went to college back when the earth was cooling. Every technical thing I learned about is now in a museum. But the things you'll find on these pages are timeless. They're lessons that will last a lifetime.

So, read on. Have a good life. Call your grandmother.

PREFACE

A university professor once noted that a student told him she decided to study broadcast journalism rather than print journalism because she didn't like to write that much. It is, of course, a misconception that there isn't much writing in broadcast journalism. Anchors and reporters don't just stand (or sit) in front of a camera or microphone and pour forth interesting information. To understand the real world of broadcast journalism is to learn the step-by-step process involved. Good writing is the heart of that process.

Our Approach

With the Broadcast News Handbook, our goal is to teach aspiring broadcast journalists how to write, how to craft the language, and how to be effective storytellers using all the technology available to them without letting technology drive the process. Together, we have more than 50 years of broadcast journalism experience. In the final two decades of the 20th century, we saw many technological advancements that affected how news is covered: videotape, microwave and satellite technology, digital editing, and the list could go on. Technology has changed and will continue to change. But the need to be an effective storyteller hasn't changed, and won't. Regardless of what the tools are, those who can use those tools well to impart interesting information will always have a place in journalism. Foremost among those tools is the language itself. We don't buy into Marshall McLuhan's contention that "the medium is the message." We think the message is the message and the medium is simply a means to get that message to an audience. Technology and journalism are intimately connected in radio, television, and online applications, but content must always drive which stories are selected for coverage and how they're covered.

Who Will Benefit from the Book

We've tried to construct a text that will be useful to beginning broadcast journalism students as well as to those who have advanced in their college training and education and even those who have entered the workforce. We believe the practical "how-to" sections of this text and the real-world advice will serve students and early career professionals well. We hope the book becomes a resource for students as they progress through their studies and for working journalists as they begin their careers in the information business. We believe this book could also be a valuable resource for news workers and managers in traditional print newsrooms as they face convergence and the need to cross train.

Special Features of the Book

The book is written by three people with decades of broadcast news experience. Between us, we've held every newsroom position there is. We approach this book from the perspective of what worked for us, as reporters, producers, and managers, and what we know will work for others. We believe the practical tips and guidelines we've included will not only help you break into the highly competitive world of broadcast news, they'll help you advance while remaining true to the ideals that led you to pursue a journalism career.

Although the book is written using three different "voices," and although each author approaches the material from his or her unique perspective, we are frankly somewhat surprised at the cohesion that has emerged during the process of writing this book. There may be minor differences in our approaches, but there is unanimity about how the product of broadcast journalists should look and the steps necessary to get to that point.

- To help readers understand and remember those steps, we've included Do's and Don'ts boxes at the end of each chapter as a quick study guide and desk reference.

- Producing and writing are so closely tied together in broadcast news that a writing book would be incomplete without a thorough look at producing. The chapter about producing was written by the member of the team who is a working news director. As with other chapters in the book, the producing chapter is filled with practical tips—both how to become an effective producer and how to make yourself stand out in the producer ranks.

- Although the book contains a wealth of information about how we do certain things, we have also included a chapter titled "Why We Fight"—a close look at the ethical component of the broadcast news business. We believe strongly in the power of the media, but with power comes responsibility. We work in and teach about one of the most important aspects of a democracy—media that are free from government control. Protecting rights as we deal with the public's right to know is a vital part of journalism.

- The book ends with two very important appendices. Appendix A is a brief compilation of tips about how to prepare your résumé and résumé tape, from someone who has reviewed hundreds of each. Appendix B is a look at some problem words that good writers must master. The language is our foremost tool, and we need to know how to use that tool extremely well. Material used in the grammar and word precision quizzes that accompany this text comes from Appendix B.

In general, the book advances from the characteristics of broadcast writing to the story selection process and writing tips that apply to all broadcast story forms. Interviewing and writing for radio chapters introduce us to the vital role of sound bites and natural sound. The book then presents three distinct television story forms: VOs, VO/SOTs, and packages. A chapter about writing sports copy addresses some of the unique aspects of covering athletics.

Supplements

A videotape will be available for instructors. The tape will include semi-raw videotape clips—both B-roll and sound bites. We will also provide story notes that, along with the videotape, will give students the material they need to write VOs, VO/SOTs, and packages. We'll also provide finished scripts that were generated by professionals. That way, students can compare what they did to what working broadcast journalists did with the same material. Please contact your McGraw-Hill sales representative for further information.

Final Thoughts

Throughout, we acknowledge that radio and TV news is a business, but also stress that it is more than that. It is a calling, both work and passion, and a means to document and be a part of history as it's made. We hope that we have imparted some of our passion for the craft of broadcast writing through this text.

ACKNOWLEDGMENTS

The authors thank a number of people for their assistance in bringing this project into being. First we would like to thank the following institutions, employers, friends and former colleagues who supplied script samples:

At WFLA-TV in Tampa, Florida:
Vice President of News Dan Bradley for permission to use station scripts, and Executive Producer Kathryn Bonfield and Sports Producer Dave Cook for their assistance in selecting them.

KGUN9-TV in Tucson, Arizona

At KRLD News Radio in Dallas, Texas:
Mike Rogers, B. J. Austin and Jack Hines

At Minnesota Public Radio in St. Paul, Minnesota:
Managing Editor Kate Smith, Political Reporter Mike Mulcahy, "Mainstreet" reporter Leif Enger and "Mainstreet" reporter Mark Steil

Numerous industry professionals provided stories and insights that added breadth, scope, and a personal touch to the work:
Melissa Antoccia of KLAS-TV in Las Vegas, Nevada
Chandra Clark of WVTM-TV in Birmingham, Alabama
Kelli Durand of WLIO-TV in Lima, Ohio
Dan Hicken of WTLV-TV in Jacksonville, Florida
Greg Kelfgun of KABB-TV in San Antonio, Texas
Joe Kovacs of WAMI-TV in Miami, Florida
Robyn Kinsey-Mooring of WTVD-TV in Durham, North Carolina
Tom Loveless of WFAA-TV in Dallas, Texas
Terry Meyers of WCBS-TV in New York City
John Miller of A.H. Belo Corp. in Dallas, Texas
Glenn Mitchell of KERA Radio in Dallas, Texas
Matt Morin of WPTZ-TV in Plattsburgh, New York
Diane Pertmer of WFLA-TV in Tampa, Florida

Several colleagues at universities throughout the nation offered very helpful suggestions and insights that helped make the book useful and relevant in a new millennium:
Dale Cressman at Utah State University
Pam Doyle at the University of Alabama
Sonya Forte Duhe at the University of South Carolina
Bill Knowles at the University of Montana

Travis Linn at the University of Nevada-Reno
Jim Upshaw at the University of Oregon

Additionally, Forrest Carr would like to thank:

Bob Steele of the Poynter Institute for Media Studies, for invaluable guidance in the preparation of the ethics portion of this book.

Al Tompkins, Jill Geisler and Lillian Dunlap, also of the Poynter, for their assistance, leadership and inspiration on the subject of ethics.

Participant of the "Doing Ethics 99" Poynter workshop, for their advice and support.

The RTNDA's *Communicator* magazine, in which earlier versions of some of this material first appeared.

The many readers of *Communicator* and *Shoptalk* who have shown steadfast support and encouragement through the years.

Lee Enterprises, Inc., the corporate mission and vision of which have created an environment in which community- and viewer-oriented journalism can thrive; and KGUN9-TV general manager Ray Depa, for being the best boss a news director could hope for.

WFLA-TV Investigative Reporter Steve Andrews, for his example and inspiration on the subject of journalism, writing, editing and ethics and, above all, for showing that it is possible to be an aggressive reporter and still treat people with professionalism and respect.

And, finally, his wife Deborah, who has allowed him to disappear into his study for long periods. Whether she has found this to be a burden or a blessing, she's graciously kept to herself.

CONTENTS

CHARACTERISTICS OF BROADCAST NEWS WRITING

Writing is easy. After all, most of us learned to do it by the time we graduated from kindergarten. However, *good* writing is difficult. Sometimes it's very difficult. If it weren't, most of us would be novelists. So what is it that distinguishes writers from good writers? In very simple terms, it's the ability to craft the language, not just use it. In this book we'll help you learn how to craft the language for a broadcast audience—to tell stories in ways that will grab attention, impart information and leave television news viewers or radio news listeners with the impression of having been at the event themselves. But before we can get to that, we need to lay some groundwork. First, let's point out some of the differences between broadcast writing and most of the writing you've done during your formal education and look at some general characteristics of broadcast style.

We Get Only One Opportunity to Make Ourselves Understood

Chances are that you've written a number of essays in your time; you might have even written for the school newspaper. In both cases, you were writing for the eye. In broadcast, you'll write for the ear. When your English teacher read through one of your essays, he had the opportunity to go back and reread sections that weren't immediately clear. Readers of newspapers, magazines and other printed material have the same opportunity. Broadcast audiences don't. (Most people, we assume, don't tape the evening news to go back and look at it later unless they or family members or friends were part of the news that day.) So, we have to make every sentence we write very clear so that audience members understand what we're talking about after having heard it only once.

Additionally, even if something looks good on the page, we don't know how it will sound until we read it out loud. Every broadcast script should be read aloud so that the writer can hear how it will sound when the words are spoken. Writing for the ear is one of the biggest differences between print and broadcast writing, but there are others.

Story Structure Is Different

Although print writers seem to be moving away from rigid adherence to the inverted pyramid style, it remains the basis of many newspaper stories, especially hard news stories. With inverted pyramid style, stories begin with the most important facts and continue with facts of lesser and lesser importance. This is done primarily to make it possible for editors to shorten stories without affecting the most important information. You might have noticed that some newspaper stories you've read seem to end rather abruptly. Most likely, that was the work of an editor trying to fit a 450-word story in a 400-word space.

In broadcast writing, we don't use the inverted pyramid style. On the contrary, television and radio news stories are written in such a way that the viewers would definitely notice something was missing if we "trimmed from the bottom" because we don't build stories in descending order of the facts. Also, the end of longer broadcast news stories should contain either a summary statement or should leave the viewer something to think about and that might be lost if the viewers started to tune out toward the end. So we need to hold their attention throughout the story. Note that a summary statement isn't necessarily intended to indicate that we know all we're going to know about that story. Often, the resolution of stories isn't known for days or even months after the event occurs. Frequently, the summary statement is to let the viewers or listeners know that the story is a continuing one and that we'll follow it to its conclusion.

Broadcast Writers Use Conversational Tone

This doesn't mean speak as you would on the basketball court or at a club with your friends, but broadcast writing is a bit less formal than print writing. You might have already noticed that this book is written using contractions. That's one of the main things that separate broadcast and print writing. More on contractions in a bit. When you write for television or radio news, the goal is to tell a story to someone who knows less about what happened than you do. You want to impress this person, but you don't want to make that desire obvious. The way to impress without appearing that you're trying to impress is to use common words but use them very well. Many of us have used some words incorrectly for so long that they sound wrong when we use them the right way. Sound confusing? Just think what the viewers and listeners might be going through. Some of them know when you use a word incorrectly or try to talk above their heads; others just have a feeling that something is amiss. In either case, you the writer have distracted the audience member momentarily. One of the things to avoid in broadcast is anything that distracts the viewers or listeners. There are already plenty of things fighting against us for their attention for us to be fighting against ourselves.

We mentioned that broadcast writing is less formal than print writing, but it's more formal than how we speak to one another. When we talk, we don't often think about rules of grammar, sentence construction and the like. But when we write, we have to think about those things. Why? Because for now, television and radio news flows one way only with no immediate interaction between audience members and reporters or anchors. Just as viewers and listeners have nothing they can reread to make sure they understand it, likewise, they're unable to ask the person speaking what he or she meant by what was just said.

Writing for Broadcast Includes Using Contractions

You don't want the anchor (one day it could be you) to sound stiff or as though she's talking down to the audience. One way to avoid this is to use contractions, because contractions are a big part of sounding conversational. But, as with most "rules" in broadcast writing, there are exceptions and you shouldn't use contractions in every instance. For example, if you want to place emphasis on something, a contraction is *not* as strong as using both words. Additionally, some contractions don't roll off the tongue very smoothly and should be avoided. Some examples are "that'll" for that will, "it'll" for it will and "there're" for there are. Avoid those three and any others that just don't sound right to you when you read the script out loud. You should also be careful with contractions that sound like plurals. If you say, "The plan's giving her reason for hope," it's unclear at first whether you're talking about one plan or more than one. Television and radio audiences only know what they hear; they can't see the apostrophe. But for the most part, write with contractions.

In Broadcast Writing, We Use Short, Declarative Sentences

This is closely related to using conversational tone. This doesn't mean that all sentences should be simple sentences along the lines of "See Dick run," but we should stick to sentence construction that makes it very evident who and what we're writing about. Hence, we rarely use complex sentences because it's very easy for our meaning to get lost in the shuffle. Broadcast writers also keep the subject and the verb as close to each other as possible. For example, "This morning, police arrested a suspect" is easier to follow and sounds better than "Police this morning arrested a suspect." We also don't often deal with complex stories as part of everyday coverage. They're difficult to tell and difficult to follow. Even in fairly straightforward stories, it's better to present a few well-developed facts than lots of little bits of information. The viewers are apt to get lost (in more ways than one) if you hit them with too much information in a short amount of time.

Active Voice Is the Choice of Broadcasters

Simply put, active voice is someone doing something and passive voice is something being done to someone or some thing. Here are examples of both:

Active. The governor gave a speech.

Passive. A speech was given by the governor.

There are occasions in which passive voice actually sounds better, but they're fairly rare. Write in active voice unless the sentence sounds strange when you read it aloud. If that's the case, try it in passive voice to see if it sounds better. But you'll rarely go wrong using active voice. We'll look more closely at active voice and its importance in Chapter 3 on leads.

Broadcast Writers Use Present or Future Tense When Appropriate

Some writing coaches and textbook writers advise the use of present tense at all times, but that just doesn't make sense. If there's a reference to World War II in your story, you certainly wouldn't write about that as if it were currently taking place. However, you should use present tense as often as you can. Remember, we want to give today's news, not yesterday's news. Also, don't use more than one tense in the same sentence; for example, you wouldn't write "Police arrest a Carrville man and charged him with arson." You could place both verbs in the past tense, but your best bet is to use the present tense with both words (unless the arrest happened some time ago and we're updating the story). There will be more about tense in Chapter 3 on leads.

Broadcast Stories Are Written in Today Language

The word "yesterday" isn't allowed in the lead sentence of broadcast news stories. If something happened yesterday (or last week) and nothing new has developed, why would we include that story on the evening news? But using today language doesn't necessarily mean using the word "today." For example, "Police are continuing to investigate" indicates that something is going on today without us having to use the word "today." Further, today language doesn't mean that we can't update something that happened yesterday. It might even be necessary to use the word "yesterday" somewhere in the story. After all, if that's when the event occurred, we can't change that. Just don't use "yesterday" in the opening sentence.

Also, keep in mind the news program on which your story will appear. Starting a story that's part of the 9 p.m. update or the 11 p.m. newscast with "this morning" indicates that either nothing has happened since this morning or we aren't out there digging for the latest information. In a world of round-the-clock news channels, program interruptions to bring viewers the latest news live from the scene and all-news radio, failing to "freshen" stories for subsequent newscasts is a major failing indeed.

How to Deal with Dates and Days of the Week

Although we don't want to use the word "yesterday" in the lead sentences of our stories, if something happened yesterday, you'll have to use the word at some point in the piece. *When* something happened is important, and we can't say it happened today if it didn't. If you make time references in a story, use these guidelines: Use the words "yesterday" and "tomorrow" if the event in question is only one day in the past or one day in the future. If it's more than one day distant, give the day of the week. Dates aren't necessary unless the event happened more than a week ago or will happen more than a week from now. For example: The bill became law yesterday. The trial begins tomorrow. The concert will be Sunday. (Note: If you write *next* Sunday, you leave a question as to whether you mean a few days from now or a week and a few days from now. Delete the word "next" if you mean the Sunday to follow, and put the date if it's a Sunday that's more than a week away.) If you use a date, it's acceptable to write it in shorthand form rather that fully written out, such as 2nd, 4th, 21st and so on.

Some news operations use the day of the week rather than the words "yesterday," "today" or "tomorrow." CNN does this frequently because a piece might run on Wednesday evening and again on Thursday morning, or it might already be Thursday somewhere in the world. If you refer to today and the piece runs again on Thursday, it's now a different day. So, keep in mind when your story will run when deciding how to refer to the day that something happened. Wednesday could be yesterday, today or tomorrow, depending on what you're talking about. But it will always be Wednesday. So, although the words "yesterday," "today" and "tomorrow" are preferred, there are cases in which you'd use the day of the week instead.

Broadcast Writers Use Last Names and Put Titles First

Except on first reference or when more than one person with the same name is part of the story, use the last name only. Hence, the first reference to a person in the story would be to Bill Smith, but use Smith in all subsequent references to that person. If Bill's brother Tom is also part of the story, it might be necessary to use the full names of both men on all references to avoid confusion. Some writers like to use the first name only, but the only time that you can get away with that is when the person you're talking about is a child. It would sound strange to refer to 6-year-old Tommy Jones as Jones. So when you're referring to children, it's OK to use the first name alone on subsequent references.

When you use a title, place it in front of the name. Again, this is to avoid confusion and keep the sentence flowing smoothly. It sounds better to say "Former Midville Mayor Jane Brown says . . ." than to say "Jane Brown, former mayor of Midville, says . . ." But please, if some government official you talk to has a title like "Texas railroad commission pipeline regulatory division engineer," shorten the title to something the viewers can digest. You're going to have to do that to get it to fit on the screen for a "super" (graphic information superimposed over the video) anyway.

There's some disagreement among television news writers about the need to verbally identify the people whose on-camera quotes we use because their names and titles will be shown in a super on the lower-third of the screen. However, a number of studies have shown that many people don't watch the news closely from beginning to end.[1] Often, people are preparing dinner, dealing with the kids, getting ready for bed or talking about work that day as they watch/listen to the news program. The viewer might even be in another room during parts of the newscast. So it isn't advisable to depend on a super as the only means of identifying a speaker.

Additionally, even with those viewers who watch the news program intently, supers don't always suffice. Any producer or show director who has been involved with television news for any length of time will tell you that when mayhem reigns in the control room (and that isn't uncommon) getting supers on the air falls far down the list of priorities. Therefore, we suggest verbally identifying each on-camera source the first time he or she is about to appear. We'll have more about introducing sound bites in Chapter 8 on voice-over/sound on tapes (VO/SOTs).

In Broadcast Writing We Use Phonetic Spelling and Avoid Foreign Names When Possible

Although broadcast writers are supposed to spell correctly under most circumstances, there are times when spelling a word correctly might result in its being pronounced incorrectly on the air. Therefore, any uncommon word should be spelled the way it sounds. This presents some special problems for closed-captioned television, but most newsroom computer systems make it possible to deal with those

---

1. See, for example, *Study of Media and Markets: Television Attentiveness & Special Events* (1994), Simmons Market Research Bureau; R. Neuman (1991), *The Future of the Mass Audience,* Cambridge, United Kingdom: Cambridge University Press.

concerns. Viewers tend to phone the station en masse when an anchor or reporter mispronounces the name of a person or place, especially if most of them know the correct pronunciation. One of the goals of writers is to keep this from happening by spelling those names phonetically. "Davis" doesn't need to be spelled phonetically, nor does "Miami." But there's no predicting how "Sarmiento" or "Kazakhstan" will come out of someone's mouth unless you indicate that those names should be pronounced Sahr-me-in-toe and Kahz-ahk-stan.

Some fairly common words should also be spelled phonetically because they have two pronunciations. On more than one occasion, an anchor or field reporter has been known to pronounce "bass" the way it should be pronounced in reference to a fish when the word was used in reference to a low tone on the musical scale. When that happens, it's embarrassing for the person whose face is on screen and for the news operation as a whole. In such an instance, write "base drum." Although the word isn't spelled correctly, the overwhelming majority of the viewers don't see the words but only hear them, and it's certainly not good for the news operation's credibility for one of its anchors or reporters to say "bass drum" (as in a drum that holds fish). Several other words are spelled the same but pronounced differently. Watch out for them. One note of warning: if seeing a misspelled word distracts your anchor, you might want to spell the word correctly, review the script with the anchor, and hope that he or she pronounces the word the way it's supposed to be pronounced. Audience members always seem to notice even the slightest double-take by someone on camera.

In reference to hard-to-pronounce names, sometimes we can do without using a foreign name at all. It might be important to mention the name of the French president, but if we're referring to the French undersecretary of defense, using the title might be enough for the viewers to understand that person's role in the story without having to deal with a difficult foreign name. However, when the name is important to the story, if you think there's a chance it will be mispronounced, spell it phonetically whether it's a foreign name or not.

When you're not concerned about a chance that a word will be mispronounced, spell it correctly. Also, don't count on a spell-check program to catch your mistakes. The computer doesn't know whether you were writing "tired" or "tried" and will accept "tired" when you meant "tried" because, to the computer, you spelled the word correctly. It's just not the word you intended to use. Computers are great tools, but they can't match the human mind on some things, such as editing copy. At least not yet.

Broadcast Writers Avoid Abbreviations and Are Careful with Acronyms

In broadcast writing, avoid all abbreviations. The fairly common abbreviation "st." can mean either street or saint. Anchorpeople have plenty to think about without having to figure out which one it's supposed to be. Some abbreviations aren't used simply because they aren't needed. This is the case with courtesy titles such as Mr., Ms. and Mrs. Generally, a person's marital status isn't important to the story. One exception to the no-courtesy-title rule is with heads of state and their spouses. It's appropriate to refer to President Clinton or Mr. Clinton, or Mrs. Thatcher or Prime Minister Thatcher. Likewise, the spouses of those particular heads of state would be Mrs. Clinton or Mister Thatcher.

It might be important to identify someone as doctor, but when it is, spell the word out rather than using the abbreviation. "Dr." is short for both doctor and drive. The same is the case with president (you wouldn't want an anchor to say pres, so don't write it that way), senator or representative. (Note: Such titles aren't courtesy titles. They're earned titles. There's a difference between the two.)

Some agencies and entities are better known by the acronyms that identify them than by their full names, and the acronyms are easier to say. For example, F-B-I is more widely used than Federal Bureau of Investigation. But notice how we write F-B-I. When you want the anchor to pronounce each letter, place hyphens between them. This is also true with A-M and P-M in references to time.

Other acronyms that are acceptable on first reference are C-I-A, N-C-A-A (but if you want the anchor to say N-C-double-A, write it that way), N-B-C, C-B-S, A-B-C, C-N-N and so on. Let your guide be the way you're accustomed to hearing it. Almost no one says American Broadcasting Companies in conversation, and most probably don't even know what E-S-P-N stands for. For local or regional groups that might not be familiar to all the viewers, give the entire name on first reference, then go to the acronym. For example, the group Save Our Cumberland Mountains might be called SOCUM on second reference.

In Broadcast Writing, Keep Hyphenated Words on the Same Line

Any words that are meant to be read together should be hyphenated to alert the anchor as to how they should be read. In addition, all parts of the hyphenation should appear on the same line. There could be a brief delay as the words are rolling up on an electronic prompter. It looks silly when an anchor gets out half of a hyphenation but has to wait for the other half to appear. For the same reason, a sentence shouldn't carry from one page to another.

Hyphenation is called for when two or more words are used as a unit to describe something. "A long-running trial" could come out sounding as if we're talking about a lengthy trial about running (a long running trial) without the hyphenation.

Broadcast Writers Use No Symbols

Unlike print writers, we don't use any symbols in broadcast. All references to dollars, cents, percent and other such words should be spelled out. We also don't use the number sign, the "at" sign, the ampersand (symbol for the word "and") or any other symbol you can come up with. Even the point in one-point-two million dollars should be spelled out. If symbols were included in scripts, it could cause the news reader to pause momentarily trying to figure out exactly what has been written. That, of course, would break the flow of the story and might even make the anchor look or sound foolish.

In Broadcast Writing, There Are Different Guidelines for Dealing with Numbers

Quite often, the precise amount or number of something is unimportant in broadcast. Certainly, if 163 people are killed in an airplane crash, the number is important. But it's better to say a budget of nearly two million dollars than to say a budget of one million—865 thousand dollars. Additionally, filling a story with too many figures and statistics brings the flow of the story to a screeching halt and sends the viewers scrambling for their remotes. Most of the time, round off numbers.

When you write numbers in broadcast, it's important to make them easy to read. Here are some simple guidelines.

Numbers 1 through 9—write out the word (some news operations prefer that you write out the words through eleven)

Numbers 10 through 999—use numerals

Numbers higher than 999—use a combination of words and numerals. For example: 37,915,776 should be written 37 million—915 thousand—776.

Write phone numbers and years using all numbers because that's how we're accustomed to seeing them. For example: 610-555-0201, 1776, 1492.

Often, Addresses and Ages Aren't Important in Broadcast Writing

Chances are that most of the viewers in a given market wouldn't know where 1600 Eagle Street is, but they might be familiar with a certain section of town. Hence, referring to an area or pointing out landmarks close to the place where an event occurred is preferred instead of giving a street address. Likewise, a person's age usually isn't important unless we're talking about a 10-year-old college graduate or a 73-year-old snow skiing champion. However, there are exceptions. When a local person has been killed, it might be necessary to give the age and an address so relatives of other people with the same name as the dead person aren't alarmed for no reason. Also, when someone meets an untimely death, the age adds some context, as when a 28-year-old dies of a heart attack. Remember, in broadcast writing there are few rules that came down from the mountain on stone tablets—only guidelines.

Making Corrections to Copy

The standard markings used by print writers and editors to indicate changes in a script can be very confusing to an anchor trying to read a story on the air. The final version of the script should contain no such markings. Also, even if something is corrected on the hard copy of the script, it still has to be corrected in the computer. Most newsroom systems send the script directly to the prompter, and if you don't make the corrections electronically, the anchor will be seeing an uncorrected version of the script. Producers should make any corrections that are necessary on the computer, send the revised story to the prompter, and print out another copy for distribution to the anchors and all other news personnel who get copies.

Broadcast Writing Is Punctuated Differently

The most common forms of punctuation in broadcast writing are the comma and the ellipsis. The comma indicates a standard pause, the ellipsis indicates a slightly longer pause. The ellipsis is often used for effect. Additionally, words that the anchor should emphasize are underlined. Hence, this short sentence could be read three different ways:

Sue loves you.

Sue *loves* you.

Sue loves *you.*

The way you write the sentence is the way it's going to be said.

Other than the comma, the ellipsis, question marks and periods, we use few punctuation marks in broadcast. Remember, broadcast writing is meant to be heard, not read. You should write copy to make it as easy to read as possible. The easier it is for an anchor to read, the easier it will be for audience members to listen to.

Quotations Are Handled Differently in Broadcast

In broadcast writing, we rarely use direct quotations in the script, but normally paraphrase instead. Most people don't speak as succinctly as we're supposed to write, so we paraphrase what they've said in as few words as possible, being careful, of course, not to change the meaning. In those few instances when a writer feels compelled to use a direct quotation, it's important to make the sentence flow as smoothly as possible, as is always the case in broadcast writing. For example:

> THE PRESIDENT SAID . . . I WON'T SIGN THE BILL UNLESS IT'S AMENDED TO INCLUDE PROVISIONS FOR LOWERING THE DEFICIT . . . MISTER CLINTON ADDED THAT HE DOESN'T EXPECT THE REPUBLICAN MAJORITY IN THE HOUSE TO ADD THOSE PROVISIONS.

Setting the direct quote off with an ellipsis tells the anchor (and the listener or viewer) that what is about to be said stands apart from what has been said up to this point and from what will be said afterward. However, if you sense that the audience members might be confused, set off the quote by adding "in his words" after "the president said." However, definitely avoid these pitfalls: "The president said, quote," and "end quote" at the conclusion of the sentence.

Again, however, we rarely quote in text. If what someone has to say is important enough for us to quote that person, we'll get a taped comment. In a visual medium such as television it's better to see and hear the person who makes the comment rather than quote the person in the script. The same is true for radio, except, of course, the visual part.

Broadcast Writers Are Careful with Pronouns

Pronouns are acceptable in broadcast writing, but only if there's no question to whom the pronoun refers. Clarity is vitally important to broadcast news, and pronouns can create a problem in that regard. For example: "The police officer tackled the fleeing suspect. He's a former football player." In this sentence, it's unclear who the pronoun refers to, the officer or the suspect. It's likely that the writer used "he" to refer to the officer, the person who did the tackling. However, there's room for doubt, and that's something that broadcasters can't afford to raise in the viewers' minds. In this example, it's best to delete "he" and restate the noun.

Broadcast Writers Use Attribution before Statements

If we don't tell the viewers or listeners beforehand who made a particular comment, stated a fact or offered an opinion, it sounds as though those things are coming from our anchorperson. For example, "Sally Johnson extorted thousands of dollars from X-Y-Z Bank during a three-year period, according to bank officials" sounds as though we're making an accusation until the viewer hears the end of the sentence. Inverting the sentence takes care of that. "According to bank officials, Sally Johnson extorted thousands of dollars from X-Y-Z Bank during a three-year period" lets the viewers or listeners know right away that bank officials are making the charge, not the members of the news team.

Almost everything we know about a particular story comes from someone else and should be attributed. Exceptions would be that an event is taking place somewhere, at a certain time, costing a certain amount. There's no need to attribute common facts, but most other information can't stand without the writer needing to tell the audience its origin. Words and phrases such as "alleged," "accused," "convicted" or "charged with" help us in this regard. If we say someone is a convicted murderer, it's obvious that person was convicted by a jury, but even in that circumstance, we don't know for sure that the person did the crime. Plenty of people have been on Death Row for years and were later found to be innocent. Hence, we advise against saying someone did something unless a television news crew captured the event on videotape and there's no doubt that the person we're talking about is the person we see on the tape.

Conclusion

Former network anchorman David Brinkley was once asked if he considered himself a journalist or a broadcaster. Brinkley replied that there's no difference because good writing is good writing. In a sense, that's true. If you can write good print copy, you can easily make the transition to broadcast writing. But, as you've seen, there are some differences between the two media in how we arrive at good writing. The guidelines listed above don't change the language, but do slightly alter how we use it. All the guidelines are designed to make the copy easier to read and therefore, easier to listen to. Remember, the key in broadcast writing is *don't make viewers/listeners work to get their information*. As a writer, you should do all the work so that the audience members don't have to do any. Otherwise, they'll turn to a newscast (or other programming) that requires less effort.

⌐/ General Do's and Don'ts

Do
- Be clear and concise.
- Make life easy for the anchor.
- Write like people talk (to a degree).
- Be careful with pronouns.
- Attribute.

Don't
- Forget that you know more about stories than audience members do.
- Depend on the computer to catch mistakes.
- Fail to make corrections on the prompter as well as on hard copy.

SELECTING STORIES AND STARTING TO WRITE

I n radio and television newsrooms across the country, some of the youngest people in the operation are writing stories and making decisions about which stories should be included in the newscast and in what form. It isn't uncommon for associate producers and assignments desk personnel to start right out of college, even in some of the largest markets in the country. So you could be helping make major decisions sooner than you think.

Chandra Clark knows all about that. Because she got a lot of experience by interning and working part-time during her college days, she was able to land a job as a producer in the Tuscaloosa market right after graduating from the University of Alabama. Eight months later, she was the executive producer at the other station in town. That station merged its news operation with two other central Alabama stations nine months after that, and Chandra was tapped to produce the new operation's first newscast in what was now the 39th largest market in the country. She was 23.

She skipped the midnight sign-on party so she'd be well rested for the big day. She arrived at 7 a.m. to prepare for the 5 p.m. (Central Time) newscast. The network was airing a golf tournament that afternoon and, of course, it went to a playoff. The delay in getting the newscast on the air added to an already intense environment. As the minutes dragged on, the people in the control room were getting more and more anxious. The news director, the executive producer, the station vice president, the general manager and the president of the parent company were in the cramped room, standing behind Chandra. The golf tournament was *still* on. Chandra got on the IFB communication system (which she had used only during rehearsals) with one of her field reporters to ask about the outcue to his live shot package insert. He told her the outcue was "Trust in God and everything will be OK." Everyone in the control room burst out laughing, easing the tension, at least momentarily. The show finally went on, nearly 27 minutes later than scheduled. Chandra says producing hasn't gotten a whole lot easier since then.

Terry Meyers is another young person who rose through the ranks quickly. At 21 and fresh out of college, Terry landed a job as an assignments editor in the 35th market and says it was "sink or swim." She had to make dozens of decisions a day and had a nervous feeling in her stomach when the news began each afternoon, hoping she didn't miss any big stories that the other stations got. She moved into producing and worked in the 24th market, the sixth market, and is now an executive producer in the nation's largest media market, New York City. She got that job a mere seven years after graduating from college.

The experience she got on the assignments desk laid the groundwork for successively bigger jobs in bigger markets, and decision making has become increasingly more difficult with each move. There are so many stories to cover, you can't possibly get to them all. Terry says it's critical to look at all aspects of a story, especially what's in it for the viewers. Because she's young, that can be difficult. Sometimes she's not that interested in stories that people older than her might find interesting, and she may not be as knowledgeable about some things as they are. Also, she works with people who have been in the business a lot longer than she has, and through the years some of them have thought she was too young or didn't have enough experience to make the right decisions.

Sometimes she can get input from others in the newsroom about whether to air a particular piece of graphic video, or whether a story warrants a package or not, but other decisions have to be made in seconds and she has only her instinct to go on. She reads a lot (at least five newspapers every morning) and she watches and listens to news veterans, and that certainly helps, but she continues to fight the "age battle" and has to prove herself again and again. You might have to prove yourself as well, but if you have the talent, the determination, the drive and the people skills needed to be a news decision maker, even hardened news veterans will come to appreciate you, despite that baby face of yours.

Chandra and Terry are examples of where you might be in this business in a few short years. Neither works in front of the camera, but each is a critical cog in the news machine at her station. If you like being involved in the big picture and don't mind being "on the hot seat," think about pursuing producing or assignments desk work. You could find yourself in a big market before long and making important decisions about what is and isn't news.

In this chapter, we'll look at the factors assignments managers and producers consider when deciding which stories are worthy of inclusion in radio and television news programs, and we'll start to get down to the nitty-gritty of writing for broadcast news. We'll look more at the joys of producing live news in a later chapter.

A highly respected network news anchor once noted that the script for a half-hour news program wouldn't fill the front page of a major newspaper. Most television and radio stations air more than 30 minutes of news a day, but the point remains the same. Newspapers have a lot more room for stories than broadcast news operations have time for stories. Hence, there are fewer stories on television and radio news programs than in newspapers, and most broadcast stories are shorter than most newspaper stories.

Television news stories might last for only 10 or 15 seconds and rarely run longer than a minute-and-a-half to 2 minutes. Radio newscasters face similar time constraints. So, broadcasters have to be very choosy when it comes to deciding which stories make it on the news. There are several factors that influence what's been called the "gatekeeping process"—deciding which stories are selected from the hundreds or even thousands that are possible on a given day.

Newsworthiness

Newsworthiness is a highly subjective matter, but people in the news business must decide every day which stories are the most deserving of coverage. Excluding weather and sports, only 15 to 20 stories are reported in a 30-minute television newscast. Even 24-hour radio news programs are limited regarding the number of stories that can be broadcast. The decision regarding which stories are included and which are rejected is based on what those in the newsroom think those in their living rooms or cars are most likely to watch or listen to. Attracting viewers is undeniably part of the equation. Because of that, those involved in the news business strive to present what's been called "infotainment"—information presented in an entertaining way.

Some critics have charged that television news is too entertainment-oriented—stressing flash and trash over substance—and some of the criticism is warranted. But news programs must compete for the viewers' attention with other television programs, the Internet, movie rentals and a myriad of other choices. Hence, the finest information in the world is of little value if no one is watching. If television news is guilty of turning the equation around and producing "enterma-tion"—entertainment with only a dash of information—then all the criticism we could heap on those who think entertainment is the first mission of news is deserved. But presenting information in a way that will make your station stand out (while maintaining fairness, accuracy and balance) is simply good business. We think well-told stories are informative, interesting, and entertaining, and hope that you'll embrace higher ideals while recognizing that we work in the information *business*.

Before writers, editors, videographers and others involved in news gathering can begin the process of telling stories in compelling ways, someone has to decide which stories will be covered. The assignments manager, show producers, the executive producer and other newsroom managers are often the ones who make these coverage decisions, with input from reporters and other personnel. The decisions are based on a nebulous concept called "news judgment," but there are ways to make the process more objective than relying on a "gut feeling." Many of the factors television and radio news workers take into account when selecting stories are the same criteria used by newspaper editors, but others are different.

Proximity

Where an event occurs is important. If a six-car pileup delays traffic on a major local thoroughfare for hours, that's likely to make the news. If the same accident occurred elsewhere in the state, it's unlikely the story would air on your market's local news program. An old maxim in television news says that one local death is worth (in terms of news interest) five elsewhere in the state, twenty elsewhere in the country, and hundreds elsewhere in the world. It might sound cold, but it's assumed that what happens locally is more important to local viewers than what happens elsewhere. Of course, there are many other factors that influence the decision to include those stories that happen in other places, such as how the deaths occurred, the prominence of the people involved and other factors, but all other things being equal, local stories take precedence over stories from elsewhere.

In the earliest days of broadcast news, proximity was of paramount importance for a very practical reason. If something happened very far from the station, it was simply impossible to get to the scene and cover it, drive back, process film or edit audio tape, and get the story on the air. Therefore, news operations were geographically limited by the technology. That changed dramatically with the introduction of electronic news gathering and satellite news gathering technology. Now it's possible to get video and/or audio from almost anywhere in the world and to get it pretty quickly. What's been called "a river of video" is there for the picking from any number of organizations that supply video to local television stations for a fee, or from cooperating stations that might even be affiliated with different networks. Many cooperatives (called consortia, one would be a consortium) exist in both radio and TV, and some stations belong to four or five of them. So, proximity might not be as important as it once was because a local station's reach extends so much farther, but it's still pretty important.

Timeliness

Some news observers contend that timeliness is even more important on today's local news scene than it was in earlier days, because of the technology. Local stories can be covered live and with very little time needed to get a microwave truck operating once the news crew arrives on the scene. Local stations can arrange to get a live report from another part of the region or the world, and can get that on the air just as quickly as the local news operation in that area can. A story being reported live in Los Angeles can be on the air live in Miami (and plenty of other places) simultaneously and within minutes after news managers learn of it.

All this has led some news outfits to operate as if something that happened this morning is no longer news at 6 p.m. So local news has gone from not being able to get something on the air at 6 p.m. if it occurred after 4 p.m. to being able to get something on the air if it happens during the news. Many news workers across the country believe timeliness has taken on too much importance in television news. A nationwide survey of news directors and senior reporters conducted in the late 1990s indicated that many respondents in both groups think that plenty of local news operations give far too much attention to stories that happen to occur close to or during the news hour. Stories that might have been covered briefly (if at all) had they occurred earlier in the day are afforded live coverage early in the news programs (both "going live" and placing a story early in the newscast indicate the story is important) simply because they lend themselves to live coverage.[1] So timeliness is an important factor, but news managers have to guard against letting timeliness outweigh all other factors and

---

1. C. A. Tuggle and S. Huffman (1999), "Live News Reporting: Professional Judgment or Technological Pressure? A National Survey of Television News Directors and Senior Reporters," *Journal of Broadcasting & Electronic Media*, 43(4), pp. 492–505.

their good news judgment. But even in the dark ages of television news, timeliness was important. No one wanted to present information that viewers had already read in the newspaper.

Impact

Clearly, one of the things that news managers consider when deciding which stories to cover is which ones will impact the greatest number of listeners or viewers, whether directly or indirectly. A cure for cancer, the abolition of the income tax or the surprise resignation of the city's mayor would certainly affect almost everyone in the audience to one degree or another. But KABB Executive Producer Greg Kelfgun warns against reacting to breaking impact stories at the expense of everything else.

Greg says you have to go after the big stories, and go after them hard, because this is a competitive business and nobody wants to get beat on the big story of the day. Many producer job ads now ask for evidence of that producer's "owning" the top story. But Greg says the pursuit of the big story often leads producers and other managers to lose sight of the rest of the show. When the big story breaks, you have to immediately start thinking about not only how you'll cover it but also how you'll shuffle everything else. Remember, you still have other stories that deserve quality treatment, and for some of your viewers, one of those stories might be the most important one of the day. The story about a third grader using the Heimlich maneuver to save his teacher's life deserves a featured place in the newscast. Greg says station personnel go crazy trying to "own" the top story, but the idea is to put together a winning newscast, not just beat your competitors on the top story of the day.

Emotional stories can also affect large numbers of viewers. A story about a young child battling a life-threatening disease, a "good Samaritan" story in which a person does something good for another with no tangible reward, or the death of a celebrity who millions found interesting (as was the case in the death of Princess Diana) are all examples of emotional stories that attract attention and impact the audience.

How many people are involved in an event also affects whether it receives coverage. When a rock concert fills a large stadium, it's apparent that a lot of people are interested enough to pay good money to hear the musical group and gives an indication that many viewers might be interested in a story about the concert, even if they couldn't attend for some reason.

Prominence

One of the things that made the Princess Diana story of interest was her prominence. A person's standing in society or recognizability plays a role in making stories about that person newsworthy. For example, should your instructor be involved in a minor car accident, it's unlikely that story would make the evening news. However, should the governor be in town on the same day and be involved in the same fender bender, then we have a story. It's not that your instructor isn't an important person, but many more people know who the governor is and something minor that happens to her is of more interest than something minor that happens to most of us "average" people. So, when the president of the United States gets a dog, we hear about it on network news.

The same is true with athletes, rock singers, movie stars and other entertainers. They're among the country's most widely known residents, and even mundane things that happen to them are of interest to some people. If that weren't true, tabloid newspapers and television shows would quickly be replaced by something else. What producers and assignments editors have to do is avoid letting a person's celebrity be the *only* factor they consider when deciding if a story is newsworthy: the shows about what's happening in Hollywood come on *after* the news.

Conflict

Disagreement makes for good copy and even better video. Confrontations between protesters and police are interesting because the viewers don't know what might happen next. A shouting match at the city council meeting is likely to draw coverage, but the passage of uncontested ordinances probably wouldn't. Good broadcast writers know how to highlight conflict without embellishing it. However, showing conflict simply for the sake of showing it isn't good decision making. Unless we provide some context, we've done the viewers a disservice. As with all the other factors that go into deciding whether something is newsworthy, conflict shouldn't stand alone. Otherwise, we'd show 30 minutes of bar fights every night, and viewers might confuse the news with a national talk show known for violent outbursts from the guests.

Unusual or "Human Interest" Stories

Stories about "average" people are interesting if those people do unusual things. A story about a college student who collects the pictorial covers of a popular sports magazine becomes more interesting when the viewers learn that the student has nearly 1,000 magazine covers and that all are signed by the athletes pictured on the covers. If a local person has a few unpaid parking tickets, that might not be of interest, but if he had 200 unpaid tickets and was thrown into jail, that would probably attract some attention.

Also, many television news producers seek out interesting and unusual stories to place at the end of news blocks or at the end of the program. These stories are typically called "kickers" and involve something amusing or cute, such as a waterskiing squirrel or a ladder-climbing dog. Such stories aren't likely to impact anyone's life, but they do give the viewers a little bit of relief from what some complain is too often 30 minutes of death, destruction and corruption.

Simplicity

Complex stories are often dismissed as "print stories" by television news decision makers. It isn't because such stories are necessarily uninteresting, but it takes time to tell complex stories, and because they're complex, they're also difficult for the viewers/listeners to follow. A minor change in the tax law might affect a large number of viewers, but such a story would likely receive minimal attention on television because the details would be difficult to present and absorb. It has been said that television news is little more than a headline service. In many ways, that's probably right. But other than occasional investigative pieces, local news isn't designed to offer a lot of detail on stories, and news workers might even alienate a portion of the audience if they tried to pack too much detail into short stories. However, complex (even seemingly nonvisual) stories can be told on TV news. So don't dismiss stories automatically if they don't seem simple: make them simple. Relate difficult concepts to common things, such as comparing information flowing through a computer chip with highway traffic. This gives viewers a concrete representation of an abstract idea. Also, remember graphics. They help with pacing and are a very good way to relate information for which you have no video.

Can We Get Video?

Television is a visual medium, and pictures are worth thousands of words. To be sure, stories sometimes make the news when there's no video to accompany them, but such stories would be very short and would probably include a promise from the anchor to bring pictures to the viewers as soon as the video becomes available. But in many cases, a story for which video wasn't available wouldn't make the news. Frequently, a story is dropped when video is available but simply isn't very compelling. Maybe this shouldn't be a part of the equation, but it is. Again, however, we strongly suggest that decision makers consider all factors when deciding whether to air a story, and not drop it simply because of a lack of video. The most important question to ask is, Is this story important to our viewers or listeners? There is no quick and easy answer. It takes thought, research and intuition. Consider carefully and decide wisely. What's selected for presentation and how it's presented are vitally important.

There's one other thing to consider related to visuals. Television news operations use file footage extensively. The station might not be able to get video of a famous entertainer being arrested for soliciting prostitution, but would probably have clips of his television show on hand to illustrate the story. The video that's used affects the way a story is written, of course. More about the importance of writing to available video in Chapter 7.

What Else Is Happening?

One of the most difficult things to deal with in television and radio news is that producers have a set amount of time to fill, regardless of what's happening in the world. Of course, for a huge story news managers can choose to stay on the air beyond the normal end time of the news program, but in most circumstances, the news ends at an appointed time and certainly never before that time arrives. One television news operation used to end its program by having the anchor say, "And that's all the news we have time for."

So, in a typical 30-minute TV news program or five-minute hourly radio update, there's room for only a certain number of stories. Whether a particular story is included in that mix sometimes depends on what else is being covered. Coverage of a plane crash might knock out other stories that on slower news days would be included. One day the news might be 90 percent local and only 70 percent local the next day because major stories are happening elsewhere and not much is happening locally. Holidays, which are often very slow news days because businesses and institutions are closed, bring out all the standard holiday stories because there's little or no breaking news to cover. With TV, on those days when a lot is happening, it's not unusual for the time allotted for weather and sports to be trimmed (rarely commercials, though) in order to free up more time for all the news. So the decision of whether a story makes it on the news can depend on other stories against which the story must "compete" for attention.

Such was the case for Robyn Kinsey-Mooring and her colleagues at the ABC affiliate in the Raleigh-Durham market when Hurricane Floyd hit the Carolina coast. In some ways, it was easy for producers and other decision makers to decide what to cover—power outages, rooftop rescues, cleanup efforts—all important and visual stories. But what do you do with non-hurricane-related stories that at other times would wind up in the A block or might even lead the show? Because of hurricane and hurricane aftermath coverage, Robyn and her cohorts were forced to give short shrift to the groundbreaking for a controversial mega-mall; a plea agreement for a man accused of kidnapping, raping and beating a local principal; and an involuntary manslaughter trial in an outlying part of the coverage area.

The new mall had already been the subject of much debate because it was being built in an area where many residents thought development was already out of control. Because of the hurricane, the groundbreaking wasn't even mentioned until a week later, when, in a 15-second voice-over (VO), the viewers found out that construction was already under way. The rape and beating case ended quickly with the plea bargain, and a story that had been covered heavily because of concerns it raised about safety in area schools garnered 20 seconds of airtime with file video. The weeks of aftermath coverage meant that the news operation couldn't devote resources to the manslaughter trial on a daily basis (the case was the result of a hunting accident), so that trial was covered as a voice-over/sound on tape (VO/SOT) one day and the video was used as file for all subsequent stories.

Robyn says these were all important stories that should have received more attention, but they just didn't pull enough weight in the grand scheme of things to compete with 48 dead, thousands homeless and the eastern portion of the state under water for weeks. Deciding how to allocate resources is never an easy process, and it's even more difficult when one major story dominates.

What Are the Viewers/Listeners Talking About?

If snow is predicted to fall later in an area that rarely receives snow, many viewers or listeners are likely to watch/listen to the news program to find out what the chances are. If a widely known celebrity is set to visit the area, members of the audience are likely to be curious about the appearance and plans being made to accommodate the person. News managers use focus groups and other research methods to try to figure out what the viewers are interested in and what they might want to know. Often, though, a good gauge of what the viewers are talking about is what everyone in the newsroom and in other departments is talking about.

A Final Note on Gatekeeping

There are many factors that play a role in the gatekeeping process in television and radio news. There's no way to say whether one is more important than another, because there are often several at work at the same time. Also, one of the factors listed above might sway news managers to include a certain story, but another factor might prove to be the most important in the decision behind whether or not to include a different story.

For television producers and assignments managers, paying close attention to which stories are included each evening is important for a number of reasons. Since 1964, Roper surveys have shown that most Americans have said they get most of their news from television and would believe the television version of a story if other media had different accounts of the same event. At the height of the Persian Gulf War, 81 percent of Roper poll respondents indicated that they got most of their news from television and 54 percent said they got *all* of their information about the world from television news.[2] Many others get at least

---

2. "Poll: Most Got War News on TV" (1991), *Gainesville (FL) Sun*, May 2, p. A8.

some of their information from drive-time radio news. Some have questioned the accuracy of these polls and whether the way the questions are worded leads respondents to answer in certain ways. But if these polls are even close to being an accurate reflection of how Americans get their news, those of us in broadcast news have a big responsibility to include the most important stories in the limited time available.

Additionally, a long line of research has shown that the media (television in particular) often set the agenda for what's considered important. Researchers McCombs and Shaw noted that the media might not tell us what to think, but are remarkably successful at telling us what to think about.[3] The other side of that coin is that when stories aren't included, television news decision makers are saying, in essence, that those stories aren't as important as the ones that are included. People become interested in pursuing careers in television or radio news for a number of reasons. One can only hope that being part of one of the most important conduits of information in the information age is a major reason that young people become interested in the field.

The Page F Test

Deciding which stories to include in the newscast is only part of the battle. The next step is to present those stories in the most clear, concise way possible, and that goes back to writing. What we suggest is that you write a script, go ahead and get something on the page, and then apply the Page F test to it. Then have someone else (usually a producer in TV) do the same thing. If it doesn't pass all five parts of the test, then it isn't written as well as it should be written. Even the best writers in history were rarely completely pleased with the first draft of their writing. The five parts of the Page F test are:

P—Are the words precise?

A—Is the story accurate?

G—Is every element germane?

E—Are all actors treated equitably?

F—Does the story flow?

Precise Words

We're sure that you've heard people who are struggling in their attempts to learn English say that it's not an easy language to pick up. There are a number of reasons for this. Those of us from the United

---

3. M. McCombs and D. Shaw (1993), "The Evolution of Agenda Setting Research: Twenty-five Years in the Marketplace of Ideas," *Journal of Communication, 43*(2), pp. 58–67.

States use a lot of slang and clichés, the language is full of words that sound alike but mean different things, and the language is full of words that we think mean the same thing when there are subtle and not-so-subtle differences between them. For example, do you know the difference between anxious and eager? If you ever come across two words that mean exactly the same thing, rid your vocabulary of one of them. Why would we need both?

Toward the end of this book you'll find a section containing words and phrases that are often misused (Appendix B). Sometimes, textbook readers tend to read only what they have to read and skip appendices. We strongly encourage you not to do that in this case. The section on word use is very important because you'll never be a very good writer if you don't use words correctly. You might be able to fool most of the people most of the time, but it's likely that someone in the audience will catch every word usage mistake you make. How credible will you be as a purveyor of information in the minds of people who've caught you misusing words? You might even be surprised at how many words you think you know how to use correctly that you actually use incorrectly. So, the first part of the Page F test is to make sure that each word you use means exactly what you think it means.

Accuracy

Many people who teach or practice journalism will tell you that if what you write isn't accurate, your credibility and that of the news operation are sure to suffer sooner or later. Even if every word you use is precise, your story might not be true. All of us were kids at one time (believe it or not), and we know that there are shades of untruth. Often, you can get away with something really bad by admitting to something a bit less heinous. But that's not the way it is in journalism. We must tell the truth, the whole truth and nothing but the truth. The viewers count on us to tell them what went on as best we can without letting our own biases interfere. They also count on us to do the legwork necessary to ensure that what we report is actually what happened.

Of course, very few newspaper writers or broadcast journalists set out to deceive the public. But if we pass on something as fact without doing any digging to find out if it's true, our laziness serves the same purpose. People want to trust what they hear on the news. Unfortunately, they've been given a lot of reasons in the past several years not to.

Germane Information

In addition to being accurate, what we write has to be germane; it must be relevant to the story. All broadcast writers have a common enemy: a lack of time. A rush to get things on the air can lead to fact errors, and because of the limited time we have to tell stories, the information we choose to include must be the most important information. Is the age, sex, marital status or race of a person germane? Does the information add understanding, or does it just take up space? If a presidential candidate is caught in an affair, is that germane? It might be relevant in a story about the candidate's character and might not be in a story about the candidate's stance on a flat-rate income tax.

Part of the failure to include only relevant information comes from the writer's inability to decide what the story is about. Many broadcast news stories today are a little bit of this followed by a little bit of that, with no theme running through the story. Report on one thing. Is your story about the huge crowds at the auto show or the newest technology on display? We're not saying that you can't mention the technology, because that's probably one of the things that attracted the huge crowds. But decide what the theme of the piece is and *concentrate* on that.

Are All Groups Treated Equitably?

Treating groups differently can take many different forms. Using sexist language is one of them. Not only might certain terms alienate members of the audience (and every news director will tell you we need all the viewers we can get), but they aren't very precise. Words such as fireman, policeman and congressman are throwbacks to a time when women didn't occupy those roles. Many of us still tend to think of certain jobs being filled by men (doctors, for example) and others by women (such as nurses). Of course, men and women fill roles today that were once the exclusive domain of the other sex. So don't let archaic thinking slip into your writing.

Now, don't get us wrong. We're not talking about being politically correct, which has come to mean "don't do or say anything that has the remotest chance of offending someone." Hence, old people are referred to as "chronologically challenged," short people are "vertically challenged" and corrupt people are "morally challenged." If someone is corrupt (and we have proof), then the person is corrupt. But a firefighter isn't necessarily a fire*man.*

Also, in terms of being equitable, there are almost always two sides (or more) to an issue. If you devote two-thirds of your story to one side of the issue and only a third to the other side, one group thinks you're siding with the other. It's especially important to make sure both sides are heard on issues that generate intense feelings, even if one side seems to be in the minority. It could be that most people agree with the second position but just aren't very vocal about it. Don't let the number of activists involved sway your thinking about which is the most widely held opinion on an issue.

Does the Story Flow?

Even if your words are precise, your story is accurate, the information is germane and everyone has been treated as equitably as possible, you still might not have a very good piece if it doesn't flow. Each thought must flow logically into another. If you don't work to make the sentences flow, the viewers can be caught off guard when you introduce new information without showing its relationship to the information that's already been presented.

"Tie-writing" is the term used to describe how we get stories to flow. We have to tie one thought to the next, and that one to what follows it and so forth. One place within stories that this often doesn't occur is going into and coming out of sound bites. We'll address this particular concern in Chapter 9 on packages.

Conclusion

A lot goes into making a good piece of broadcast copy. In addition to the points of style we've already covered about how broadcast copy is written, we also have to be concerned with the content, what is written. We don't have the luxury of being able to spend hours on a piece of copy to make sure it's the best we can make it; at times it's a luxury to be able to review it once. So, much of what we do in terms of self-correction has to happen almost automatically. That begins to be the case only when we've written a lot. We trust that sooner than later you'll grasp how to deal with various story forms and broadcast writing guidelines as you continue writing—a lot.

🗁 Do's and Don'ts When Starting to Write

Do	Don't
• Think like a viewer.	• Let your own biases come into play.
• Be precise, accurate, germane and equitable, with flow.	• Let the entertainment part supersede the information part.
• Decide what the story is about before you start writing it.	• Disregard the need for strong grammar and word precision skills. (Read Appendix B.)

WRITING GREAT LEADS AND OTHER HELPFUL TIPS

I t's a truism that "everyone knows a story written for television or radio must be conversational." But casual observance of the news in any media market shows that the skill of turning that truism into reality isn't so common. In this section, we'll use several guiding principles and some examples to show how to write in a fashion that succeeds in being conversational while also doing a good job of delivering the news.

A well-written story will contain three basic ingredients:

- The writer captures the essence of the story in the lead.

- The copy itself doesn't sound like it's been *written* at all. It will sound, in fact, like one side of a conversation, exactly as if the anchor or reporter is talking to someone, rather than *at* someone.

- The writer presents the facts in narrative storytelling format.

29

In writing copy, you must always keep in mind our basic mission in broadcast news: relay needed information to the viewer, making yourself clear *on the first attempt.* Remember, you only get one pass at it.

The Art of the Lead

A story "lead" is, quite simply, its first sentence. Arguably, it's also the story's single most important element. In broadcasting, the lead accomplishes much the same task as a headline in the print world. For the consumer, it's the "point of purchase." The viewer/listener will make a decision whether to pay attention to the story based on the strength of the lead, in much the same way a reader decides whether to scan through a given newspaper story based on the headline. However, there's one huge difference between print and broadcast customers. If the print customer doesn't like a story headline, he or she probably won't put down the newspaper but will simply skip to the next story. A television viewer faced with the same situation is likely to pick up a remote and zap the entire newscast into oblivion.

The State of Oblivion is arguably a good place to visit on occasion, but you don't want to live or work there. For one thing, wages are pretty low. To avoid such a fate, when writing a lead you should:

- Grab the viewer's attention right away by capturing the essence of the story.
- Don't make the lead hard to digest by loading it down with too many facts! You'll write a "nonfactual lead."
- Write in present or future tense.

In addition, you should apply the same rules and techniques in the lead that pertain to copy writing in general, including:

- Write in active voice.
- Use narrative storytelling technique.
- When appropriate, use creative techniques to make the copy sparkle. But don't overdo it!
- Write conversationally! Use short, declarative sentences. Employ the "Mom Rule."

We'll explore each of these points in the pages ahead. The last point is the most important of all, and that's where we'll begin our discussion.

Writing Conversationally: The "Mom Rule"

Broadcasting isn't like the print media. In the print world if a reader doesn't understand a sentence, paragraph or story on the first attempt, he or she can go back and reread it. That's not an option in broadcasting. As mentioned in Chapter 1 and at the beginning of this chapter, we must get it right the first time. To accomplish that, we must write the way people *listen*, and to do *that*, we must write the way people *talk*.

An easy way to prepare yourself for that is to remember the Mom Rule. Ask yourself: if you were sitting down at the dinner table to tell this story to your mom, what would you say? We hope you'll want to speak in sentences that are grammatically correct but not rigidly formal. You'll be friendly and conversational, using short, declarative sentences. You'll get to the point right off the bat.

Apply that rule when you're speaking to the viewer/listener. Visualize the copy as your part of a conversation with someone standing right in front of you. Keep your sentences short: take a breath! Make your tone friendly and informal, but not so informal as to be chatty, gushy or silly.

The Mom Rule doesn't apply just to writing leads; it also applies to general copy writing. We'll talk more about the Mom Rule and see how to apply it in some of the examples that follow.

Capturing the Viewer's Attention: The Essence of the Story

The most basic definition of a newsworthy story is one that the viewer or listener finds beneficial or valuable. Remember, they're making a decision about your story (whether you like it or not) during the lead. In writing and leadership seminars I've attended, I've often heard this analogy, which I find helpful: remember that every single viewer or listener is tuned in to the same radio station. Its call letters are WII-FM, or "What's In It For Me?" If your lead doesn't answer that question *immediately*, you may lose the viewer.

So the lead is, in essence, a sales pitch of sorts. Make it a good one. The sale is important to you: no sale, no viewer; no viewer, no ratings; no ratings, no revenue; no revenue, no paycheck. To close the sale, you must immediately convince the viewer of the value or benefit of the story. Sometimes this is obvious and easy for the writer to do; often, it's far from it. One thing is clear: in order to capture in your lead the essence of what makes your story newsworthy, you must know it yourself.

The Mom Rule can assist us once again. The best way to zero in on the essence of the story is to imagine that you're having a conversation about it with your mom. What is the single fact that you would find to be the most interesting? On what point would the conversation focus? How would you begin the conversation?

Here's an example, loosely based on an actual news story. The scenario is that three weeks ago in Miami (a city in your state but not in your market) police arrested Kathy Newsmaker and charged her with involuntary manslaughter for the death of her baby. Kathy had left the child locked inside her car while she went inside to speak to a neighbor for "just a moment." But she was gone for more than an hour, and when she returned, the child had died from exposure to the severe heat inside the car. You have previously carried stories about this in your local newscast. Now, this afternoon (about an hour before airtime) a story crosses your news wire stating that the district attorney has decided to drop all charges against Kathy. The DA says her investigation showed that Kathy was in general a loving mother and that the baby's death was simply a tragic accident and not in character for Kathy.

Your mission: to write a lead to this story that captures its essence and makes a connection to the viewer, without resorting to lurid writing or tabloid-style sensationalism.

This is similar to the lead that actually aired on one Florida TV station:

TODAY IN MIAMI THE DISTRICT ATTORNEY ANNOUNCED SHE WON'T PURSUE A MURDER CASE AGAINST 38-YEAR-OLD MOTHER KATHY NEWSMAKER.

Among its sins (it's in the past tense, too long and not conversational) this lead inspires a response along the lines of "So what? Who's she?" The lead does key on what happened today, but doesn't even come close to touching on the essence of what makes this story newsworthy.

Going by the exercise suggested above, if you talk this story over with your mom or imagine yourself doing so, chances are you'll have no trouble at all focusing on the one thing that makes this story relevant. You'll begin with the fact that has the greatest impact on you, and in this case, it's an emotional impact: "Mom, can you believe it? That Miami child killer got off!" What you've just expressed is the same factor that makes this story newsworthy to the average viewer: the expectation that Kathy would pay a price for her mistake, and the surprise and disappointment that she won't. To be meaningful and relevant to the viewer, then, your lead must address that same issue.

It would be convenient if you could write a lead such as this:

A LOT OF MIAMI RESIDENTS ARE SHOCKED AND OUTRAGED TONIGHT: A WOMAN ACCUSED OF KILLING HER BABY HAS WALKED FREE.

However, because this story is just breaking and no one has had an opportunity to react to it, you can't honestly say anyone is shocked and outraged. Instead, you have to focus on the *development*, which may (or may not) later lead to those outraged feelings, and get to the point right off the bat:

A MIAMI WOMAN WHO WENT TO JAIL FOR LEAVING HER BABY LOCKED IN A HOT CAR IS FREE TONIGHT. THE DISTRICT ATTORNEY SAYS THE CHILD'S DEATH WAS NOTHING MORE THAN A TRAGIC ACCIDENT.

There's also another way to do this. You can write *specifically* to the viewer's unspoken expectations:

YOU MIGHT THINK THAT IF A BABY DIES WHILE LEFT LOCKED INSIDE A HOT CAR . . . SOMEONE WOULD GO TO JAIL. BUT IN ONE MIAMI CASE . . . YOU'D BE WRONG.

This last example has the advantage of being much more conversational, and because it speaks directly to the viewers'/listeners' emotions, it will be relevant to a wider circle of people. However, it must be acknowledged here that not every journalist is comfortable with this style of writing. Some feel that speaking directly to the viewer in this manner "crosses the line" in the direction of being editorial. As a news writer, you must follow the dictates of your conscience and of your newsroom's policy. Keep in mind, though, that the most common failure of broadcast journalism is the failure to make a connection with the viewer or listener. The story example outlined above is newsworthy precisely because it contains a "surprise"; the viewer's expectations about the likely outcome of this story aren't being met. The most effective and memorable copy will *directly* address those expectations. Many journalists are comfortable reciting the dry facts only. To really communicate, however, you must go beyond that dry recitation of facts and frame the story in a way that showcases its relevance to the viewer. This isn't editorializing; it's *humanizing*. Used properly, it's perfectly appropriate. Of course, having spoken directly to the viewer's expectations, the story must then go on to give a fair and balanced explanation of what happened and why.

Present or Future Tense—Without "TV Speak"

Most producers, writers and reporters have it drilled into them that they should write all leads in present or future tense. This is one point that is almost universally acknowledged in local television and radio newsrooms across the country. The reason is simple: as discussed in Chapter 1, if it's happening now, or will be happening soon, then it's news. If it happened hours ago, it's old news and fading fast. If it happened yesterday, it's history. Yesterday's news doesn't hold a great deal of value except to historians. If this weren't so, then no one would use yesterday's newspaper to line parrot cages. Yesterday's broadcast news has even less value; you can't even wrap fish in it. The easiest way to telegraph to your audience that your newscast is fresh, new and therefore valuable is to talk about what's happening *now* or what *will be happening* in the near future—using present and future tense, respectively.

Now here's where many broadcast news writers go astray, particularly those writing for TV. Many a producer will write a past-tense lead, then stop, suddenly realizing that in the postshow meeting the news director or executive producer will hold up any past-tense leads to criticism and ridicule. So, our producer scratches his or her head for a moment, then, without employing any creativity or considering whether the result will sound natural and conversational, simply changes the tense of the verb from past to present. The result is a mangled, bastardized form of English known as "TV speak." Some have also come to deride it recently as "foxism," but this probably isn't fair, because the practice predates the Fox network and is not, in my observation, peculiar to any one network or network affiliation. But whatever you call it, it's about as pleasant as fingernails screeching across a chalkboard.

Example Scenario

You're working in the Tucson market and are writing a story about a local bank robbery. Here are the facts of the story: a gunman held up a bank and got away with some cash. After running out the door, for no apparent reason the gunman shot at a passerby on the sidewalk. The passerby, Otis Armstrong, was about to step into the bank to cash a check. When the shot was fired, he dived to the sidewalk and wasn't hurt. Police say it was a miracle the bullet missed Armstrong, and officers credited him for his alertness and quick reflexes in ducking for cover. The bank is processing the security film and will release it in the morning.

A traditional, unimaginative past-tense lead might read something like this:

A TUCSON BANK WAS ROBBED THIS MORNING . . . AND THE GUNMAN GOT AWAY.

But wait! It's past tense! So the producer, suffering from a sudden, acute attack of unimaginativeness, simply changes the verb "got" to the present tense "gets" and comes up with:

A TUCSON BANK IS ROBBED THIS MORNING . . . AND THE GUNMAN GETS AWAY.

The above sentence is indeed in the present tense, but the problem is that it doesn't sound natural. In fact, it's ridiculous. It's written in TV speak. The writer made a half-hearted attempt to follow the present-tense rule, but in doing so gave no thought or creativity to the effort and simply changed the tense without regard to how it would sound. Think about it. When was the last time you sat down to dinner with your mom and said, "A Tucson bank is robbed this morning"? The answer is never. No one talks that way. This style of writing might be appropriate for a tease, but not for the story itself. In "fixing" the past-tense lead, the writer actually has made the situation much worse. It's better to use past tense conversationally, even in a lead, than to use present tense unnaturally.

The best way to fix it is to start over from scratch. Ask yourself three questions:

1 Who are the participants in this story?
2 What are they doing now?
3 What will they be doing later—tonight, tomorrow or next week?

The answers to these questions will tell you how to rewrite the lead.

In this particular example, who's in the cast of characters? The list includes:

- Police
- The employees developing the security film
- The bank teller who was robbed
- Witnesses
- The gunman
- Otis Armstrong
- The viewing public (never forget the viewers!)

A list of things happening right now might include:

- Police are looking for the gunman.
- The gunman presumably is trying to avoid capture.
- The victim who was nearly shot is telling his story to friends and in general is glad to be alive.
- Police are investigating the incident.
- The bank is processing its security camera pictures.

A similar list of things that will happen in the future regarding this story might include:

- The gunman will or will not be caught.
- The bank will release its security photos.
- The bank will reopen tomorrow with business as usual.

A good writer can fashion any and all of these facts into a present- or future-tense lead. The best and most effective lead will also be the one that focuses on the most interesting human element. In this case, who in the cast of characters has the most interesting and colorful story to tell?

Present-Tense Examples

ONE TUCSON MAN IS RECOVERING FROM A FRIGHTFUL EXPERIENCE THIS AFTERNOON.

THIS HAS TURNED OUT TO BE A DAY ONE TUCSON MAN WON'T SOON FORGET.

OTIS ARMSTRONG'S GRANDCHILDREN WILL BE HEARING ABOUT THIS DAY FOR YEARS.

(Note: for this last example, don't make this up. You can take the liberty of assuming Otis will tell his grandkids about this, but do make sure Otis has grandchildren!)

Future-Tense Examples

WHEN OTIS ARMSTRONG RETURNS TO WORK TOMORROW . . . HE'LL HAVE ONE
AMAZING STORY TO TELL HIS FRIENDS.

POLICE HOPE EVIDENCE TO BE RELEASED TOMORROW WILL HELP THEM
CATCH A CROOK.

And just to show that even the past tense can on occasion be effective if it's written conversationally and employs narrative storytelling:

ONE SECOND OTIS ARMSTRONG WAS WALKING DOWN THE STREET WITHOUT A
CARE IN THE WORLD . . . THE NEXT . . . HE WAS DIVING FOR COVER.

And finally, another present-tense lead, this one with a touch of word play and alliteration:

POLICE ARE BANKING ON A BATCH OF PHOTOS TO HELP THEM BAG A BANK BANDIT.

Keeping It Short: The Nonfactual Lead

How many facts should your lead contain? Here's a startling thought for you: the best leads may contain *no specific facts at all*. Many writers are tempted to launch into the body of their story right out of the starting gate. Thus we might see a lead like this:

AN AMERICAN AIRLINES 737 WITH 57 PASSENGERS ON BOARD DISAPPEARED
FROM RADAR SHORTLY AFTER TAKEOFF FROM BUENOS AIRES THIS MORNING . . .
SPARKING A MAJOR SEARCH BY THE ARGENTINE AIR FORCE.

It has too many facts. We don't need to know in the very first breath how many passengers are on the manifest, the airline company involved, the circumstances surrounding the disappearance, the location and who's conducting the search. This sentence has so many facts in it competing for attention that the viewer can't possibly remember them all. *Keep it simple:* save the details for the body of the story. Again, ask yourself: How would you say this to your mom? Would you sit down and say, "Hey, Mom! An American Airlines 737 with 57 passengers on board disappeared from radar shortly after takeoff from Buenos Aires this morning, sparking a major search by the Argentine Air Force!" Probably not. If so, you've been watching too much bad TV news. Chances are you might say something more like, "Hey, Mom! Did you hear about the plane crash?" Your lead should get the viewer's attention in a very similar fashion:

WE HAVE BREAKING NEWS OUT OF ARGENTINA THIS AFTERNOON. A MASSIVE
SEARCH IS UNDER WAY FOR A MISSING JETLINER.

Such a lead also serves a preview function. In essence you're saying to the viewer, "Listen up. You're about to hear a story about a plane crash." With this style, when you do begin presenting the facts, the viewer is prepared to accept them, instead of being clobbered over the head without warning.

Beyond the Lead: General Copy Writing Tips

"Selling the story," though critically important, isn't the only purpose of the lead. It must also set up and support certain tasks and styles to be accomplished in the body of the story. The lead must begin the "preview and review" function. It must support narrative storytelling technique. And, like all copy throughout the newscast, the voice should be active, not passive.

Preview, View and Review

Your mission, as stated, is to be clear the first time. The best way to reach any destination is to have a clear road map. When you're writing copy, that road map consists of a framework providing a clear beginning, middle and end to the story. This is also known as "preview, view and review," or "Tell 'em what you're going to tell 'em, tell 'em, then tell 'em what you told 'em" rule.

Exactly how to accomplish this in practical terms varies widely from story to story. A nonfactual lead written according to the guidelines we've discussed will serve as a preview for the story. In the jetliner example above, the lead makes it clear that we're about to hear a story about a missing jetliner. The body of the story should contain all the pertinent facts. Wrap up with a line that summarizes the current status of the story or looks ahead to what might happen next, such as:

AUTHORITIES SAY THE SEARCH FOR THE MISSING JETLINER WILL CONTINUE
THROUGH THE NIGHT.

Or,

IT'S NOT KNOWN WHETHER ANY OF THE MISSING PASSENGERS IS AMERICAN.

Or,

THE AIRLINE IS NOW IN THE PROCESS OF CONTACTING RELATIVES OF MISSING
PASSENGERS.

Each of these sentences serves to reinforce the idea that the jetliner is missing (which we've already said) and that concern about it is ongoing.

For a major story involving one or more sidebars, it's never a bad idea to write a copy story specifically for the purpose of summarizing and recapping the situation, to run after the final sidebar.

Narrative Storytelling

To know how to tell a story, you must first know what the story is. The basic definition of any story is simply this: it's something interesting, remarkable or unusual that happened to somebody.

Sounds simple enough, right? But casually glancing at/listening to many local newscasts will show that some reporters don't stop to define their stories before they sit down to write. The resulting product is confusing, incoherent and unfocused. To prevent yourself from falling into this trap, ask yourself this simple question: What is the story *about?* If you can't answer that question *in one sentence,* then you need to rethink your report and narrow the focus. In doing so, define the "something" that happened (the traditional "what, when, where and why") and the "someone" at the center of the story (the fifth "w," the "who").

Usually, the best way to relate a story is to tell it the way it happened, in chronological order, preferably through the eyes of a central character (the someone). It's the same style used in most fairy tales and novels. "Once upon a time there was a fair maiden who lived in the forest. And then yah dah yah dah yah dah happened. And then they lived happily ever after." Narrative storytelling works because the events unfold in their natural order in a fashion that's easy to follow and comprehend. When writing, think of yourself as Mark Twain, Margaret Mitchell, Stephen King or Anne Rice. The principles and challenges you face in your writing are very similar to those they faced in theirs. Your task, too, is to tell a story, to spin a yarn, to engage your customers in a narrative exercise that will leave them with a firm understanding of the events you're trying to relate *as if they had lived it themselves.*

But wait! When writing for TV, news directors, chief photographers and some consultants will insist that the "best pictures should go first." Is this good advice? The answer is not always. Putting the best pictures first doesn't always make the best story and can, in fact, make the story harder to follow.

Here's an example. In the Tampa market one day all the TV stations were competing to cover a hostage situation. Two teens had broken into a house in which an elderly man lived. The police SWAT team surrounded the house. They broke a window and threw in a telephone. The kids refused to negotiate. Eventually police fired tear gas through the windows, broke down the door, stormed the house and dragged the hostage takers out by their hair in full view of TV cameras. Later, police found the home owner dead.

Some reporters opened their stories in a very predictable way: they began with the dramatic video of police breaking down the door and storming the house. One reporter chose a different route. He began with video of the police surrounding the house. Then he told the story in narrative style, revealing a new fact with each sentence as it had actually occurred, allowing the drama to unfold for the viewer as it had unfolded in real life. The story won an Emmy award in spot news reporting that year. The judges found it clear and compelling. Chances are the viewers did, too.

But as with all rules, there are exceptions. Sometimes narrative storytelling principles conflict with other concerns. In most newsrooms, for instance, it's important for stories in the late evening newscast to begin with the freshest, most updated video. When such a conflict arises, here's a rule of thumb: go ahead and put the new pictures first, but then immediately cut to an earlier part of the story and pick it up from there in the proper chronological order. Here's an example:
(Open with natural sound, flames)

> THESE TOWERING FLAMES WERE A FIREFIGHTER'S NIGHTMARE. FOR HOURS THIS AFTERNOON . . . THE MEN AND WOMEN OF FIRE COMPANY 33 BATTLED THE RAGING FIRE. THEY BRAVED SEARING 120 DEGREE HEAT. BUT FAR MORE DANGEROUS THAN THAT . . . WAS THE SULFURIC ACID CONTAINED IN THE BURNING TANK TRUCK. THIS ORDEAL BEGAN FOUR HOURS EARLIER . . . AT THE U-SAVE GROCERY STORE ON BRUCE B DOWNS BOULEVARD. THAT'S WHERE TRUCK DRIVER MACK SIMPSON BLUNDERED INTO A HIGH SPEED POLICE CHASE. . . .

If you have to break from the chronology, try not to deviate from it more than once. Your viewers can probably handle one clearly defined flash-back or flash-forward, but don't ask them to follow you through a whole series of them.

When writing your story, it's crucially important that you not only relate the events in chronological order but also pick a strong central character. The best and most memorable stories are those told through the eyes of a person to whom we can all relate. In Chapter 9 on packages, we refer to this as the diamond approach. That's why in the bank robbery story outlined earlier in this chapter, passerby Otis Armstrong makes a good choice for the central character—what happened to him could have happened to any of us.

A final point about narrative storytelling. Although the traditional "five W's" are very important, don't forget the "s"—the "so what?" Make sure your story contains context, perspective and meaning for the viewer/listener. In the case of the bank robbery, don't just relate the basic facts; answer the "so what?" question. Were patrons in danger? Is the bank taking any extra steps to improve safety? How many other bank robberies have taken place at that branch? In that neighborhood? Are bank robberies on the rise? Are your deposits safe? What does all this mean to the viewer?

Write in Active Voice

There are several reasons why passive voice isn't well suited for news copy. For one, it just doesn't sparkle; it sounds dull and drab. Two or three back-to-back passive sentences can kill a story dead.

Which of the following examples sounds more crisp and memorable to you?

Example A

JOHN WAS SHOT BY FRED. FRED WAS QUICKLY ARRESTED BY POLICE. THE QUICK RESPONSE BY POLICE WAS PRAISED BY THE MAYOR.

Example B

FRED SHOT JOHN. POLICE QUICKLY ARRESTED HIM. THE MAYOR COMPLIMENTED THE OFFICERS FOR THEIR QUICK RESPONSE.

But the real sin of passive writing is that it makes your story more difficult to comprehend. Passive voice makes narrative storytelling technique difficult or impossible because it interferes with attempts to present the story in chronological order. It presents the target of the action before showing the person or thing that initiated the action. We see the result before the cause, the exact opposite of the way it happened in real life. In our example of Fred doing evil to John, in real life the first thing that happens is that Fred acts, pulling the trigger, and then John falls with a gunshot wound. But if you write it in passive voice ("John was shot by Fred"), you're showing us the second action first (John being shot), the first action second (Fred pulling the trigger), and then trying to go back and piece it all together. It's confusing. Put enough passive sentences in your story and you'll make it an incomprehensible quagmire.

Finally, passive voice leads journalists to adopt passive habits in pursuing the facts. It allows them to omit major information—such as who did it. For example, "JOHN WAS SHOT." Who did it? Maybe the reporter knows, maybe not. But if you write this sentence in the active voice, it's *not possible* for you to leave out the subject. You can write "Fred shot John" or even "Someone shot John," but it's impossible to write an active-voice sentence without some reference to the person or thing responsible for the action. With passive voice, one or more of the actors may be in the shadows. Active voice places all the actors on stage.

Sensitivity

Let's face it: we live in a "politically correct" world. Speaking personally, I've seen newsrooms change dramatically in recent years. Behavior that would get you canned today was once prevalent. We've all had to learn to be more sensitive, both in our personal behavior and in the copy we write. We've all had to learn to think before we speak and to filter our copy for potential offensiveness before putting it on the air.

Whatever your political views might be, trust me: this is not a bad thing. Here's why: if your copy makes a connection to 95 percent of your audience but alienates 5 percent of it because you've inadvertently offended someone, then it's 5 percent less effective than it should be. But the bad effects don't stop there. That 5 percent of your audience that you've just offended may feel disenfranchised. They may not watch your station again. Worse, they may not watch *any* station again. Who was it who wrote, "No man is an island"? If anyone is alienated, we're all worse off.

Say what you will about how sad it is that no one has a sense of humor anymore and the like, but the fact is that our society is what it is. People *do* get offended, and we have to deal with that fact. Here's a good rule of thumb that has served me well through the years: never offend anyone *by accident.* If you're going to offend someone—and let's face it, good journalism does that on occasion—make sure you're doing it on purpose for a very good reason. On every other occasion, potentially offensive copy is simply an accidental roadblock to good communication.

So how do you know copy will be potentially offensive? Your own gut instinct, if you listen to it, will tell you about 75 percent of the time, maybe less. The rest of the time, you have to rely on feedback from co-workers and, most especially, from viewers.

Here's a quick personal example. When I was an 11 p.m. producer, I once wrote a piece of copy that began something like this: "It was another black day on Wall Street." Now, this piece of copy was in no danger of winning me a Pulitzer Prize to begin with. The "black day" cliché was in wide use at the time (and still is), and I didn't think anything about it. But after the newscast, I received a call from a viewer. The gentleman was very polite and very well spoken. He simply wanted to know if I knew that many people were offended by use of the word "black" to describe all things negative. Truthfully, this thought had never occurred to me. Ever. Certainly, I hadn't meant it in a racial way. But my intentions didn't matter. The effect of my words did. I stopped using the word that very day and have never used it in that context again. Every time I see it in someone else's copy, I think of that viewer.

Again, the point remains: why offend someone if you don't have to? Find other words. The New Golden Rule applies in this case: Treat Others As They Want To Be Treated. Every case is different, of course. But to the extent that it's possible and practical for you to follow it, do so. Your copy will be that much more effective.

Basic Creative Techniques

You don't have to use a lot of creative writing techniques to write good copy for television or radio. In fact, normally you should be suspicious and wary of too much creativity. Colorful adjectives and flowery prose can, if not used properly, make a story sound contrived, hyped and trite. Or worse, these techniques can convolute a story to the point that it can't be understood by the normal human being. Even so, some creative techniques, when used sparingly and in moderation, can add to the story and make it more understandable and memorable.

Alliteration

Alliteration is the practice of taking a number of words beginning with the same consonant and grouping them together in the same sentence or phrase. For example:

POLICE ARE PLANNING TO PUT A PERSISTENT PURSE SNATCHER IN THE POKEY.

This technique has the virtue of making your sentence instantly memorable and even entertaining. The danger is that it's also a very easy technique to overdo and abuse. It's fairly safe to use with light stories but riskier with hard news. In either case use it with moderation.

Parallel Writing with Word Play

Parallel writing is simply the act of linking two actions or situations for the purpose of comparing or contrasting them. Often, the connection is made with a word play—that is, using a pun or a double meaning of one word to link the two ideas. Its purpose is to make a quick and obvious connection between different actions or concepts.

Example 1

IN IOWA . . . TEMPERS ARE RISING ALONG WITH THE WATERS.

This is a play off the word "rising," one verb used to place two very different but linked concepts into parallel: the act of land being flooded and people getting angry about it.

Example 2

THE SKYRISE APARTMENTS CAME WITH A SKY HIGH COST TO THE ENVIRONMENT.

This is a play off the word "sky" or, more specifically, a play off the concept of "rising to the sky." Again, it places two very different but linked concepts into parallel: the act of building an apartment complex and the act of damaging the environment.

This technique isn't available or effective in every situation. The key is to look for two parallel actions that you can then link together with a common verb, phrase or concept.

The Rule of Threes

The idea behind the Rule of Threes is that people remember ideas more easily if they're presented in groups of three. Examples abound in everyday conversation: "reading, writing and 'rithmetic," "earth, wind and fire," "Tom, Dick and Harry," "wind, sea and rain," "morning, noon and night," "blood, sweat and tears," to name a few.

The Rule of Threes is especially effective when used in conjunction with parallel writing. This involves using a group of three words or phrases to draw a comparison or contrast to a second group of three words or phrases. The danger is that this technique, like alliteration, is more difficult to bring off properly and more likely to sound contrived. When it works right, however, it can be effective. For example:

> DONALD SMITH SWEARS HE BEGAN HIS DAY LIKE ANY OTHER. HE CLAIMS HE WOKE UP . . . SHAVED . . . AND HEADED OFF TO WORK. BUT THE F-B-I TELLS IT DIFFERENTLY. IT CLAIMS HE WOKE UP . . . PUT ON A FAKE BEARD . . . AND HEADED OFF TO ROB A BANK.

(Rule of Threes: waking, shaving and heading off)

> INSTEAD OF SPENDING THEIR DAY IN SCHOOL LEARNING READING . . . WRITING . . . AND 'RITHMETIC . . . POLICE SAY THESE GANG MEMBERS SPENT IT IN A CAR RIDING . . . RACING . . . AND ROBBING.

(Combines alliteration and parallels three expected activities with three unexpected ones)

Metaphorical Writing

This is the technique of using a physical situation, thing or activity to symbolically describe something else. For example:

> THE ATTORNEY GENERAL SAYS EMPIRE MINING WAS INDEED DIGGING FOR GOLD . . . BUT IN THE WRONG PLACE: THE POCKETBOOKS OF ITS INVESTORS.

(Metaphor: "digging for gold")

> THE COMPANY NEVER FINISHED THE POOL. AND THE NEWSMAKERS WEREN'T THE ONLY FAMILY TO GET SOAKED. THE A-G SAYS NOT ONE OF THE FIRM'S DOZEN OR SO CONTRACTS HELD WATER.

(Metaphor: double use of actions associated with the word "water")

Exaggeration

This is known in literary circles as "hyperbole." A bit of well-placed exaggeration serves to paint your subject in vivid and therefore more memorable terms. This is another one that's easy to overdo; be judicious. It works best with kickers. For example:

- "Roach the size of a Rolls Royce"
- "Killer rabbit"
- "Kamikaze pelican"

Human Terms

Stories dealing with a great number of facts and figures often get lost on the average listener or viewer simply because he or she can't relate to them. It's your challenge to translate those figures into terms people can understand. This might take a little quick arithmetic on your part, but the results are well worth it. For instance, suppose you're doing a story about oil exports and find that the gasoline usage has gone down by one million gallons a year. The average person can't comprehend the concept of one million gallons of gasoline. So ask yourself this: What does one gallon of gasoline mean to you personally? How much gasoline do you burn each week? Roughly 20 gallons? If you use 20 gallons of gasoline a week, it would take you 50,000 weeks to burn a million gallons—that's 962 years! Now you get the picture—and you can put it in just those terms for the viewer:

> IF YOU BURN ABOUT 20 GALLONS OF GASOLINE A WEEK . . . A MILLION
> GALLONS WOULD LAST YOU 962 YEARS.

Exercise

At this point, we're going to use some of the principles outlined above to take apart and fix a poorly written story.

Here's an example of how not to write:

> AN APPARENT ONE-CAR ACCIDENT HAS CLAIMED THE LIFE OF A LOCAL MAN.
> POLICE SAY FOR SOME REASON A RED 1987 FORD TAURUS DRIVEN BY 38-YEAR-
> OLD JOHN SMITH OF 1237 GONER ROAD IN TUCSON WENT OUT OF CONTROL ON
> PRESTON LANE . . . FLIPPED . . . ROLLED DOWN AN EMBANKMENT . . . AND
> LANDED UPSIDE DOWN IN A DRAINAGE DITCH FILLED WITH WATER FROM LAST
> NIGHT'S STORMS. APPARENTLY THE DRIVER WASN'T KILLED BY THE IMPACT BUT
> RATHER DROWNED AFTER BEING TRAPPED IN THE WRECKAGE. IT HAPPENED
> ABOUT SIX THIS MORNING. THE WRECK WAS WITNESSED BY ANOTHER
> MOTORIST. THE CAUSE OF THE MISHAP IS BEING INVESTIGATED BY POLICE.

The second sentence alone is so filled with facts, adjectives and dependent clauses that in one breath, the writer is telling the viewer:

1 Where the facts came from (attribution)
2 The name of the driver
3 The age of the driver
4 The driver's home town
5 The driver's address
6 The make of the vehicle involved
7 The model of the vehicle involved
8 The year of manufacture of the vehicle involved
9 The color of the vehicle involved
10 The name of the street involved
11 That police don't know the cause of the accident

12 That the car flipped and rolled
13 That it landed in a drainage ditch
14 That is landed upside down
15 That the ditch was full of water
16 That it rained last night

That's 16 facts in one sentence!

And its length isn't this sentence's only sin. It also begins and ends in passive voice. In grammatical terms, the subject of this sentence is the 1987 Ford Taurus, but in actual fact the subject of the story is John Smith, and the story is about how our subject met his grisly and untimely end. Because the subject of the sentence doesn't match the subject of the story, the viewer is hard-pressed to figure out which is which, and thus finds it harder to understand what's going on.

Though this copy is technically accurate and grammatically correct, its style is atrocious. Yet copy just like it airs on TV and radio stations every day (this is taken from an actual example of a story that went out on one station's air). How can we fix it?

For one thing, the second sentence is so loaded with facts that it can be broken up into an entire paragraph, and that's what you should set out to do. Each major fact should get its own separate sentence, rather than one sentence attempting to convey several major facts.

Again, apply the Mom Rule. How would you relate this story if you were telling it to her? Chances are you'd say something like, "Hey, did you hear about the guy who ran off the road into a drainage ditch last night and drowned?" Why would you start that way? Because the unexpected, gruesome fate of a guy who died unexpectedly while doing nothing more offensive than driving down the road is the single most interesting and memorable aspect of the story. It's something that could have happened to anybody—which happens to be precisely what makes this story newsworthy. The lead to your story therefore should accomplish the same purpose as the opening gambit to your conversation with mom.

After capturing your mom's attention with that opening line, chances are she'd respond with a question like "No! What happened?" At this point, you'd likely continue your story, starting at the beginning and continuing in chronological order until you reach the end of your story—the outcome of which you've already revealed in your opening remark. Your news copy has to accomplish essentially the same thing. Here's one way to do it, applying the above rules:

LAST NIGHT'S STORMS ARE PARTIALLY TO BLAME FOR A TRAFFIC DEATH THIS MORNING. A TUCSON MAN DROWNED WHEN HIS CAR RAN OFF THE ROAD INTO A FLOODED DITCH. IT HAPPENED ABOUT SIX THIS MORNING ON PRESTON LANE. ACCORDING TO POLICE . . . THE CAR WENT OUT OF CONTROL . . . RAN OFF THE

ROAD . . . FLIPPED . . . AND ROLLED. IT LANDED UPSIDE DOWN IN A DRAINAGE DITCH STILL FILLED WITH RUNOFF FROM LAST NIGHT'S THUNDERSTORMS. THE DRIVER DROWNED. ANOTHER MOTORIST SAW THE WHOLE THING HAPPEN. . . BUT THE CAUSE OF THE CRASH REMAINS A MYSTERY. POLICE HAVE IDENTIFIED THE VICTIM. HE'S 38-YEAR-OLD JOHN SMITH OF 1237 GONER ROAD IN TUCSON.

This particular version of the story has all the facts of the first, except the make, model and year of the car, which aren't particularly pertinent. The sentences are short and conversational, and each contains a smaller number of facts. Everything is written in active voice, with action following the subject rather than vice versa. Note that it doesn't contain many of the creative techniques outlined earlier; they aren't necessary in this instance. The story is much easier to understand in one take than the previous version, and its style much more closely matches the form a two-sided conversation about the same event would likely take.

Conclusion

As we've shown you, there are a number of techniques you can use to make your copy memorable and effective, but the most important thing to keep in mind is that you must not emphasize creativity at the expense of clarity and brevity. Don't let efforts to jazz up your writing get in the way of delivering information that the viewers or listeners can understand on their first attempt. Remember the caution about alliteration, word plays and the like. *Don't overdo it.*

🗁 Do's and Don'ts for Writing Leads and Other Copy

Do
- "Sell" the story.
- Use preview and review.
- Use the "Mom Rule."
- Make stories relevant to listeners/viewers; remember WII-FM.

Don't
- Start writing until you decide what the story is about.
- Put too many facts in a lead.
- Write in "TV speak."
- Break from chronology more than once.

DEADLY COPY SINS AND HOW TO AVOID THEM

Four Words That Kill Good Broadcast Copy

"Allegedly"

> **Question:** When is it safe to "call names" on the air?
>
> **Answer:** Hardly ever. Not even if you say "allegedly." On-air name calling is what funds Caribbean vacations for libel lawyers.

The words "alleged" and "allegedly" are the single most abused and misused words in television. Why? Because too many writers believe the words stand as shields protecting them from litigation and freeing them to make statements they couldn't otherwise make. Unfortunately, this feeling of protection is a delusion. According to Gregg Thomas, First Amendment lawyer with the prestigious firm of Holland and Knight, the word "has no value." Thomas says reporters who liberally sprinkle the word "allegedly" into their copy are practicing "condom journalism." "The word is vastly overused," he says, "because somebody feels it has some pro-phylactic effect" and allows writers to "avoid responsibility for mak-ing a declarative statement." But the word doesn't impress judges or juries. "It offers no protection whatsoever," Thomas says.

Name calling is one area in which writing in a conversational style—the way people really talk—can get you into serious trouble. Why? Because when it comes to general conversations about figures arrested, charged or convicted of heinous crimes, members of the public tend to assume the person involved is guilty and speak about him or her accordingly. As a journalist, you don't have that option—not even if you couch your name calling with the word "allegedly" and its cousins.

Example

Let's say you're writing a story about a high-profile child molestation case in which the defendant, John Doe, to the surprise of many, was able to come up with enough cash to make bail. A casual conversation with Mom about this incident might go something like this:

CAN YOU BELIEVE IT? THAT CHILD MOLESTER GOT OUT!

A casual conversation with close friends might be even more direct:

CAN YOU BELIEVE IT? THAT DIRTBAG DOE GOT OUT!

As you sit down to write your own lead, you're faced with a prob-lem. One, you want to write in the same conversational style, but you realize (we hope) that you can't use the word "dirtbag" or any like it. Also, you want to be careful not to convict the defendant on the air. So, you write something like this:

JOHN DOE . . . THE ALLEGED CHILD MOLESTER . . . IS OUT OF JAIL.

There are several problems. One, the sentence isn't conversational; aside from professional journalists, few people use the word "alleged" in casual conversation. Two, it's sleazy; in this sentence, through use of the word "alleged," we're calling Doe a really ugly name without attribution, without allowing him to face his accusers. Three, what if Doe didn't do it? If your facts aren't straight, the word "alleged" will give you about as much protection as an umbrella in a hurricane. Because you didn't make an attribution, a jury is more likely to decide that you were simply careless with the facts—and jurors might even attribute the accusation to you *personally.*

The problem is that whenever you call some specific individual a name—such as "criminal," "killer," "child molester," "embezzler" and the like—essentially you're drawing a conclusion. If the facts overwhelmingly support that conclusion, then you're probably safe. But if the facts are at all in dispute—as they almost always are in criminal cases—then that's another matter.

There's another problem with the word "allegedly." It's a lazy word that cheats the audience of details. It's a shortcut around the facts. Strike the word, and insert the facts. Let's take the case of John Doe, the alleged child molester, and the example lead "JOHN DOE, THE ALLEGED CHILD MOLESTER, GOT OUT OF JAIL TODAY."

Which of the following conclusions can we comfortably and safely draw from that sentence?

1 The defendant's name is John Doe.
2 John Doe got out of jail today.
3 Police have charged Doe—or, at very least, have charged him in the past—with molesting at least one child.

Answer

Only 1 and 2. If you also drew conclusion number 3, you're not alone. Probably a good portion of the audience would have drawn the same conclusion. However, that conclusion can't be drawn from the lead as presented, and it's a good example of why the words "allege" and "allegedly" are so dangerous. The lead doesn't make plain who's making the allegations or give any hint as to how strong the case might be. Who says Doe is a child molester? Police? His neighbors? Sidewalk graffiti? From the lead presented above, any of the following could be true:

- The DA's office brought the charges; it's a strong case, and prosecutors are angry Doe is out.
- An individual police officer made the arrest and filled out a complaint, but the DA hasn't had a chance to study the paperwork and has no idea whether there's a case.
- Doe's next-door neighbor made the complaint and swore out a warrant for Doe's arrest, but the DA hasn't yet been able to substantiate her allegation.
- Doe is under indictment.
- Doe isn't under indictment; the grand jury hasn't seen the case yet.
- The DA privately believes there's no case and told the magistrate that he or she wouldn't be opposed to letting Doe out on bond and, in fact, plans to drop the charges after the publicity dies down.

If police have indeed charged Doe with the crime of molestation, then you're safe. But if not, then you're potentially in trouble. Even if police haven't charged Doe, you might get away with the above copy—for one story. But what happens when the 11 p.m. producer rewrites your copy for his or her newscast? He or she might draw a false conclusion from the sloppy copy you wrote. Thus you might get a lead story for 11 p.m. reading, "JOHN DOE . . . A MAN POLICE SAY IS A CHILD MOLESTER . . . IS FREE TONIGHT." This sentence is now completely divorced from the truth, and you and your employer are in trouble.

Here's another way to look at it. As mentioned, your job is to write to the facts. Take this sentence: "DOE ALLEGEDLY MOLESTED A 3-YEAR-OLD GIRL WHO LIVES NEXT DOOR." Which fact are you trying to present here? That Doe did it? Or that someone says he did? Unless you were there personally, you can't say whether Doe did it. Therefore, you can only say that someone *says* he did. Your story, then, is about the *allegation,* not about the act of molestation. Let me say it again: you're writing about an accusation, not a crime. This is a crucially important point, and it's paramount that you remember it to clarify your thinking and writing on the matter. The molestation is, for all you know, fictional. Stick to the facts, and the facts are that someone is accusing John Doe of molesting someone. Don't structure your sentence as if Doe actually did it, with only the word "allegedly" making the difference between an accusation and an on-air conviction. Structure your sentence and story around the accusation itself. Tell us who's making the accusation, then delve as much as you can into the quality and soundness of that accusation. Bring out the players: tell us who they are, what they have to say and how likely they are to be telling the truth. Forget the words "alleged" or "allegedly." Tell the audience what you know, with specific attribution: "SEVEN NEIGHBORS ACCUSED HIM OF MOLESTING THEIR CHILDREN. BUT TONIGHT JOHN DOE IS A FREE MAN."

Dropping the word "allegedly" will accomplish three very important goals. First, it will force you to write a much more clear, concise story. Second, your story will be much more conversational in style and therefore more understandable and memorable. And last, but certainly not least, it will stick to the facts and therefore be true. As any lawyer will tell you, the only *absolute* defense in a libel case is the truth. By taking a little extra time to present the facts, you'll be doing a better job with your audience and you will be less likely to get into trouble. The word "allegedly" stands in the way and serves no purpose. Lose it.

The threat of legal action shouldn't be your only motivation for dropping the word "allegedly." Regardless of whether you get sued, the abuses this word invites simply aren't fair to the person named. The Sixth Amendment of the U.S. Constitution gives every person the right to face his or her accuser. Journalists sometimes short-circuit the spirit of the law by hiding behind the word "allegedly." Drop the word. Come out from behind cover. Spell out who the accusers are with specific attribution. It's the fair and socially responsible thing to do.

If none of the above arguments convinces you, consider this point. As a beginning producer or reporter, you're much more likely to land a job and advance up the career ladder if your résumé reel doesn't contain eight uses of the nonconversational word "allegedly" within one 90-second period (which, so far, stands as a record among tapes I've reviewed personally).

"Suspects"

If "alleged" is the single most abused word, then "suspects" has to be a close second. A suspect is a specific, *named* individual who is charged, jailed or wanted in connection with a specific act. There is no such thing as an "unknown suspect." It's an oxymoron, a self-contradictory phrase describing something that doesn't exist. For a person to be a suspect, police or investigators have to know who he or she is. They must have a specific name in mind or on paper.

If someone holds up a bank but police have no idea who the person as, "THE SUSPECT POINTED A GUN AT THE TELLER AND DEMANDED MONEY." You can refer to the perpetrator as a man, woman, bandit, robber, gunman, gunwoman, street person or whatever (but please don't use the word "perpetrator"—see the Do's and Don'ts at the end of this chapter). Note that in this case you *can* use red-letter, name-calling words such as "bandit" and "robber"; you're not calling anyone names on the air because *you haven't named anyone*. But if the robber is unknown, you can't refer to him or her as a suspect. The reason is simple: if police don't yet suspect anyone, then there are no suspects!

You're not convicting anyone on the air if you write words like "WITNESSES SAY THE GUNMAN FIRED TWO SHOTS . . . KILLING THE VICTIM INSTANTLY," even if police have named a suspect. But you can't substitute the word "SUSPECT" for "GUNMAN" without careful and proper attribution. If there's a dead body with a bullet hole in it, and if it was a case of murder, then there was a gunman, and you can write about him and even speculate about him. What the gunman did or didn't do isn't the dispute in this case. The dispute, and the issue to be addressed in court, is whether the suspect was the gunman.

Bottom line: if there was a crime, then there was a bad guy. You can write about him generically and call him any names you want, provided of course that your story is factual. Where you have to be extremely cautious is when you begin saying that a *specific individual* was the bad guy. "Bandit," "robber," "killer" and the like are generic terms not describing any specific individual. "Suspect" is a specific term describing a specific individual, an individual who has rights and, presumably, a lawyer just aching to sue you. But if the specific individual is unknown, then there is no suspect.

Thus you can't write a sentence such as "THE SUSPECT IS ON THE LOOSE" if police have no idea who he is. Instead, you have to write "THE BANDIT IS ON THE LOOSE."

Conversely, you can write "THE SUSPECT IS IN JAIL." But you can't write "THE BANDIT IS IN JAIL" unless you've never been sued and are curious to see what it's like.

A final point about attribution. The only truly safe stories are those that attribute the facts and accusations to an official source, such as police officers, fire officials or prosecutors. In 49 of 50 states (South Carolina being the only exception) journalists have a qualified privilege to quote government officials and official documents. Generally speaking, you can't be sued for reporting what a police officer or prosecutor says, even if it later turns out the official was wrong or even lying. But the further you get away from official sources, the more dangerous the game becomes. Handle witness accounts very carefully when reporting accusations against individuals. In libel terms, *their* speech is *your* speech. If a witness makes an untrue libelous statement, *you* are liable and can be sued.

"Apparently"

Consider the following sentence:

APPARENTLY SMITH LOST CONTROL OF HIS CAR . . . WHICH RAN INTO A DITCH.

The only thing apparent here is that the writer doesn't have a clue what really happened. Did the steering fail? Did the driver swerve to avoid a moose? Was it a mob hit staged to look like an accident? Did the driver commit suicide? Who knows? The only thing we know for sure is that we don't know. In this case, the writer is using the word "apparently" to camouflage the fact that he or she has no facts and is just making a guess about what really happened.

Remember, it *is permissible* not to have the answers. In such cases, 'fess up. Tell the viewer you don't know. Explain what you do know, and outline the current speculation on what may have happened. Here's a fix of the above sentence using these guidelines:

THE CAR RAN OFF THE ROAD AND CRASHED IN A DITCH. BECAUSE ROAD CONDITIONS WERE DRY . . . POLICE ARE AT A LOSS TO EXPLAIN IT.

Or,

THE ROAD WAS DRY AT THE TIME. POLICE ARE NOW CHECKING TO SEE WHETHER THE CAR'S STEERING FAILED.

There *are* some perfectly acceptable uses of the word "apparent" and its derivatives. It's OK to use the word, for instance, to introduce a speculative conclusion, provided the conclusion is supported by the facts. For example:

IT APPEARS LETTUCE MAY SOON COST YOU A BIT MORE. WHOLESALE PRICES HIT AN ALL-TIME HIGH FOR THE SECOND WEEK IN A ROW TODAY. THE NUMBERS CRUNCHERS SAY IF THAT TREND CONTINUES . . . IT WILL SHOW UP AT THE GROCERY COUNTER SOONER OR LATER.

"Undetermined"

The fourth most worthless word in television is the word "undetermined" in connection with a bank robbery or other theft. One, it's not conversational. When was the last time you turned to someone and said, "The robber got away with an undetermined amount of cash"?

Two, it's not factual—or at least, it's not always factual—and it leaves the viewer with a false assumption that the amount of money missing will be determined. Guess what, folks. Often they know *exactly* how much money the bandit got away with, for the simple reason that he probably has a "bait bag" with a dye bomb inside it and a well-known amount of bait cash. If they don't know, they'll find out very quickly. But believe this: *They might never tell you how much cash the bandit got.* There's a very simple reason for this, and it's a good one: revealing the amount of cash the bandit took is the worst form of advertising for the bank. The bandit may have escaped with a nice wad of cash. If the bank reveals the amount, it's essentially throwing out a challenge for other robbers to try to match or surpass the previous robber's haul.

As a matter of policy involving the public's safety, it makes sense for newsrooms to support this concept of not revealing the amount taken for bank robberies and other armed robberies. The exceptions are cases when the robber got very little, or a whole lot, such as Brinks holdups running into the millions, and the amount taken will be well-publicized elsewhere.

Therefore, drop the word "undetermined." It adds nothing and isn't conversational. If you feel it's crucial to make some reference to the cash amount—and there's some indication that (1) the amount is relevant, (2) police really don't know how much was taken and are trying to find out, and (3) they're going to share this information with you—then you should write specifically to that point. For example:

POLICE DON'T KNOW HOW MUCH CASH THE BANDIT GOT . . . BUT THEY DON'T THINK IT'S MUCH. THE BANK IS COUNTING ITS LOSSES AND HOPES TO HAVE THE ANSWER BY TONIGHT.

Summary—Example of a Completely Worthless Sentence

THE UNKNOWN SUSPECT ALLEGEDLY POINTED A GUN AT THE TELLER . . .
DEMANDED MONEY . . . AND APPARENTLY ESCAPED WITH AN UNDETERMINED
AMOUNT OF CASH.

Miscellaneous Do's and Don'ts for Writers

Many of these points have been made elsewhere, but we present them
here in bullet form to emphasize their importance.

Do's

- Do make frequent use of synonyms.
- Do make frequent use of time-specific references, such as "this
  morning," "this afternoon," "tonight."
- Do make frequent use of "you" inclusive words, such as "you,"
  "us," "we."
- Do introduce the people you're interviewing. Don't rely on a
  super to do it for you. Hint: you don't necessarily have to give
  the person's proper name as long as you give us some
  indication of what relevance he or she has to the story. For
  example: "SOME RESIDENTS FEEL THE MURDER WAS
  JUSTIFIED" is a perfectly fine introduction to a bite with a
  neighbor. If you do use both the person's proper name and his
  or her title in your track, it's important to put the person's
  relevance to the story first. So give the title first, then the name.
- Do use good grammar when referencing groups. Many people
  confuse singular and plural when referencing a group with a
  pronoun. In the form of English spoken in the United States,
  collective nouns take the singular. So when writing for a U.S.
  audience, a group is an "it," not a "they." For example: "THE
  UNION SAYS THEY'RE GOING TO STRIKE" isn't correct.
  Make it "THE UNION SAYS IT WILL STRIKE."
- Write in active voice.

Don'ts

- Don't begin successive sentences with the same word or words
  if it can be avoided. This makes your copy sound labored and
  uninspiring.
- For the same reason, don't use the same word to describe an
  object again and again in close proximity.

- Don't use clichés (such as "up in arms," "packing winds" and the like). There are exceptions. Sometimes, the cliché can serve a higher purpose, such as setting up a word play. For example: "RESIDENTS ARE UP IN ARMS ABOUT A CONTRACTOR UP TO NO GOOD." Sometimes you can turn a cliché around to your own purposes, in essence making fun of it. For example: "Crunching the scales" as a derivative of the cliché "tipping the scales."

- Don't use "police blotter" terms, such as "perpetrator," "at large" and the like. They're not conversational and will hamper your efforts to connect with your viewer. Plus, they'll make you sound like Dick Tracy.

- Though there are few "nevers" in this business, here's a safe one: never, ever, ever refer to a criminal or suspected criminal as a "gentleman," as a substitute for "the man." For example: "WITNESSES SAY THE GENTLEMAN KILLED THREE SCHOOL CHILDREN AT RANDOM . . . THEN FLED." Most references of this nature that wind up on the air are done live, off the cuff. Avoid this like the plague. If, on the other hand, the perpetrator was well-dressed, then devote a separate sentence to that fact. Don't call him a gentleman! His actions give lie to your words. Or worse than that, it sounds as though you're sympathizing with him.

- Don't present a confusing mishmash of pronouns without clear antecedents. When you use the words "he," "she," "it," "him," "her," "they" and so forth, make sure we know who you're talking about. For example: "LAST NIGHT . . . JOHN SMITH ATTACKED THE MAYOR'S CREDIBILITY. TONIGHT HE'S TAKING HIS CASE TO THE PUBLIC." Who's taking his case to the public? Smith? Or the mayor?

- Don't leave out the verb! For example: "QUESTIONS IN THE BAY AREA CONCERNING MISCONDUCT." This isn't a sentence, much less a lead. There are occasions when sentence fragments such as this one can work—provided that's the way someone would really talk. This isn't one of them. When in doubt, put in a verb.

- Don't put the allegation ahead of the attribution. For example: "ALL POLITICIANS ARE JERKS. SO SAYS BILL SMITH OF THE CITIZENS' GROUP 'TAX WATCHDOGS.'" For a split second, the anchor reading this sentence appears to the audience to be the one with the bad opinion of politicians. Don't place him or her in that precarious position.

- Don't make careless generalizations. For example: "RESIDENTS OF HUDSON BAY ARE SHOCKED ABOUT THE MURDER OF AN ELDERLY WOMAN." For all you know, she may have been a witch and they're all dancing on her grave. Unless you've talked to each and every resident, this sentence is a dangerous and possibly untrue generalization. On the other hand, if you or a reporter has talked to some shocked residents, then you can comfortably write "THE MURDER OF AN ELDERLY WOMAN HAS SHOCKED A LOT OF PEOPLE IN HUDSON BAY."

- Don't use "TV speak." (See the extensive discussion on this subject in Chapter 3.)
- Don't begin a lead or any other sentence with a dependent clause. For example: "HIS HAIR HAVING BURST INTO FLAME, FRED BEGAN BOBBING FOR APPLES WITH NEW ENTHUSIASM."

INTERVIEWING: GETTING THE FACTS AND THE FEELINGS

Interviewing members of your community, important people visiting your community, or newsmakers you travel to visit is a vital part of the broadcast writing and reporting process. Interviews provide background information for your story, and they provide sound bites for your package or VO/SOT, or the radio equivalent of those television news story forms. It's important to remember that one of the unique strengths of broadcast news is its ability to transmit the experience of what happens at the scene of an event to members of your audience. The people you interview and what they say to you are key parts of that process.

Interviews are essentially conversations with members of your community or those who have something to say that your viewers/listeners would find important or interesting. And when your story is broadcast, you share those conversations with your audience. So you want to let the people you interview tell about what's happening. Let them tell the story themselves from their point of view, to the degree that they can. You want to let their personalities come through so that people watching or listening will feel something for them. The average person wasn't at the scene of the story and doesn't understand what happened. Through your interviews, you can take the viewers/listeners to the scene to experience what happened and understand it through the words of those who were there.

The people you interview are the people whose voices will be heard in your newscast. So remember to talk and listen to a diversity of "regular" people in your community. Don't rely entirely on the experts, the officials, the usual voices. As a reporter, you can give voice to the voiceless in your community by interviewing them for your stories.

Those you choose to interview and the tone you take when you interview them will also contribute to the image your audience will have of you as a reporter and of your station as a local business. It's often the case, particularly with beginning reporters in smaller markets, that the reporters are young, single, from someplace else, and looking to move on to a larger market as soon as possible. This is the opposite of what's true of many of the members of the viewing/listening audience, who tend to be older, married with children and a mortgage, born in the community, and planning to stay in this town that's their home and workplace. So stop and think and ask about who's in your audience, what their lives are like, and what their concerns and interests are.

There are several steps to take to get yourself ready to conduct an interview and to do the interview itself. These include:

Thinking Ahead

When you're thinking about which people to interview, ask yourself: "How do I make this story real for my viewers and listeners? How do I make a difference in my community? And how do I tell this story clearly and in a compelling way?" You don't want to get in an interviewing rut, going to the same experts and officials time after time, although this is easy and quick and sometimes unavoidable. Take some time to be thoughtful and creative in choosing whom to interview. Some interview subjects are given to you, not chosen, as in news conferences and emergency situations. But other situations offer you more opportunities to choose from among a broad spectrum of citizens.

If water rates are going up, you might think in terms of interviewing the people who come to the window at city hall to pay their bills, or the person who receives the water bill payments at the window or who answers the phone and listens to comments from local residents about the rate increase. You might ask that person what people are saying to her when they pay their water bills. If the story is about the economy, you might first ask your neighbors and colleagues, "Do you know anybody who's out of work, who's been laid off, or who's looking for work?" People who are out of a job and looking for work will have firsthand knowledge about the state of the economy as it affects their lives. These individuals can add depth, perspective and context to your story, which "official sources" may not be able to provide.

Interviews with affected individuals "humanize" your stories. For example, if the welfare allowance for a woman with two children is raised from $188 a month to $201 a month, a mother of two can put a human face on the story by telling you what $13 more a month will buy.

Being Prepared

You want to prepare for your interview by learning as much as possible about your subject in advance. That means research. Read what you can about the subject so that you'll be familiar with it. Ask other people in your newsroom and station what's important to ask about the subject. Brainstorm with them, to the extent that time constraints allow. The person you'll spend the most time with on any given TV story is your photographer. He or she can help you prepare by suggesting questions and offering perspective. Talk with your photographer as you plan each story, and work together as a team.

You want to have some idea what you're going to ask and in what order before you go out on a story. Prepare at least a few questions, and write them down to use as a memory jog if you get nervous or draw a blank. You don't want to be "married" to these questions and follow them blindly in spite of what the interviewee says, but you do want to have a focus beforehand on your story. Too often, students and young professionals go into an interview with a list of questions and essentially read them to their interviewees. When that happens, it *isn't* a conversation. But a list can be helpful, because you don't want to be fishing around and asking questions about everything in the hope of getting a usable sound bite. Interviews have a dual purpose. They're a way for the reporter/writer to gather information, and they're a way to gather usable sound bites. Do the information-gathering part of the interview off camera and the sound-bite-gathering part on camera.

In the information-gathering part of the interview, what people tell you provides details and even language you can use in your story. NBC correspondent Bob Dotson was one of the many reporters who covered the Union, South Carolina, story about Susan Smith, who drove her car into a lake with her two young sons strapped into the back seat. One of the recovery divers told Dotson that the first thing the diver saw in the submerged car was "a tiny hand pressed against glass." Dotson used that detail and those words at the top of his report.

When you're writing your TV news package or radio wrap, you'll be weaving together the words in your narration track with natural sound and with sound bites (and video in the case of television) you've gathered in the field. So the writing for your story actually begins in the field as the interviews and natural sound are being recorded. Before you go out into the field, you want to be prepared and know your subject so that you'll know what you're talking about and asking about.

If your interview is part of a spot news story, and there's no time to prepare, you'll be drawing on the base of knowledge you've accumulated from reading your local newspaper, reading news magazines and books, surfing the Internet, meeting people in your community and keeping up with their topics of concern and conversation. So always pay attention to what's in the news, and pay attention to what the controversies and disagreements and issues are within your community. These are daily habits you want to cultivate. They'll serve you well over time.

Interviewing is equal parts art, craft and science. And the first question you ask can dictate the entire experience. If people are offended by what you ask them or by the tone in which you ask it, it will color the whole interview. If people feel they know and can trust you, things will go more smoothly. So, people skills are essential. Tell the person up front who you are, which station you represent and what you're doing. For example, "I'm Jane Smith from Channel 2. We're doing a story about the heat. We'd like to talk with you about how it's affecting your company, family, business, health"—whatever the focus of your story is. Don't tell the interviewee beforehand what the specific questions will be. That leads to rehearsed answers. Just tell him or her the topic of the questions. Use a professional and conversational tone of voice.

You must also remember to ask questions that can be answered, and that can be answered with something *other* than yes or no. What made the Chris Farley interview skits on *Saturday Night Live* so hilarious was Farley's own bumbling, nervous attempt at being an interviewer. He would ask long rambling "do you remember when" questions. All his interviewees could answer was yes or no. We learn nothing from such interviews.

Knowing the Mechanics of Interviewing

Remember to look straight in the eyes of the person you're interviewing and maintain eye contact with him or her. Strong eye contact seems to help divert the person's attention away from the equipment, which makes for a less nervous interviewee. Don't fidget with your notes or with your hair or wave the microphone around. When possible, use a clip-on microphone. When interviewing for TV, ask the person you're interviewing to look at you, not at the camera. Your back will be to the photographer, who will get a shot over your shoulder of the interviewee's face.

The microphone should point toward the interviewee and be about 6 inches below his or her mouth in normal situations. In a situation in which there's loud ambient noise, such as a cheering crowd at a football game, put the microphone closer. (Clip-on mics don't work well in these situations.) As you ask your questions, point the mic at yourself and record your own questions because you may want to use them in the edited piece. However, be sure to have the mic directed at the interviewee for all of his or her comment. If the mic is moving back toward the interviewee as he or she begins to answer, the audio might not be usable.

As often as possible, conduct the interview at the scene of the event or in the setting of the story, whether in the factory or the classroom or the orange grove. Be sure to find out your interviewee's full name, how to spell it, and how to pronounce it correctly. Write down his or her phone number in case you need to call back later. If the person is an "official," get a title.

In the interview itself, you want to be direct, clear, straightforward, empathetic and respectful. You want to be frank, sincere and courteous. You want to ask precise, specific questions, one at a time. You want to show interest in what the person is saying by looking directly at him or her. And you want to actively listen to what the person is saying to you. That's the only way you can come up with logical follow-up questions. In many ways, this kind of active listening is really watching, for you must pay attention to any nods of the head, frowns, clinching of the teeth or tightening of the facial muscles that may tell more about the interviewee's true reactions than what he or she is saying to you. Also keep in mind that people sometimes lie or "shade" the truth.

Your questions should be direct, simple and open-ended. Asking people open-ended questions allows them to show what they know. You want to get them talking, by asking questions that start with why, how and what. Ask them, "What is the proposal designed to accomplish?" Or "What is your understanding of how the accident happened?" Or "What do you love about your hobby?" Or "Where does the agency's report fall short?"

You must also understand what the interviewees mean by what they say, and you may need to ask for clarification to make sure. You may need to say, "What do you mean when you say . . .?" Or "Tell me a little bit more about that." Or "Give me an example of that."

Ask questions that cause the person to think, to reflect, to search and, if necessary, to clear up any discrepancies in earlier statements he or she may have made on the same subject. Challenge the interviewee to respond to different viewpoints or to answer critics by asking, "How do you respond to Councilman White, who says that this is only a short-term fix and won't solve the problem long-term?" Or "Why are you so determined to push this legislation through when there's so much opposition to it from the teachers' union?" Attribute challenges such as these so that it doesn't sound like you're the one making them.

You may also need to ask the people you interview to summarize what they've just said in one or two sentences, especially if they tend to ramble on or talk in long run-on sentences. You may need to interrupt them and re-ask the question if they go way off track. You need short answers—sound bites—you can use in your story. Because you'll be using audio/videotapes or disks to record your interview, and you or someone else will be editing it later, you can ask the question a second time if the interviewee flubs up the answer the first time. Or you can ask the question another way. Or you can ask it a third time. Take the time to get the most understandable, succinct statement you can. Tape is inexpensive. After you've asked all of your questions, ask if there's anything the interviewee would like to add. Then wait.

Leave some editing "space" during the interview. Let the person you're interviewing finish answering each question and pause for a couple of seconds before you ask the next question or interrupt the speaker in some way. This can be tough to learn, but it becomes important in the editing booth when you're working on deadline. You don't want to "step on" the sound bites. Also, don't listen out loud by saying "OK" or "Uh-Huh" in response to everything your interviewee says. You don't want to sound as if you're agreeing (or disagreeing) with what the person is saying. If you're off camera, you can slightly nod or tilt your head to confirm to the person you're interviewing that you're listening and paying attention.

You want to stay in control of the interview and not let yourself be used. This is particularly important in live situations. One California TV reporter, interviewing a member of the Hell's Angels motorcycle gang, live, was shocked when the biker grabbed the microphone away and began swearing during the 6 o'clock news. In hindsight, perhaps the reporter should have anticipated such an outcome. But once the biker had the microphone in his hand, the reporter was helpless to end the interview. It was up to the director and producer in the control room to end it instead and for the anchor to apologize. Remember, you hold the microphone. You stay in control. There are other, less extreme situations to watch out for. At times, politicians and others who are accustomed to being interviewed frequently won't answer the question you ask; instead they'll respond with something they want you to use in your story. You might ask the governor what's being done to curb illegal immigration, and the answer he gives you may be that he's working hard to provide tax relief for home owners this year (a part of his campaign platform). So pay close attention to what he's actually telling you. If you think a politician is avoiding a question, ask it again. And again. Then ask him why he's avoiding the question.

If you're writing a 90-second TV story, you'll be looking for sound bites that run about 10 seconds in length; that's about one sentence long. If you're writing a 4-minute story, you'll be looking for sound bites that may run 20 seconds in length; that's about two or three sentences long. Radio sound bites range from about 5 to 15 seconds in length and are usually in the lower end of that range. Sometimes you'll be looking for a long series of quick sound bites from your interview subjects. If you're interviewing college students about where they'll be traveling for spring break, you may just ask them that one question, "Where are you going for spring break?" When the sound bites are edited together into the final piece, the answers will then be: " Cancun . . . Austin . . . home to Miami . . . London . . . Phoenix . . . I'm staying here to study." In this case, one- or two-word answers are all you're looking for.

If your station has cameras or audio recorders with a time code, it's helpful to set your watch and the camera/recorder time to real time, so that you can just glance at your watch and make a note of the time when you hear a sound bite that's one you're pretty sure you'll want to use. This makes the editing process go more smoothly and quickly. It's particularly important when you're working on a daily deadline or when you're covering a trial, for example. You may wind up with four or five field tapes.

It's also helpful for television reporters to carry audiocassette recorders with them to their interviews. This way, reporters can pick out their sound bites by listening to the audiotape while they're riding back to the station in the van. When choosing a sound bite, remember to listen to the phrasing of the sentence. You want to cut the sound bite at the end of a phrase or the end of a sentence when the voice falls. You don't want to cut someone off in midsentence, when the voice is rising.

Because you or someone else will most likely be editing these interviews later, it will be important for your photographer to shoot some cutaways of you (in TV interviews) when the interview is finished. These are essentially shots of you listening to your interviewee. When the photographer is shooting these, ask your interviewee another question so that you can look at her knowledgeably and listen attentively. Hold the mic as you did for the actual interview. Don't nod your head, shake your head, laugh or smile or talk while the photographer is shooting these cutaways. Just listen attentively. The cutaways will be used in the editing process, and you want to be shown listening, not agreeing or disagreeing or laughing at what your interviewee is saying.

Most interviews are conducted with both you and your interviewee standing or with both of you seated. The point is that you want your eye levels to be equal. If you're interviewing a person in a wheelchair, you sit in a chair. If you're interviewing children, be extra patient with them, and get down to their eye level by sitting in a chair or getting down on your knees. If you're interviewing an NBA center, you might need to stand on a step stool or have him sit while you stand!

Dressing Appropriately

If you're going to interview a U.S. senator in her Washington, D.C., office, wear a suit. If you're going to interview a West Texas rancher, jeans and boots would be appropriate. If you're doing a live television report outside in Minnesota in the winter, you might want to wear as much clothing as you can scrounge up. Sometimes, informal attire for celebrities may give the interview a casual feel, and conversely, semiformal attire for people not usually the subject of interviews may be viewed as a sign of respect. Wear something sensible to work every day, and keep a pair of khaki slacks and some hiking boots in a suitcase by your desk for those times you're sent at a moment's notice to cover a fire or flood or chemical spill.

"Managing" the Interviewee

The camera/audio recorder intimidates many who are unfamiliar with it. And most "regular" people have never been interviewed or been on camera before. You may need to put your interviewees at ease and "warm them up" by asking a few easy questions to begin interviews. You don't want to start immediately with the toughest question you have, the one most likely to end the interview once it's asked. The photographer/sound tech can use this "warm up" time to double-check that the microphone is working and to help the interviewee get comfortable.

In the case of TV, remind the person you're interviewing to look at you during the interview and to ignore the camera and crew as best he or she can. It will then be up to you to be fair with this person and to establish your own rapport with him. No one wants to look "bad" during an interview or to stumble over words or to lose composure. No one appreciates leading questions. No one wants you to put words in his mouth. And no one likes to feel she's been "tricked" by the media. If the interviewee is in a tough spot, he may be anticipating a tough question, so don't wait *too* long to ask it. Often, people will rise to the occasion when they're asked really pointed questions. You don't have to ask hard questions in nasty, vitriolic ways. Overly aggressive, rude, dishonest reporters have left some members of the public with a wary attitude toward media practitioners, and they may be defensive until they get to know you individually as a member of the media in your market. Winning their trust can take some time.

Keep in mind also that not everyone wants to be interviewed and not everyone is good at it. And, because of company policy, some employees are essentially forbidden from talking with members of the media, and they'll be putting their jobs on the line if they talk to you. That's a powerful deterrent for them.

Your goal as a reporter is to inform the people in your community, not to panic or titillate or mislead them. When you're working on your story, you're working to answer the basic journalistic questions of who, what, when, where, why and how. When you're in the field and conducting interviews, you want to find out all the information you can about the story you're writing. If this is a conflict story, you want to identify spokespersons for all sides of the issue and talk with as many of them as possible.

But keep in mind that you absolutely do *not* want to turn your photographer's gear into a hundred-pound pencil and notepad. You're going to have to listen to this tape later and log all of it, and you don't need or want 60 minutes of interview for two quick, 10-second sound bites. Many questions are for background information, and you can take written notes on those off camera: information such as how old the person is or how long she's worked for the company. But others are for sound bites, and you want those to be sharply focused, narrow questions done on camera. You want to ask: "What did you see?" "What did you hear?" "What did you think?" "What did you feel?" "What led you to make that decision?" "What will you accomplish with this new program?" "What bothers you about that?" "How did you. . . ?" "What was it like to be. . . ?" These questions are open-ended and don't presuppose an answer. In contrast, it isn't informative to ask someone, "Isn't it about time we begin to clamp down on these violators?" That leads to a one-word yes/no answer and makes it appear the interviewer already has an opinion on the matter.

If at all possible, you want to avoid questions that result in yes/no answers. For example, if you ask someone, "Is it hot enough today?" his answer might be yes or no. But if you say to him, "The weather's so hot today, how would you describe it?" you'll get a sound bite you can probably use. This is especially true when interviewing children. If you ask a child "Are you having a good time in preschool?" her answer might be yes or no or simply a nod of the head. But if you ask her "What do you like best about preschool?" you'll get an answer such as "playing with computers" or "coloring in my coloring book" or "playing with my friends." In some cases, such as stonewalling by a politician or local official, if yes and no are the only answers the individual will provide, it can be effective to edit all the no's or yes's together into one long sound bite. Next time, the politician may give you more of an answer.

Telling Their Stories

Reporters can relay details more succinctly than "average" people, because reporters are trained storytellers. What reporters can't relay as effectively are the thoughts, feelings, attitudes and reactions of the people they interview. That's what sound bites are for. Your interviews are a way to get at what's in a person's mind, expressed in his or her own words. As often as possible you want to look for people who are telling this story, rather than people who are telling about this story. In other words, look for eyewitnesses you can interview. Look for those people who are directly affected by an action or event. Look for those who can provide the color, the details. Then let these people tell you what they went through, what it was like, what they see as the problem. (We'll have more about this in Chapter 9 as we look at the diamond approach to structuring a package.)

As a reporter, you're the one who can best summarize the objective information in the narration track or stand-up of your story. Those you interview are the ones who can best tell the subjective information about how they felt, about what they experienced, about how they live on $201 a month. They can tell you the ideas, the reactions, the opinions, the feelings, the fears, the challenges.

Being Sensitive

Beware of asking "how do you feel" questions when interviewing those in shock or in grief. Members of the audience often *know* how the grief-stricken feel. They can see how the person feels by looking at his face in your video, or by remembering a tragedy in their own lives. You'll appear immature at best and insensitive at worst for not knowing how it feels to lose a family member or neighbor or friend to a violent or sudden death. Think of something more informative to ask. "Give sorrow words," said Shakespeare, and many in grief can articulate their loss. But they and those around them may be in a daze, struggling to retain their composure and to understand what you're asking. Kindness and tact and patience will serve you well in these situations. You may want to approach someone in this situation without the camera/recorder. Any crew members with you can stand back a bit while you go up to introduce yourself. You might say, "What's happened is awful. And we're sorry to bother you right now. But we'd like to talk with you about what's happened."

Most people will do it, if approached in the right way. It's actually easier to get a "yes" response in person than by phone, so go ahead and approach people in this situation in person. If the person's son has been killed in an automobile accident, you might say, "We're so sorry about what happened. We'd like to talk with you about your son. What was he like? What did he like to do? We'd like to tell our audience what he was like as a person. Do you have any pictures you could share with us?" Or "What happened is a tragedy and I know you must be devastated." Sometimes people will just pick up on such a statement and start talking about what their son was like. If they're comfortable with you, they'll open up. But keep in mind that people know their rights—they know that they don't have to talk with you—and if you're standing on their private property, they know they can ask you to leave and expect you to comply.

Be sensitive to people and their situations. Many spot news stories are tragic, traumatic. They involve fires, murders, fatal accidents. Your interviewees are human, and you're in their faces with a microphone and maybe a camera too. This is their family or livelihood you're asking about. This is their home or business you're in. People are perceptive. If you're sincere and caring, your interviewees will pick up on that. If you're merely feigning sympathy, they'll pick up on that too. The interviews you've already conducted will have shaped your reputation as a reporter in the community. People will remember you from your previous work. Many will feel they know you and may already like and trust you. Of course, if this is your first interview, you're just starting to build your reputation in the market. How you handle those first few tough interviews will go a long way toward setting your reputation with the viewers/listeners in the market you're in.

Diana Pertmer has been a news reporter at WFLA-TV in Tampa, Florida (*www.wfla.com*), for more than 20 years. She knows from personal experience how much common courtesy and human kindness matter in these situations. Her most memorable interview wouldn't have ever happened had she not extended a simple courtesy on the worst day of one man's life. She and her photojournalist partner arrived at the scene of a violent murder.

A killer had somehow slipped inside the home of a young teenager, savaged her and escaped. Her family discovered the horror, and never set foot in the house again. Detectives on the scene told the news crew the parents were with the next-door neighbor. So when a man who fit the description of an anguished father walked to a car, Diane asked if he was the victim's dad. He said no, a relative. She asked if anyone in the family, considering the terrible circumstance, was available to answer a couple of questions. He said no. As he turned away, Diane told him she and her partner were sorry they had to be there and asked that he express their sympathies to the girl's parents.

She later learned that man was the girl's father. He agreed to an exclusive on-camera interview, because he said the news crew respected his family's grief and placed it above the demands of TV news. Diane says her experience underscores an important truth in reporting: compassion does not conflict with fairness. Both values create a foundation of trust usually necessary to negotiate an interview. Television is intimate. People in grief should feel that sharing their loss on TV won't be exploited.

But ordinary people thrust into extraordinary circumstances often have their own reasons to speak publicly in an interview. The father of the murder victim pleaded for help in finding the killer. He also shared memories of his daughter, an important acknowledgment that her life, however brief, mattered to others and should be recognized. Victims managing unwanted media attention after suffering a loss will often agree to an interview, if only to talk about what the loved one meant. It's helpful to request the family designate a spokesperson if emotions are especially raw.

Diane believes the most successful interviews come from demonstrating genuine interest in the person and the subject, no matter what the story is. In answering Diane's questions after his daughter was murdered, the victim's father offered a warning made compelling by his courage in going public: watch your children, warn them of the dangers out there, and never fail to tell them you love them.

Knowing the Power of Silence

Reporters can sometimes concentrate so much on the questions they're asking that they forget to *listen* to what their interviewees are saying. So this is a reminder to listen to the words your interviewees use. Listen carefully to the language they use to describe something. And remember also to *wait* during those "pregnant pauses." If you ask someone a question and she doesn't answer it right away, stay quiet and continue to look at her. Don't be too eager to jump in with the next question just to fill the silence and to keep the conversation going. Let the person you're interviewing pause and think for a moment, and then let her finish speaking. Sometimes the silences and the pauses themselves are as telling as the answers you thought you'd get. Sometimes the nonanswers and the evasions are more informative than the answers. In a memorable Barbara Walters interview with one of O. J.

Simpson's attorneys, there was an excruciatingly long pause before the attorney finally answered Walters' question about whether he believed O. J. Simpson is an innocent man. He never answered yes or no, but instead made a long statement that sometimes the guilty go free to prove a greater point and to right a greater wrong.

Checking Your Bias

The people you'll be interviewing are who they are: they look the way they look, and they are the age they are. Don't assume every business tycoon is a man. Don't assume every nurse practitioner is a woman. Don't make similar assumptions about race or age or anything else. Don't derail your interview by making inappropriate opening remarks, such as "I had no idea you would be. . . ." That says more about you than it says about the person you're supposed to interview. Just ask your questions. And don't assume that all men or women or teen-agers or Christians or motorcyclists think alike on any given topic. You're interviewing this person about what this person thinks or saw or experienced.

Reading between the Lines

As we alluded to before, people in the spotlight who are frequently interviewed sometimes develop a style of answering questions that allows them to use the media for their own purposes. You may find yourself in the position of asking a politician, for example, what he or she plans to do about a specific situation. Rather than answering the question, the person may respond with a sound bite about a totally different (but favorite and popular) subject and may then leave the room, pleading time constraints. This leaves you in the position of having only the one sound bite the person gave you, a sound bite that is completely off the subject but one the politician wants on the air.

Also, listen to what politicians don't say. The politician may say, "I categorically deny being in Laos on July 17th." The truth may be that the senator was in Laos on July 16th, and you'll have to read "between the lines" for your answer. So be prepared, be persistent and pay attention to what's being said to you. Remember that there's a difference between persistence and rudeness. You want to be persistent in searching for answers. Being rude won't help you find them. You want to be assertive but not abrasive. You'll be working in this market for some time, and you don't want to burn too many bridges before moving on to another market, if that's the career path you follow.

You're in a high-profile job. People will remember how you treat them, or someone close to them, or they'll hear about someone else's experience from neighbors or friends.

"The Get"

In the 1990s, an aggressive style of interview pursuit appeared and was quickly dubbed "the get" by veteran reporters. This term describes the stakeout and aggressive pursuit of someone—the get—for an exclusive interview. In this situation, there's ferocious competition from other reporters in the market or at the other networks. Examples of this style of pursuit would be Connie Chung's interview with skater Tonya Harding, and Diane Sawyer's interview with pop star Michael Jackson and Lisa Marie Presley when they were married.

Locally, it may be the person held hostage for hours by a deranged gunman. These are the people *everyone* in the media wants *to get* for an interview. And the results are exclusive and promotable, even if not particularly informative. Reporters who are successful in this style of interviewing often win the trust of the person and gain access to him or her through personal touches extended in notes, phone calls, and brief conversations. The reporter's reputation and stature may also be a factor. But this is, nevertheless, a style of continual, relentless pursuit. If you do it, you may be praised for it. Or you may be blamed for it.

Another controversial style of interviewing is the "ambush," wherein a reporter runs up to someone as he's leaving his home for work and starts firing questions unannounced. This may be all you can do if the person consistently refuses to schedule an interview with you, but it catches the person off-guard and the answers may not be particularly informative.

As a reporter, you'll find there are competing values within your newsroom. Think about them when considering whom to interview and how to go about it. Here's a list of news values that most can agree with: integrity, accuracy, fairness, responsibility, sensitivity, accountability. But these news values compete and conflict with others that are equally important and valid to your news director: being competitive, being timely, being compelling, being commercially successful in the ratings, being marketable, being promotable. If your organization has a mission statement, it may provide some guidance to you about what's really important at your station. If the mission statement declares "We will seek every opportunity to destroy our competitors," you'll be moving in one direction with your interviews and your reports. If the mission statement pledges the newsroom "will bring to light the good news, so we can celebrate, and the bad news, so we can work together to correct the problems we encounter," then you'll be going in a different direction and can explain to your interviewees the reasons behind some of your questions.

Get out in your community and listen to what "real" people are saying. You can listen to what people are saying when they're standing behind you in the grocery store checkout line. You can listen to what people are saying when they're talking with each other at high school basketball games. You can listen to what people are saying when they're talking with each other at the gym, at the gas station, at the table next to yours in the restaurant or coffee bar, or in the chair next to you in the beauty salon or the barber shop. Many people complain that media types don't even go out to community events to find out what average people are up to. You get the idea. Get out there, and wherever you are, listen. You'll learn what's important to people in your community. And you'll increase your list of people in the middle, not just those on the fringe or in "official" positions, whom you can call for an interview. You'll then have enterprise story ideas and interview subjects for your newscast, stories that will differentiate your station, and you, from competitors.

News directors and assignments editors love enterprising reporters who come up with many of their own story ideas. Let people in the community help in this regard. In big markets, the community isn't just the city of license. It may be the surrounding beach communities, or communities of commuters, or certain demographic communities. As a reporter, you're a contact person, a conduit to put informed people in your community on the air so that others can hear their voices, thoughts and opinions. You have the power to do that. And you want to use it wisely.

Also, don't forget to listen to the people who work at your own station in departments other than news. Ask the receptionist, members of the sales staff, the engineering staff or the housekeeping staff about news story ideas and interview possibilities. These people have most likely been at your station and in your community much longer than you have. They all have networks of family and friends and business associates. As a group, they're most likely more diverse than your circle of friends. They can help you decide whom to interview and what questions to ask, especially when you're just getting started in a market.

We've covered a number of points in this chapter, from planning the interview to managing the interviewee to actively listening to what's being said. Here's a quick checklist of things to remember when you're getting ready and when you're conducting a news interview.

📁 Do's and Dont's When Interviewing

Do

- Think ahead.
- Be organized and prepared.
- Research the topic and the people.
- Dress appropriately.
- Be courteous.
- Maintain eye contact.
- Interview in a conversational tone.
- Leave editing space after answers.
- Attribute charges to the person making them.
- Read between the lines (especially when interviewing politicians).
- Listen.

Don't

- Ask yes or no questions, especially of children.
- Be "married" to your questions.
- Give up control.
- Show agreement or disagreement.
- Tell the interviewee what your specific questions will be.
- Forget to ask for clarification.
- Ask really tough questions right away.

WRITING RADIO NEWS

Radio is the fastest and most widely dispersed mass medium. It's ubiquitous. It's everywhere. Because you can listen to the radio in places where you couldn't watch TV or read a newspaper, it's the medium through which much of the public is first informed when big news breaks. Radio news is a high-energy production of highly condensed information. A radio newscast may run only four minutes, but it may contain a dozen to fifteen stories.

"Hyperkinetic" best describes radio news on many commercial stations these days. Short, rapid-fire stories, a high story count and a driving rhythm are what one hears most often on the car radio during morning and evening drive times. Radio news at the top of the hour is often followed by traffic and weather reports, sports updates, medical reports, commentary, possibly a syndicated piece or a business report, and then the cycle repeats itself on the quarter-hour and the half-hour. Most stories are only a few seconds long.

Sound is the driving force of radio, and good-quality audio is very important. The voices of the reporters and anchors, the natural sounds from the scene of events, and the eyewitness sound bites with those who are there are the essential ingredients of radio news. It's important for the radio journalist to remember that sound itself attracts. Just ask any eavesdropper. Sounds have a romance. Consider how the sound of a cricket at night establishes mood in a radio drama. Or the sound of thunder or of rain. Radio is a medium that employs the magic of sound. Radio made America a land of listeners in the early 1920s. And America remains a nation of listeners today, a captive audience in automobiles commuting to and from work each day.

There are two kinds of radio news stories: "reader/actualities" ("RAs") and "wraps." An RA will be read by the anchor, who will read the opening copy, punch a cart or disk, which is the audio recording of the actuality or sound bite, and then read the closing copy. A wrap includes the anchor lead and a voiced report from the reporter along with an actuality (sound bite); a wrap is the equivalent of a news package in television. This terminology can vary slightly from shop to shop. In some newsrooms, a reader or "R" means the anchor reads the copy, a sound bite or "S" means the anchor reads a story that includes a sound bite, a voicer or "V" means a reporter delivers a story that includes a sound bite or bites and is prerecorded. Many stations are digital now and play the audio cuts right out of the computer or from a mini–disk player. But some stations still use cart machines, which are essentially audiotape players.

Most radio news stories on commercial stations are *very* short. As a writer, think in terms of 30 seconds for each story; that's about five sentences long. A story that runs 35 seconds will raise an eyebrow at the editor's desk. Generally speaking, each radio news story opens with a couple of sentences of copy, followed by a sound bite or clip of natural sound that runs between 5 and 10 seconds, and ends with a closing sentence or two. Write the bare minimum you need. You have to be clear, but you also have to be concise and short.

The radio news writer needs to remember: (1) to write in the present or future tense—this news is being heard in the current moment; (2) to write with a sense of urgency or a sense of the event itself; and (3) to choose the sound bite with the most "zing." The shorter the sound bite in radio, the better. Three seconds is long enough *if* the bite delivers the message. For example, the opening copy reads "Dallas Mayor Ron Kirk is pleased." Then bring up the sound bite: "Boy! Howdy!" Then continue the copy for the story and explain why the mayor is so happy.

As is the case in television, a good lead can make a radio news story. It's what gets the listener's attention in the first place. So think carefully about the words and sounds you're planning to use at the beginning of each story.

It's almost always necessary for the radio news writer to identify the person speaking in the sound bite or actuality. For example, write "Prime Minister Tony Blair said the death of Princess Diana is a great loss for the nation" leading into his sound bite. In radio, the idea is to let the listeners hear the voices and the sounds in the news. It's up to the writer to explain to the listeners why those voices and sounds are important.

Radio reporters work in relative anonymity compared with television reporters, because a lot of radio interviewing is done using the phone. If you can get someone on the phone, you can probably get that person to agree to a taped interview. Radio reporters can locate possible interview subjects by using city directory cross-referencing systems. If a man is holding children hostage at a day care center in town, the radio reporter can cross-reference the address of the house across the street from the day care center, look up the phone number and name of the people living in that house, call them up and ask them to describe for the listening audience what activity they can see going on across the street. Most people are willing to do this. If these eyewitnesses don't want their names used on the radio, the reporter can identify the person speaking as a "neighbor" or "someone who lives directly across the street from the day care center."

In a large-market radio newsroom, there are news editors, news reporters and anchors/personalities. In a small market radio station, one or two people may wear all the hats, serving alternately as anchors, reporters and editors. The news editors are similar to assignments editors and to producers in television. They're concerned with the newscast itself, the individual stories in it and how the stories fit together. They're also consciously concerned with getting and keeping listeners, the audience for their advertisers. The editors both assign stories and produce the newscasts. Producing includes putting the stories in order, lining them up so that they flow together naturally. News editors are interested in story count; the more stories in the newscast, the better. That means the shorter the stories, the better. Editors will edit reporters' copy to make the newscast as a whole flow together; they'll add segue lines to some stories; they'll rewrite and cut where necessary.

Some radio news reports are assigned, some come from the "futures" file and others come from reporter enterprise. Radio news is a team effort; it's collaboration. Radio reporters have to produce a lot of copy. They have to "crank it out" on deadline. This pressure to produce, to get stories on the air as quickly as possible, is enormous. And it's relentless, because the clock is always ticking.

Radio reporters are often expected to write four or five different news stories a day. And they're expected to write multiple versions of each story, using different audio cuts or sound bites. This may add up to 20 different stories a day. That's 20 different pieces of copy. So radio reporters have to be able to write fast and to write a variety of leads for their copy. Their days are long and unpredictable. It's hectic, concentrated work. There are few breaks, and there are no long lunch hours. Radio news reporters often eat while they work, or they eat while they drive. As they drive between assignments, they're rethinking the story they just covered, deciding on definitive leads and choosing which audio cuts to use.

Radio news keeps its writers and reporters busy. One reporter says, "It's like feeding a shark. You keep feeding it, or it eats you." It's a high-energy job, and you need lots of stamina to do it. The hours are long, and there are constant deadlines. You have to be fast, you have to be organized and you have to write short.

Writing short is a challenge. It's much tougher than writing long. It takes practice because there's so much you have to leave out. That increases the burden of deciding what the important details are that you must put in. A radio story is reminiscent of the old "Dragnet" Sergeant Friday statement: "Give me the facts, ma'am, and only the facts." There's no time for any more than that.

Radio reporters rarely know what they're going to be doing as the day progresses. When spot news happens, they go there, and they *stay* until they get the story—whether it's to the river where searchers are looking for a body or to a day care center where a gunman is holding children hostage and police are set up to wait him out. Live reports from the scene of such events can be called in over the phone. Many radio stations have microwave trucks equipped with a transmitter called a Marti unit. Engineers can hook up "the Marti" and have studio-quality sound over the microphones. But this takes time and planning, so most daily radio spot news stories are called in over a landline phone or a cell phone.

To help keep up with what's going on in the world, news editors and reporters listen constantly to the police scanners in the newsroom, and they keep an eye on the television monitors on the wall. The newsroom phones are set on speed dial for calls to the police dispatcher, the sheriff's office, the fire department or other agencies when a story breaks.

Radio reporters say they love "being in the know" about news events. They have access to the rich, the famous and the infamous for interviews. They travel and have front row seats at many history-making events. And the job is different every day. After all, the "unexpected" is what makes news. Radio reporters meet world leaders, national leaders and celebrities. They go places, see people and have access to people and places they normally wouldn't have. If you like to observe, it's the perfect place to be. It's fun, it's interesting, it's exciting and there's not as much equipment to lug around as in TV. The everyday tools of the trade are portable: a writing pad or laptop computer or word processor, audiotape or mini–disk recorder, cell phone, beeper and "patch" cords for audio jacks on public address systems. Other helpful equipment includes umbrella, ball cap, extra shoes, sunscreen and a big water jug. (The umbrella can even serve as a makeshift sound booth on the scene.)

Mike Rogers has made his career in radio news. Here are four scripts written by Rogers at KRLD News Radio 1080, Dallas/Fort Worth, Texas. KRLD is a CBS-owned-and-operated station; its format is News/Talk with Top-40 overtones, and its Internet site is *www.krld.com*. Mike Rogers' stories are often delivered with more "attitude" than regular news stories. He often calls his reports "The Other Side of the News." The first two scripts are two versions of the same story. The next two scripts are two versions of another story. These are reader/actualities, designed for the on-air talent to read, hit the actuality cart or disk, and finish reading.

6DEGREE1

AIR DATE=9SEPT 98

TALENT=RMR

CART=W-01

KILL=7PM

SIX DEGREES IN CYBERSPACE

EVER HEARD THE THEORY THAT EVERYONE ON EARTH IS SEPARATED FROM EVERY OTHER PERSON BY NO MORE THAN SIX RELATIONSHIPS ??? IT'S CALLED THE SIX DEGREES OF SEPARATION . . . AND NOW THERE'S A WEBSITE THAT ALLOWS US TO FIND OUT IF IT'S REALLY TRUE. ANDREW WEINRICH (WINE-rich) IS PRESIDENT OF SIX-DEGREES-DOT-COM.

CART=W-01

OUTCUE='. . . CONNECTING THEM ALL TO EACH OTHER.'

RUNS=:13

[VERBATIM] The goal is to provide Internet users with tools that allow them to network . . . to interact . . . to build what we call their personal virtual communities. We do that by giving them contact managers and connecting them all to each other.

THE SIX DEGREES WEBSITE NOW HAS ONE MILLION MEMBERS . . . EACH CATEGORIZED BY NAME . . . ADDRESS AND OCCUPATION. WEINRICH SAYS HE'D EVENTUALLY LIKE TO FORM A NETWORK OF EVERY INTERNET USER IN THE WORLD. . . . .

6DEGREE2

> AIR DATE=9SEPT98
>
> TALENT=RMR
>
> CART=W-02
>
> KILL=7PM
>
> NETWORKING ON THE NET

KEVIN BACON'S NOT A MEMBER . . . BUT A MILLION OTHER PEOPLE HAVE JOINED A NEW WEBSITE THAT TESTS THE SO-CALLED 'SIX DEGREES OF SEPARATION' THEORY. IT STATES THAT EVERY PERSON ON EARTH IS NO MORE THAN SIX RELATIONSHIPS AWAY FROM ANY OTHER PERSON. ANDREW WEINRICH (WINE-rich) IS PRESIDENT OF SIX-DEGREES-DOT-COM . . . WHICH TAKES A LIST OF YOUR FRIENDS AND ACQUAINTANCES . . . AND PROVIDES YOU WITH A LIST OF 'BLIND DATES' . . .

> CART=W-02
>
> OUTCUE=' . . . A TREMENDOUS AMOUNT OF POWER.'
>
> RUNS=:15

[VERBATIM] A blind date is by definition what we call your second degree. It's not someone I know. It's someone that knows someone I know. If we can build a database where we can capture all of this information and allow people to identify relationships to the people they don't know through the people they DO know, we can provide them with a tremendous amount of power.

WEINRICH SAYS THE SIX DEGREES WEBSITE CAN BE USED FOR ON-LINE NETWORKING . . . BECAUSE EVERY MEMBER IS LISTED BY NAME . . . ADDRESS AND OCCUPATION. . . .

PET-INS1

> AIR DATE=10SEPT98
>
> TALENT=RMR
>
> CART=TH-01
>
> KILL=7PM
>
> HEALTH INSURANCE FOR FIDO

IF ONLY IT WERE THIS SIMPLE FOR HUMANS. A COMPANY IN OHIO IS NOW OFFERING HEALTH INSURANCE . . . FOR YOUR PET. RUSSELL SMITH IS A CO-FOUNDER OF PETS-HEALTH INSURANCE. HE SAYS VISITS TO THE VET ARE USUALLY EXPENSIVE . . . BECAUSE PETS CAN'T TELL YOU WHEN THEY'RE SICK. . . .

CART=TH-01

OUTCUE=' . . . SO IT CAN GET VERY COSTLY.'

RUNS=:14

[VERBATIM] By the time you realize there's something there when you take the pet in, typically you have some additional treatments and re-visits that come after that, so it can get very costly.

PETS-HEALTH PAYS 80 PERCENT OF YOUR VETERINARY BILLS. THE MONTHLY PREMIUM RUNS ABOUT 20 DOLLARS A MONTH . . . SLIGHTLY MORE FOR SOME BIGGER BREEDS OF DOGS WITH BAD HEALTH RECORDS. . . .

PET-INS2

AIR DATE=10SEPT98

TALENT=RMR

CART=TH-02

KILL=7PM

PREMIUMS FOR PETS

AT WHAT POINT WILL A MAJORITY OF AMERICANS DECIDE TO PUT THEIR PET TO SLEEP . . . RATHER THAN PAY FOR AN EXPENSIVE MEDICAL PROCEDURE ??? ONE RECENT STUDY PUTS IT AT 570 DOLLARS. ANY MORE THAN THAT . . . AND FIDO'S HISTORY. BUT RUSSELL SMITH SAYS IT SHOULDN'T COME DOWN TO THAT . . . WHICH IS WHY HE'S STARTED A COMPANY THAT OFFERS HEALTH INSURANCE TO PETS. TYPICAL PREMIUM ??? ABOUT 15 DOLLARS A MONTH . . . SLIGHTLY MORE FOR CERTAIN BREEDS. . . .

CART=TH-02

OUTCUE=' . . . THE COURSE OF THEIR LIFE.'

RUNS=:14

[VERBATIM] We've identified a few breeds such as a Boxer, a Basset Hound and others that tend to have a little bit more claims or medical conditions or losses beyond the normal pet, throughout the course of their life.

. . . AND LIKE MOST MEDICAL PLANS FOR HUMANS . . . PETS-HEALTH INSURANCE PAYS 80 PERCENT OF YOUR PET'S BILLS. . . .

In the preceding examples, you'll notice that the directions accompanying the stories are fairly straightforward. Those at the beginning of the stories include the slug (title, with the number at the end of the slug giving us which version of the story it is), the date, who the reporter is, which cart to use, and the time at which to "kill" the story. These stories are scheduled to be killed or dropped after 7 p.m., which is the expiration date the writer has given them. The directions in the middle give the cart or disk number again, give the outcue (final few words) of the sound bite, and indicate the length of the bite, that brief portion of the interview that the reporter chose to include in the story. You'll notice that all the copy to be read live is in uppercase, but this can vary from newsroom to newsroom.

Here are two scripts written by B. J. Austin, a local news reporter at KRLD Radio in Dallas/Fort Worth. They are two versions of the same story. The first one is a wrap and runs a total of 30 seconds; it includes an anchor intro to the reporter's "voiced" package that includes a sound bite. The second is a reader/actuality: an anchor read into a cart audio cut followed by another read. Notice how short the stories are, how succinct the writing is, how tight the sound bites are.

> OLYMP2
>
> > AIR DATE=9/9/98
> >
> > TALENT=BJ
> >
> > CART=W 67
> >
> > KILL=7PM
> >
> > ***ANCHOR***
>
> "DALLAS" IS OFFICIALLY LEADING THE D-F-W BID FOR THE 2012 SUMMER OLYMPICS. CITY COUNCIL GAVE ITS OKAY THIS MORNING, AFTER ASSURANCES THAT PLANS TO DOME THE COTTON BOWL WOULDN'T BE SCRAPPED.
>
> > CART=W 67
> >
> > OUTCUE=SOC (standard outcue, which at this station is "KRLD Local News")
> >
> > RUNS=:30
> >
> > ***REPORTER ON CART***
>
> COUNCILMEMBERS WERE CONCERNED THAT THE "CHANCE" DALLAS MIGHT HOST THE 2012 OLYMPICS MIGHT SCUTTLE THE MORE "SURE-THING" OF A PRIVATELY FUNDED "DOME" ON THE COTTON BOWL. DALLAS MAYOR RON KIRK SAYS THE COTTON "DOMERS" ARE WILLING TO WAIT FOR INSTRUCTIONS FROM THE U.S. OLYMPIC COMMITTEE—AT A MEETING IN PHOENIX NEXT MONTH.
>
> > ***:04 AUDIO CUT OF MAYOR ON CART***
>
> "Do we need a bigger facility? If not a bigger facility, do we need a dome?"

REPORTER BACK ON CART

THERE'S ALREADY TALK OF A RETRACTABLE ROOF AND OTHER "OLYMPIC
RELATED" TOUCHES FOR THE COTTON BOWL. B. J. AUSTIN, K-R-L-D LOCAL NEWS.

OLYMP3

    AIR DATE=9/9/98

    TALENT=BJ

    CART=W 68

    KILL=7PM

"DALLAS" IS THE "OFFICIAL" LEADER OF THE REGIONAL BID FOR THE 2012
SUMMER OLYMPICS. THE CITY COUNCIL OKAYED THE PROJECT THIS MORNING,
AFTER MAYOR RON KIRK ASSURED MEMBERS THE COTTON BOWL WOULDN'T BE
SACRIFICED . . . JUST PUT ON HOLD A WHILE.

    CART=W 68

    OUTCUE=THE BEST INFORMATION WE HAVE

    RUNS=:09

"You know we're going to work hand in hand with them because we've
got a vested interest. I think it's clear to everybody on the council we want to
see the dome go forward but we want to do it with the best information we
have."

MAYOR KIRK SAYS THE PLANS TO DOME THE COTTON BOWL WILL BE
CLEARER AFTER AN OLYMPIC MEETING IN PHOENIX NEXT MONTH. ONE CITY
HALL SOURCE SAYS DEVELOPERS ARE ALREADY TALKING ABOUT A POSSIBLE
"RETRACTING ROOF" AND OTHER ADJUSTMENTS.

Although many commercial radio stations do a rapid-fire, high-story-count brand of news with stories such as these at the top of the hour, there are alternatives for those who want more. National Public Radio stations feature long-form, thoughtful pieces that may run 8 to 10 minutes in length. This makes NPR stations unique among radio stations today. If NPR reporters can make it a good "sound" story, they can turn in long pieces with lengthy interviews and lots of natural sound. For example, a bridge in Austin, Texas, has become known for the colony of bats that lives in its girders. A reporter for NPR once did an eight-minute piece on the bats and the bridge. He included the natural sound of the bats beating their wings as they flew out of the bridge at sunset, interviews with people who had come to watch the bats fly out, interviews with bat experts, and interviews at the bridge with T-shirt vendors selling a variety of books, bat caps, and other bat paraphernalia. The reporter was able to create a "word picture" of the scene for his radio listeners.

Such word pictures are what radio journalists strive to create. And we remember those written by such legendary reporters as Edward R. Murrow. This is part of the script Murrow wrote and broadcast over the CBS Radio Network on April 15, 1945, the day Allied troops liberated the Buchenwald concentration camp from the German Nazis: "As I walked down to the end of the barracks, there was applause from the men too weak to get out of bed. It sounded like the hand clapping of babies; they were so weak." You, the listener, can "see" the condition of the men Murrow is seeing through the words he has written in this script. Murrow used descriptive language in another radio script about Allied bombing in World War II. Murrow wrote that the bombs "were falling like white rice on black velvet." Good writing is in the details, the language and the choice of words.

Glenn Mitchell is a radio reporter at KERA 90.1 (*www.kera.org*) in Dallas, and he freelances for NPR. The shortest pieces he writes run about three-and-a-half minutes. Some go more than seven minutes. He says that what he writes is determined by the quality of the sound he gets in the field. He advises beginning writers to think in advance about the best questions to ask so that the end result will be good quality sound.

Before he writes his final scripts, Mitchell listens to the sound he's recorded and then he writes the script. He wants sound that's going to tell a story. Most of it will be interview sound, but some will be natural sound. If he's doing a story about a factory, he'll talk to the person who runs the factory, people who assemble the product, the engineer who designed the product, and he'll also get ambient sound of the factory machinery so that the final piece isn't just words. The ambient sound is the radio equivalent of b-roll natural sound in TV. It enhances a story and puts the listeners in the place where the story occurs.

Mitchell says in order to get good quality sound, he has to get a lot of audio. His ratio is 5-to-1: he'll record 15 minutes for every 3 minutes he actually uses, and he's a veteran at this. As a beginner, your ratio may be 10-to-1 or 15-to-1. The turnaround time for Mitchell's reports varies. It may be a few hours, or a few days. Sports stories are usually due the next morning after the game. He may have as long as a week to put together a feature story on the arts. But it's the time devoted to the stories that makes NPR news unique. From three to seven minutes is a luxuriant amount of time for a single radio news story.

NPR reporters have that luxury because public radio station newscasts may run a half-hour or more in length. Mike Mulcahy reports for Minnesota Public Radio 91.9 FM (*www.mpr.org*) in St. Paul, Minnesota. This is a story he wrote in the mid-1990s about the surprise announcement by a former governor that he wouldn't try to reclaim the office. This is a "real world" piece reported and written under tight deadline pressures. The former governor made the announcement at about 8:30 a.m. during a live interview on another radio station across town from Mulcahy's office at the state capitol. Mulcahy phoned in a live report right after the announcement, then covered the former governor's postbroadcast news conference. Mulcahy then raced back to his office and put this version together for MPR's 11 a.m. program. He did another version of the story with more reaction for MPR's 5 p.m. program that afternoon.

TODAY, FORMER GOVERNOR RUDY PERPICH ANSWERED THE QUESTION THAT POLITICAL JUNKIES HAVE BEEN ASKING FOR MONTHS. IN AN INTERVIEW WITH A MINNEAPOLIS RADIO STATION PERPICH SAID HE WILL NOT RUN FOR GOVERNOR THIS YEAR. BUT PERPICH SAYS HIS POLITICAL CAREER ISN'T OVER, AND THAT HE WILL BE A CANDIDATE FOR GOVERNOR IN 1998. MINNESOTA PUBLIC RADIO'S MIKE MULCAHY REPORTS. . . .

TAPE: (3:32)

    OUTCUE: " . . . soc

    Perpich kept listeners guessing for more than an hour before finally making his announcement. He certainly sounded like a candidate—calling incumbent Arne Carlson a caretaker governor, and Minnesota a stagnant state. He ticked off a list of events he would have tried to attract to the state during the past four years—including the Olympics, the World Cup soccer tournament, and a visit from the pope. And he ran down a list of projects he would pursue in the future—including a downtown casino, a subway system for the twin cities, and education vouchers for private school students. He said he could win the DFL primary this year—but the time is not right for him to be a candidate:

    out #1 PERPICH- "I believe that Minnesota has fallen behind in the last 4 years—but not enough for people to recognize the virtue of innovation. Thus I have decided not to run for governor. Instead I will pursue my plans and run in 1998."

    Most political observers thought Perpich would run this year. The former governor says he was planning to until about ten days ago. He says he knew many people have unfavorable opinions of him, but he thought he could counter that with television advertising. He says he realized this past weekend he couldn't raise about 70-thousand dollars he needed for the ads—and then decided not to run. He says part of his fundraising problems come from the state's new campaign finance laws, which limit donations to 2-thousand dollars per person. Perpich won't endorse any other candidate. He says the other DFL'ers in the race—John Marty, Tony Bouza, and Mike Hatch—are all good people, but he says no one in either party is talking about the international economic issues that will influence Minnesota's future:

out #2 PERPICH –"If you're poor—strike one. If you're uneducated—strike two. And then if you're a minority, especially black—strike three. I mean, what are they going to do? Wait two years? Wait five years? Things are going to get better? Where? I'm listening to what they're going to do for the economy. It's not there. It's not going to change. It's going to deteriorate. It's deteriorating other places. You're losing 15-20 dollar jobs for 6 dollar jobs. And the 6 dollar jobs are going to Mexico. That's what's happening in Chicago."

Perpich says he doesn't see how Allen Quist can lose to Governor Carlson in the republican primary. He says even if Carlson wins in September, he'll be out of money and badly beat up going into the general election. Perpich says he intends to stay in Minnesota and work as a consultant. He says he'll promote his ideas around the state during the next four years and see whether people are more receptive in 98.

I'm Mike Mulcahy, MPR at the capitol.

Rudy Perpich didn't run in '98. He died of cancer about a year and a half after this story aired, and was mourned as one of Minnesota's greatest governors.

Here are two more examples of long-form radio reporting from Minnesota Public Radio.

Friday, May 9, 1997

Trash, debris, refuse, garbage—call it what you will, it's the most visible and immediate legacy of this spring's record flooding in the Red River Valley.

In Grand Forks and East Grand Forks, entire buildings have been transformed into trash; in Fargo, used sandbags form a whole new geography at the local landfill.

Farther upstream the community of Breckenridge—hit hard by flooding— is still trucking trash off city streets, as it's been doing for most of a month. Leif Enger of Mainstreet Radio has this update.

D-CART ITEM: 1309

TIME: 4:46 plus 5 sec amb (fades)

OUTCUE: " . . . soc

258 fx a whole herd of goodhumored volunteers, laughing and dumping sand, fade under

The last of the sandbags came up in South Breckenridge this week. A hundred bussed-in volunteers formed one last human chain—this time, to lift sandbags from a neighborhood dike, pass them to the street, and empty them in the path of a waiting front-end-loader. Doug Schmidt came all the way from Long Prairie to help lay these sandbags weeks ago; he came back to help clean up.

114 SCHMIDT: "Dump it in the street, dump it in the alley, wherever they want it, we dump it. (Is there a little less pressure this time around?)

Ha ha ha, yes, for sure. It's not life or death this time—"

337 BARTH: "I'm Cliff Barth, and I'm on the city council here in Breckenridge, Minnesota, right now we're in the process of desandbagging, we've fought flood here for about a month now—tomorrow we're gonna start with debris removal, and we have a lot of it, it looks like a war zone here on the south side of Breck. (TRACTOR GOES BY, VRROOM!)

The mounds of trash here breeds similes: a neighborhood looks like a war zone. It looks like a shipwreck. Like a third-world country. Weeks after the waters went down you could stand at the railroad tracks and look down the street and see not many mounds, but a single one—continuous, serpentine, a dragon of trash."

2357 LUTZ: "Furniture, sheetrock, paneling, insulation, appliances and on and on and on—"

Jim Lutz is operations manager for Northern Waste Systems, across the river in Wahpeton.

2750 LUTZ: "I haven't seen the total tonnage reports yet, because we've not had the time to catch up with the paper, but I will tell you that the day we started on the south side, we put nine hours in, with four dump trucks being loaded by payloaders, we hauled over a hundred tons of just demolition material that day. And that only covered about four city blocks. And that wasn't complete—those houses weren't even close to being finished, they were still hauling stuff out after we left."

10327 FX DUMP TRUCKS CRUISING IN AND OUT OF LANDFILL, FADE

The Prairie View Landfill these days rumbles constantly with dump trucks. Its name is optimistic: you can see a lot of clay here, and a lot of garbage, and a few seagulls—not much prairie. But these towns are lucky in a couple of ways: for one thing, this landfill's close by—right on the edge of Wahpeton. For another, it's fairly new—there's a lot of room left. Good thing, says Brad Reilly, with all this traffic:

5528 REILLY: "Yeah—it's tenfold what's gonna go in there normally."

Reilly works for Disposal Services, the company operating the Prairie View.

5924 REILLY: "We have projected time periods that this landfill is good for, and this in the scope of things is a very young landfill. We're not even to a tenth of capacity yet—but it will have an impact, a definite, definite impact."

In fact, the burden on Prairie View landfill has multiplied exponentially. It's supposed to be a demolition landfill—reserved for sheetrock, paneling, and other construction materials less threatening to groundwater. But the record flooding prompted the Minnesota Pollution Control Agency to relax certain guidelines. Now, household trash corrupted by sewage—and that's almost everything from every basement—is also being dumped at Prairie View. The MPCA says it weighed the possible risk to groundwater against the more immediate risk—of disease from contaminated garbage sitting even longer on city streets.

5250 HAMMERING, SCRAPING, FADE

The first floor is being rebuilt at the Wilkin County Environmental office; flood waters chased some county employees to temporary quarters in a construction trailer, but environmental officer Bruce Poppel stayed dry. He's up on the second floor, tabulating the results of a recent collection drive for hazardous household trash—the kind of stuff everybody has on the basement shelves.

4040 POPPEL: "We've collected 495 gallons of oil-based paint, 660 gallons of latex paint, 440 gallons of fuel products—gas, diesel, paint thinners—"

And residents are still calling with fuel oil leaks, pesticide spills, you name it. The environment, Poppel says, took a beating from the flood.

1613 FX GRUNTING AND HOISTING

At home in South Breckenridge, a volunteer named Dave hoists boxes of soaked sheetrock up from the basement and into a waiting wheelbarrow. The driveway is mounded high with wallboard, appliances—and history. The owner of the house, Connie Nennig, was born in Fargo the year of Pearl Harbor. She was one of a set of quadruplets. She'd saved a lot of newspaper articles.

FX WHEELBARROW DUMPING—

1930 DAVE: "We wonder, ourselves, what they're gonna do with all that. But they'll find a place for it—"

FX MORE DUMPING—

Leif Enger, Mainstreet Radio

*** *** ***

DECEMBER 16, 1999

The days of the independent country veterinarian are nearly at an end. The lone doctor has been replaced by large clinics, or "animal hospitals," businesses that do everything from treating sick animals to managing farms. As livestock operations become larger, the types of medical assistance they need have changed, leaving little room for a solitary doctor with an easy farm yard manner. Mainstreet Radio's Mark Steil reports:

On several sheets of plywood in the back room of the Appleton Veterinary Clinic there's a hand-crafted scale model of the classic family farm. There's a nice red barn and a solid farmhouse; hogs, cattle, ducks and chickens fill the pens and yard. There are still farms like this here in western Minnesota, but most have disappeared, replaced by larger farms that specialize in certain crops or animals. The man who built this scale model is nearly as rare as the old-fashioned family farm itself:

NISSEN (:12): "Mostly what I'm happy about is I'm still able to get up in the morning and go to work. But my biggest drawback right now is I'm getting some arthritis in my knees and arms."

Despite the creaky joints Doctor Chris Nissen still puts nearly forty years of veterinary skills to work every day. He's the only veterinarian at the Appleton Clinic. When he began practicing nearly all his work was done on nearby family farms. But as those farms disappeared, his business changed. Now he spends more time treating dogs, cats and other pets than he does on farms. He's a relic of a simpler time on Minnesota farms, when the veterinarian was nearly a member of the family:

NISSEN (:17): "There's very few people that offer me dinner anymore. There's about a half a dozen and I accept them. But it used to be when you got done with a job you had to go in for dinner. No more. There are a few yet that do that but they're kind of old fashioned like me."

MOOING UP

On a clear December day Nissen visits a farm a few miles outside of Appleton, vaccinating and dehorning cattle:

NISSEN (:08): "Well if you're going to sell these and they get a shot you're going to get more money. Every dollar's a dollar." (Farmer: "Do it then.")

The cattle are led into a steel pipe contraption known as the squeeze chute. Nissen tows it from farm to farm behind his pickup. The cattle are driven into the chute where they're briefly immobilized. Then with a few graceful sweeps of his arms, Nissen gives the cow a couple of shots and stripes a purple de-lousing agent across its back. While he waits for the next animal, farmer Keith Schirm says changes in veterinary medicine mean it's sometimes hard to find a doctor for his cattle:

SCHIRM (:11): "We've got a vet clinic in Milbank, which is about 35 miles away and when Chris has been gone we've used them some. But it's much handier to have one right close you know."

The trend away from solo practitioners in favor of clinics has evolved with the trend toward larger farms. Nissen says he wants to continue serving the small farms that gave him his start. Working for a large operation would be nearly a full-time job. But many veterinarians are finding new opportunities with the large firms. The Fairmont Veterinary Clinic in south central Minnesota has about twenty employees including nine doctors. In nearly ten years at the clinic, Brian Roggow says the biggest change he's seen is a move toward preventive medicine. He says the era is gone when his day depended on a telephone call:

ROGGOW (:22): "The veterinarian went out, treated sick animals and didn't go on to a farm until the farmer called and had a sick animal. Now we're more of a consultancy based organization. Where we're out on farms on a regular basis working with the farmer to prevent disease so he doesn't have sick animals."

The Fairmont Clinic still does hands-on work treating farm animals, but consulting is a major part of their business. One reason that's possible is because farmers typically do the routine jobs themselves, like giving vaccination shots. Roggow says the consulting role has advanced to a point that the veterinary clinic actually manages the day to day operations of some large hog farms. He says this usually happens when a number of farmers build a livestock operation together. The new facility requires management that none of the farmers really has time for:

ROGGOW (:21): "Each individual farmer really doesn't want to be responsible for the day to day management of that unit so they hire our organization to do that. So we'll help with hiring people and monitoring the day to day operation of the business so those farmers can stay on their own specific operations and manage them but don't have to worry about the group venture that they've done."

Roggow expects that type of veterinary clinic management to increase in the years ahead. One reason for that is because he sees an entirely new field just beginning to open:

ROGGOW (:12): "I think we will probably be more closely involved with the issues of food safety."

He says consumers are demanding safer food in the wake of several highly publicized food poisoning scandals in recent years. Roggow believes veterinarians will play a lead role in implementing new livestock management programs, like better on-farm sanitation, to meet consumer demands:

ROGGOW (:21): "Working with the farmers to develop procedures so the food is going to be safer than it has been. In terms of certain organisms, the salmonella's and the E coli's that we hear in the news. Working with them so starting at the farm the animals don't have those."

MOOING, FARM SOUNDS BACK UP

Managing a large scale livestock operation takes a whole team of veterinarians and is something Chris Nissen of Appleton has no interest in. Nearly 65 years old, he's thinking of retiring in a few years. When he does he'll take with him decades of hard work, spiced with moments that still bring a smile. Like the time he lassoed a cow:

NISSEN (:20): "The guy was standing there and I got him in the lasso too. And I tied him down to the top of this cow. And of course cows don't like to have people on top of them very much. And she starts bucking like crazy, and he had all fours just sprawled out there, hollering and screaming." (LAUGHS)

Like the family farm the scale model replica in his office recalls, independent country veterinarians like Chris Nissen are a rare breed these days. But he's not mired in nostalgia. He says while traditional family farms are an American icon, they required repetitive, nearly backbreaking labor to operate. And the veterinary care they required was equally difficult. When every farmer had a few milk cows, pigs and other animals, Nissen was basically on duty 24 hours a day, 365 days a year. Many times he had to leave the warmth of his home in below zero weather to visit a sick cow. He doesn't miss that. What he does miss are the friendships he shared with those long gone family farmers. Farmers who gave names to each of their milk cows, always shared the latest family news and when the work was done, insisted that the country veterinarian come inside for dinner.

Mark Steil, Minnesota Public Radio, Worthington.

Conclusion

It doesn't matter if you listen to NPR or the local all-news radio station, one of radio's strengths is that it's portable. You can take it with you and hear it while you jog or while you drive your car. Another strength is its intimacy. You can hear the person speaking, hear the inflection in his or her voice, the tone, the emotion. You get to use your mind's eye. A child was once asked whether he preferred radio or television. He said radio. When the father asked why, the child answered that he preferred radio because the pictures are better. It's up to the radio writer to create those word pictures. The best ones become "wordsmiths." They know what words mean, and they choose the appropriate words, the most descriptive words for the story they're telling to the listening audience. Some television writers and reporters have started their careers in radio and will tell you "if you want to get into television, start in radio." There, the pictures don't get in the way.

🗁 Do's and Don'ts for Writing Radio News

Do
- Write short.
- Use descriptive language.
- Create word pictures.

Don't
- Forget to get good ambient sound.
- Forget to write in present or future tense.
- Let the shark get you.

TELEVISION NEWS STORY FORMS— THE VO

In television news, there are five basic story forms: readers (or "tell" stories), voice-overs (VOs), voice-over to sound on tapes (VO/SOTs), reporter packages, and donuts. Beginning writers and associate producers are the people primarily responsible for taking information from story notes and compiling it into story form to be read by an anchor. If a story involves no video or other visual over the face of the anchor, then it's called a reader. Sometimes, the viewers can see the anchor's face for the duration of a story but also see a graphic over his shoulder. That story would still qualify as a reader, because the viewers see the anchor for the entire story. Because there's not much production value associated with reader stories, they're usually quite short and might include a promise of video once it becomes available.

A voice-over is any story that's read by the anchor and also incorporates video, a full-screen graphic or some other visual. The term "voice-over" simply indicates that the anchor's voice is heard "over" some visual. The acronym VO usually indicates that she's talking over a piece of video. If she's talking over a graphic, many news operations label the story a VO/g to distinguish between the two. Later, we'll get to the longer story forms, such as VO/SOTs and packages. In this chapter, we'll concentrate on VOs.

Voice-over stories serve an important role in a newscast. They help the producer vary the pace of the show, while allowing us to deliver useful and interesting information in short form. VOs work very well when we cover events and a comment from someone at the event really wouldn't add that much to the story, when there's no real issue involved, or when there's only a limited amount of interesting information to impart to the viewers. A downtown street fair would probably warrant VO coverage only. It would involve nice colorful video and would be a way to highlight a part of the community; however, there's no controversy, and someone saying "I enjoyed the petting zoo" doesn't add anything, so a 20- to 30-second VO would suffice. The street fair isn't as important as other stories in the newscast, so less time would be devoted to it.

The relative importance of the story isn't the only reason for it being assigned VO status. We might be getting late-breaking video from the satellites and have no time to put together a longer piece, so we would quickly edit some of the compelling video and give the few details that were available. Perhaps a trial has generated a couple of important bits of interesting information, but not enough to warrant more than 20 or 30 seconds. The information might be good, but there just isn't much of it.

Also, what might be a full-blown reporter package on a slow news day can be reduced to VO status simply because other news takes precedence. A producer might feel compelled to include the story, but simply can't give up the time in a packed news show to make it a long piece. Something a reporter has been working on all day might occupy only 30 seconds of news time when all is said and done.

The flip side of that is what's known as "trying to make chicken salad out of . . ." (you fill in the rest). Some days, the news managers are sitting around trying to figure out what to cover, especially as the lead story, because it seems *nothing* is going on. On those days, a compelling VO can give the show a kick start and perhaps even lead to a short series of related reports. Matt Morin is a producer at the NBC affiliate in Plattsburgh, New York, and remembers just such a day.

Because it was *so* slow, the news managers were considering a story about a stolen exotic bird as the lead story on the evening newscast. But they decided to take a look at what was happening in world and national news before making the decision. About the only thing worthwhile was the outpouring of support for victims of an earthquake in Turkey. However, to that point they knew of no local groups organizing relief efforts, and no one was aware of a large population of people of Turkish ancestry in upstate New York. They decided to do some digging though, and a reporter learned that there were a few Turkish students at a nearby university and at another small college in the area.

As the day progressed, the death toll from the earthquake continued to rise. The news team learned from the Turkish students that there were other Turkish people living in the area, and the story of what they went through waiting to hear of the fates of loved ones and friends made a solid story for the reporter. So the newscast opened with compelling video of the quake site as a VO, progressed to the reporter package about how the local Turkish community was dealing with news of the tragedy, moved on to a VO/SOT about the local Turkish students and the impact on them, and then moved to a quick VO/graphic about how local residents could help through the Red Cross. The first VO included the latest information on the death toll and tales of survival, and served as a "scene setter" to pieces 2 and 3. The second VO put a wrap on the segment. The two short stories added both pace and context. By the way, the stolen bird story wound up as a VO, item number 11.

The Mechanics of a VO

Information for a VO can come from a number of sources, such as story notes compiled by a reporter or videographer, news releases, wire services, video feed services and the like. Story notes might be very brief, requiring the writer to expand on what's provided either by incorporating related information or by contacting the reporter or videographer (who might have gone on to another story assignment) for more information. The writer might also contact a source indicated in the story notes for clarification or additional information. In the case of news releases, the writer's primary task is taking the information and boiling it down to the essential elements. In the case of a script sent by a wire service or feed service, the primary task is to rewrite the information, putting a local "angle" on the story.

A Lot to Say in 30 Seconds or Less

Although there's no set length for any broadcast story, VOs on local news programs typically run about 20 to 30 seconds. In a series of back-to-back VOs, some might be as short as 10 to 12 seconds, and in rare circumstances, a VO might run as much as 40 to 45 seconds. Generally though, you can expect a VO to be about 20 to 30 seconds in length. It's not uncommon for viewers to see the anchor briefly at the beginning of a VO and perhaps again at the end. However, it's still a VO and not a reader because at some point in the story we see something other than the anchor's face.

Writing to the video is so important that we'll mention it several times throughout this book. Having the video to tell part of the story helps, but in many cases, we can't fit all the information that's available into the time limit we're given. Information *will* be left out. The key is not to leave out any major information. VOs are challenging because television news writers must capture viewer attention, impart the most relevant information of the story, and perhaps even transition to the next story, all in 20 to 30 seconds.

It's difficult to be very creative in such a short amount of time, and many of us making the transition to broadcast are caught in the "flowery words and phrases" mindset we learned when writing much longer stories and essays. The creativity in broadcast writing doesn't come in how many dependent clauses and rarely used words we can stick in one sentence. Instead, creativity often comes in the ability to tell a story so that people who don't know anything about what happened can understand what we're telling them right away. As with any good piece of broadcast writing, an informative VO gives viewers the most pertinent information and relates to what the pictures are showing.

Broadcast writers do have room to get creative with their writing, depending on the type of story they're dealing with. This is frequently the case with soft news or feature stories. We still have to use clear, understandable words and short sentences, but the English language is a wonderful tool, even when you're operating within severe time constraints. Chapter 4 contains a lot of information about writing creative news copy, but here's a quick example of how to change a lackluster story into a better one. The following very average copy is taken from an actual newscast that hit the air exactly as presented below. Note that the available video consists entirely of a giant pumpkin and the farmer who grew it. A suggested rewrite follows. We'll explain what the markings on the left side of the page mean after we look at the examples.

Pumpkin (Early Version)

	(TED)
on cam	IT'S ALMOST TIME FOR HALLOWEEN
	. . . AND WHAT WOULD HALLOWEEN BE
	WITHOUT PUMPKINS?

:00 Take cass	(vo)
nat snd under (VO)	FOLKS ACROSS THE COUNTRY ARE
	GEARING UP FOR THE HOLIDAY,
	MAKING COSTUMES, BUYING TREATS
	AND HARVESTING PUMPKINS FOR THIS
	SEASON. MILTON BARBER MAY NOT
	WANT TO BUTCHER HIS PUMPKIN
	BECAUSE IT IS A WORLD RECORD
	PUMPKIN. THE WINNING PUMPKIN
	WEIGHS A WHOPPING 743-POUNDS.
	BARBER SAYS HE'S NOT SURE WHAT
	HE'LL DO WITH THE PUMPKIN BUT HE
	DOES PLAN TO SELL THE SEEDS.
:40 cass out	

The story as written contains all the pertinent information, but it certainly isn't very memorable. The following example takes the same set of facts, presents them in a different way and still takes only 40 seconds to read. After reading both, decide which of the two you prefer.

PUMPKIN (Later Version)

	(Ted)
on cam	EVERY OCTOBER SOME PERSON
	PRETENDS TO HAVE PRODUCED THE
	PLANET'S MOST PRODIGIOUS PUMPKIN.
	THE PERSON MAKING THAT CLAIM THIS
	YEAR MIGHT HAVE A CASE.
:00 take cass	(vo)
snd under (VO)	MILTON BARBER OF PITTSBURGH IS
	PLEASED AND PROUD TO BE THE
	OWNER OF AN OUTRAGEOUSLY
	OVERSIZED ENTRY. IN FACT . . .
	MILTON'S PONDEROUS PRODUCE WEIGHS
	ROUGHLY FOUR TIMES MORE THAN
	MILTON HIMSELF. IT'S A VERITABLE
	VEGETABLE ON STEROIDS: THIS
	PUMPKIN CRUNCHES THE SCALES AT A
	STAGGERING 743 POUNDS. THAT'S
	ENOUGH TO GIVE A FOUR OUNCE
	SERVING TO EACH OF ABOUT THREE

THOUSAND PEOPLE! WHAT'S HE GOING TO DO WITH ALL THAT POTENTIAL PUMPKIN PIE? WELL, HE COULD TURN HIS ENTRY INTO THE JACK-O'-LANTERN THAT ATE PITTSBURGH. BUT WHETHER HE DOES THAT OR NOT . . . MILTON DOES HAVE ONE THING IN MIND. HE MAY WELL WIND UP TURNING THE WORLD'S BIGGEST PUMPKIN INTO THE WORLD'S BIGGEST PUMPKIN PATCH. MILTON PLANS TO SELL THE SEEDS.

:50 cass out

Providing Directions

Writing a VO so that viewers can understand the story (and perhaps even get a kick out of it) is only part of the writer's responsibility. Other people in the news operation also have to understand what the writer has in mind in relation to the video or other visual elements of the story. If the story is structured so that viewers are supposed to see the anchor and an over-the-shoulder (OTS) graphic for the first sentence, the script has to indicate that.

Television news scripts are set up in split-page format. The right side of the page is what the anchor is supposed to read. It also includes a bit of information to help cue the anchors as to who reads the story and when the video appears. That information is placed in parentheses and isn't in uppercase, so the anchor knows not to read it. (Some stations do it differently, putting the anchor copy in upper/lowercase and directions all uppercase. The key is to set directions and copy off from one another somehow.) The left side of the page contains directions for the control room personnel. If those directions are incomplete or missing, the show director has to guess at which point to incorporate the tape, or if there's even a tape associated with that particular story. Having the tape appear too soon or too late throws off the flow of the story. Anchors can adjust their read rate when the tape is a second or two early or late, but several seconds of discrepancy almost always result in noticeable errors on the air. You don't want your anchor to be talking about "this little boy" at the time that the tape is showing a female police officer.

In the pumpkin example above, the writer intends for the viewers to see the anchor (Ted) for a brief period of time before the video appears. That's what the "on cam" marking means. The director will then "take" the video at the point indicated on the script. The anchor knows that his face is no longer on the screen at this point, because of the (vo) indication on the right side of the page. So, he can read directly from the hard copy of the script and keep an eye on a video monitor at the same time to make sure the script and the video are matching. If they aren't, he can vary his read rate.

We line up the directions on the left with the place in the copy at which the directions are supposed to be applied. Go back and look at the pumpkin example. We've asked the director to take the video when the anchor is saying "folks across the country" in the "before" example and when the anchor is saying "Milton Barber of Pittsburgh" in the "after" example. We've also indicated on the script that the video is accompanied by natural sound, the sound of the people in the pumpkin patch, for example, and that the natural sound is to be played "under" the anchor's voice. When the director calls out "take VTR three" (in this example, the tape in question is being played through VTR three), she also indicates to the audio person to "track" it, meaning to play the accompanying sound.

All tapes start at :00, so when the director takes the tape he or she also resets a timer in the control room. Writers also indicate how much time is on the tape. In that way, if the timer is up to :38 on a piece accompanied by a 40 second tape and the anchor still has two sentences to read, the director knows it's time to quickly cut back to the camera shot of the anchor before the tape goes to black on the air. In an effort to keep this from happening, writers and producers time the part of the script intended to be "under" video beforehand and ask tape editors to provide 8 to 10 seconds of tape beyond what's needed.

So, if someone read the "before" pumpkin example and it took :30 to read it, the tape editor would be asked to provide :40 seconds of tape. That video pad is critical, and we indicate the amount of tape provided including the pad. This alleviates a lot of panic in the control room. A quick production note: The 10 seconds of pad isn't a new shot but a continuation of the shot that covers the final seconds of the VO. Just as we don't want the video to run out, we also don't want the shot to change just before the director punches out. So the final shot on a 40-second piece of tape would run from about :25 or :26 all the way to :40—or as close to :40 as that one shot will get you.

Also, notice where the "cass out" (short for cassette out; some news operations use "tape ends" or other similar wording) marking is positioned. It comes at the bottom of the script. This indicates that once we've taken the tape, it's supposed to continue until the end of the script. If instead we had wanted to see the anchor for the final sentence of the script, we would have positioned the "cass out" marking at the end of the preceding sentence and added an "on cam"marking at the beginning of the final sentence. It's very important to include these directions, and we'll introduce you to others as we discuss other television news story forms. Remember, television is a visual medium and news writers have to provide information to the folks on the technical side so that the pictures and the words will match up.

Writing to File Footage

Many VOs include file video rather than fresh footage shot that day. The problem with writing to file footage is that it simply doesn't happen in many instances. A writer or producer might have a general idea of what a particular piece of file tape shows, but rather than looking at the tape and writing today's story specifically to it, the writer composes a story and hopes that the file tape fits. Often, it doesn't. Using our earlier example, what if a shot of a police officer comes up during the part of the story when the script is mentioning a little boy? The only way to know if that might be a problem is to look at the piece of tape and tailor the writing to fit what the viewers will see.

Even in the cases when we know the tape doesn't show what the script is mentioning, there are ways to downplay the discrepancy. For example, let's assume that Johnny Famoussinger was killed in a plane crash half an hour before airtime, and no video of the crash site is available yet. We might choose to use file tape of a recent concert, but of course that has no direct relation to today's story. Making a reference to the specific video we have at the beginning of the story makes the use of this piece of file tape more acceptable. The story would begin something like this:

Singer

	(Gayle)
On cam	POP SUPERSTAR JOHNNY
	FAMOUSSINGER IS DEAD.
:00 Take cass snd under (VO)	(vo)
	SHOWN HERE AT A CONCERT LAST
	MONTH . . . FAMOUSSINGER IS SHOWN
	HERE . . . HE WAS RETURNING TO
	GOTHAM CITY FROM THE WEST COAST
	EARLY THIS MORNING WHEN HIS
	PRIVATE JET WENT DOWN IN A REMOTE
	PART OF THE ROCKY MOUNTAINS . . .

Making a reference to the video we're seeing makes it more acceptable for use in relation to a story that has nothing to do with the concert. It's important to write to the video throughout, but in cases like this we have no video to go with today's story other than the file tape. So, a direct video reference at the top is about the best we can do. Failing to reference the video can lead to some confusion. In this example, we'd be talking about Famoussinger returning when the footage is of him singing. Giving the viewers the visual reference at the top alerts them that what they see is what they're going to get.

Now let's look at a few more examples. First, a reader story.

Boys Ranch
_____

	(—— Colleen—- -)
SS: BOYS RANCH	ARIZONA BOYS RANCH HAS FILED
	AN APPEAL TO KEEP THE STATE FROM
	SHUTTING DOWN THE PROGRAM FOR
	DELINQUENT YOUTHS. THE BOYS RANCH
	ACCUSES THE STATE OF WRONGLY
	REFUSING TO RENEW ITS CHILD-CARE
	LICENSE. THE GROUP'S ATTORNEY
	CLAIMS THE STATE SINGLED OUT THE
	MARCH DEATH OF 16-YEAR-OLD
	NICHOLAS CON-TRER-AZ BECAUSE IT
	DOESN'T LIKE THE PROGRAM. THE BOYS
	RANCH HAS BEEN IN OPERATION FOR
	49 YEARS.

The only marking we've provided for the director on this example (other than the title of the story) is the notation "SS: BOYS RANCH." That lets the director know that the story begins with the anchor (Colleen) on camera and an image out of the still store machine appearing over her shoulder. Because no other markings appear, the director knows no tape is involved and that we'll see the anchor's face for the duration of this short story. "SS" stands for still store, and this particular image will include the written title "BOYS RANCH." Colleen knows not to read her name even though it appears on the right side of the page because it's in parentheses and is in upper and lowercase. The procedure at this station is to put the script in all uppercase.

Now we'll look at a few examples of different ways of dealing with VOs, either as individual stories or as part of a story set.

Periodontal
_____

	(—— Colleen——-)
On cam	THERE'S A NEW WEAPON TO HELP
	KEEP YOUR TEETH HEALTHY.

ENG NATVO	(——-vo——)
LENGTH :30	THE FOOD AND DRUG
	ADMINISTRATION HAS JUST APPROVED
	AR-TI-DOX . . . A NEW, PAINLESS
	TREATMENT FOR PERIODONTAL DISEASE.
	IT COMES IN THE FORM OF A TOPICAL
	GEL AND IS CONVENIENT TO USE. THE
	CURRENT TREATMENT USED TO FIGHT
	PLAQUE PROBLEMS AND BACTERIA
	REQUIRES ANESTHESIA AND CAN BE
	PAINFUL.
ENG OUT	

Notice that some of the markings we've provided for the director on this script are a bit different from what we've used before. All stations in this country speak the same language; it's just that the dialects can vary. The wording used for the various directions is usually a function of the newsroom computer system used in that particular shop. Some of the more common software programs for writing television news are NewsStar, AP NewsCenter and Basys. In our earlier examples, we noted the place where the tape is supposed to start with the marking "take cass." This station uses the marking "ENG NATVO." In the next example, that point will be indicated by the marking "M2/VO." They all mean the same thing: this is the place to start the tape. The way we indicate the place at which the director should punch out of the tape in this story is with the marking "ENG OUT," which means the same thing as "cass out" or "tape ends." In one station, "ENG" means a videotape; in another, that's indicated by "cass"; and in others, it's indicated by the particular type of videotape the station uses, such as "M2," "beta," "SVHS" and the like.

You'll notice that the time for the tape is indicated near the beginning of the script rather than at the end. It's simply a matter of getting accustomed to the conventions used in a particular station. Although the wording and the positioning of the director cues are sometimes a bit different, we give the director the same information in all of these examples: whether or not the anchor appears on camera, if a tape is involved, and if so, where it starts, where it ends and how long it is.

Daviscourt
___

	(**GAYLE**)
SQ/SS	(** SQ/SS **)
	ADAM DAVIS AND JOHN WHISPELL
	HAVE NEW ATTORNEYS TONIGHT. BUT

	THEY STILL HAVEN'T ENTERED PLEAS TO THEIR MURDER CHARGES.
M2/VO	(**M2/VO**)
	THE 19-YEAR-OLDS ARE CHARGED WITH MURDERING CARROLWOOD REALTOR VICKIE ROBINSON LAST MONTH. ROBINSON'S 15-YEAR-OLD DAUGHTER VALESSA IS ALSO CHARGED . . . SHE'S ENTERED A NOT GUILTY PLEA. THIS MORNING, A HILLSBOROUGH JUDGE ASSIGNED BOTH MEN COURT-APPOINTED LAWYERS. THEIR ARRAIGNMENT WAS DELAYED UNTIL THE NEW LAWYERS GET FAMILIAR WITH THE CASE.
M2/ENDS :35	

This example is essentially the same as the one that came before it. We begin with Gayle on camera and an image from the still store (SS) squeezed (SQ) to fit over her shoulder. We then punch up the tape at the indicated spot, and it continues until the end of the story.

Orimulsion

	(**BOB**)
SS/CK/WALL	(**SS/CK/WALL**)
	THE FIGHT TO BURN ORIMULSION AT A PARRISH POWER PLANT IS OFFICIALLY OVER TONIGHT. TODAY, FLORIDA POWER AND LIGHT CALLED IT QUITS.
M2/VO	(**M2/VO**)
	FOR YEARS THE POWER COMPANY HAS TRIED TO GET PERMISSION TO INTRODUCE THE CONTROVERSIAL FUEL. ORIMULSION IS A MIX OF WATER AND A TAR-LIKE SUBSTANCE THAT'S MINED OUT OF A RIVER IN VENEZUELA. IT DOESN'T FLOAT AND MIXES WITH WATER. THAT MAKES IT MUCH MORE DIFFICULT TO CLEAN UP IF THERE'S A SPILL.
M2/ENDS :35	

At the beginning of this VO, we're doing something a little different. Instead of having something out of still store squeezed over Bob's
shoulder, we're going to position him in front of the chroma key (CK)
wall and electronically place the still store image on the wall behind
him. This is how weather maps, radar and satellite images are projected behind the weathercaster. As a way to enhance the pace of the program and show off other parts of the news set, many stations (and
network newscasts) have begun using the chroma key wall for much
more than weather.

Let's look at one final example of how VOs are used. Often, a number of related stories are placed back to back, and we transition from
script to script without seeing the anchor between stories.

World Tonight

	(—— Colleen—-)
	MAKING HEADLINES IN THE WORLD
	TONIGHT . . . TWO RIVALS TEAM UP
	. . . TO FLY AROUND THE GLOBE . . .
	AND HISTORIC TALKS IN NORTHERN
	IRELAND . . .
ENG NATVO	(—- vo—-)
	FOR THE FIRST TIME EVER . . . THE
	POLITICAL LEADERS OF THE PROTESTANT
	AND CATHOLIC COMMUNITIES IN
	NORTHERN IRELAND SAT AND TALKED
	. . . FACE TO FACE. DAVID TRIMBLE AND
	GERRY ADAMS SPOKE OF WIDE GAPS
	BETWEEN THE TWO SIDES . . . AND
	SAID THEY WOULD USE THE TALKS TO
	GET TO KNOW EACH OTHER. THEY'VE
	PLANNED MORE MEETINGS.
WIPE ENG NATVO	(—- wipe vo—-)
	(—- Colleen—-)
	(—- vo top—-)
	STEVE FOSSETT AND RICHARD
	BRANSON ARE TEAMING UP . . . TO TRY
	TO FLY A BALLOON AROUND THE
	WORLD. BOTH MEN HAVE FAILED
	SEVERAL TIMES TRYING TO MAKE THE
	FLIGHT ON THEIR OWN . . . BUT SAY

```
                                TEAMWORK WILL GIVE THEM AN
                                ADVANTAGE. THEY SAY THEY'LL TAKE
                                TURNS FLYING THE BALLOON.
WIPE ENG NATVO                      (—- wipe vo—-)
                                    (—- Colleen—-)
                                    (—- vo top—-)
                                A FRESNO, CALIFORNIA CORNFIELD
                                HAS TOURISTS TRYING TO FIND THEIR
                                WAY OUT OF A MAZE . . . THE MAZE IS
                                IN THE SHAPE OF THE STATE OF
                                CALIFORNIA . . . WITH A STAR TO
                                SHOW FRESNO'S PLACE IN THE STATE.
                                THE WALLS ARE 10 FEET HIGH . . . AND
                                THERE ARE 85 PLACES WHERE VISITORS
                                HAVE TO TRY TO FIGURE OUT THE
                                RIGHT WAY TO GO.
ENG OUT
```

In this example we start with Colleen on camera and give a brief idea of the stories coming up. We get to the first of the three stories in standard fashion, but then transition to the subsequent stories by wiping from one tape to the next. Colleen continues to read, with video starting right at the top of stories 2 and 3. Some of the markings here might seem redundant, because if we're wiping to a new VO, it stands to reason that the second VO will start right at the top. But it's better not to look confused, and often in a series of stories like this, each is on a separate page. So it helps to reiterate at the beginning of tape 2 what the instructions were at the end of tape 1.

Conclusion

By now it should be clear that we have much more to deal with than just the words we write, even when structuring the most basic television story—the voice-over—and the markings become a bit more extensive when we get to VO/SOTs and packages. Although the production element of what we do is important, the bottom line is still the ability to craft the written part of the story. Use of over-the-shoulder inserts, chroma key, wiping between tapes and other production techniques can add to the presentation of stories. But no amount of jazzy production can rescue a poorly written piece.

Do's and Don'ts for VOs

Do	Don't
• Write to the video.	• Leave out times and other cues.
• Grab viewer attention right away.	• Write generic copy for generic video.
• Make sure everyone on the team knows what we're doing.	• Leave out any major information.

TELEVISION STORY FORMS—THE VO/SOT

As the acronym implies, the VO/SOT begins as a VO, which you're quite familiar with by now. But, as also implied, the VO/SOT involves an additional element, the SOT (sound on tape) portion. The SOT (often called a sound bite, or simply a bite) is a brief snippet of an on-camera interview that's edited to follow a certain amount of voice-over video. So, the VO/SOT involves more than one voice: the anchor's voice and one or more brief comments from an interview source or sources. Some news operations use the acronym VO/B rather than VO/SOT so that they can indicate if more than one bite is included. So, a VO/B/B would include two different bites. However, many operations still use VO/SOT because the number of sound bites on the tapes isn't what's really important to the people in the control room. What's really important is the length of the SOT. More on that when we discuss marking VO/SOT scripts.

The Role of a VO/SOT

A VO/SOT lets producers vary the pacing of a news program and allows us to give a little more airtime to a story than if it were a VO, but not as much as to a package. A VO/SOT should be used when we're covering an event and something a participant or observer has to say carries some emotion or impact that would be lost if we paraphrased the comment for the anchor to read.

Melissa Antoccia is a producer in Las Vegas. One of the photographers at her station covered an overnight house fire and got a few comments from the public information officer (PIO) for the fire department. (It isn't uncommon for a photographer to shoot and conduct brief interviews by himself or herself.) The video was compelling—the house completely in flames, firefighters working hard to put out the fire—but most of what the PIO had to say was general information about what happened, so Melissa was thinking VO.

However, one comment stood out when Melissa was logging the tape, and she decided to make the piece a VO/SOT. The PIO said that the people in the house were very lucky to get out and credited some neighbors who knocked on the windows of the house and woke up the sleeping occupants, probably saving their lives. The emotion in the voice of the PIO was sincere and imparted a sense of how truly lucky the people in the house were. Some of that emotion would have been lost had the anchor told that part of the story.

This raises a concern that Melissa is quick to point out. Generally, an official spokesperson isn't as emotionally involved in a story like this as the people affected are, and a bite from one of the neighbors or one of the occupants would have been better still. Many news operations are overly dependent on "official" comments. Work to get bites from the people who are directly affected. PIOs are generally very helpful to news crews, but there's no way they can share the emotion that someone else experienced because of losing a home or suffering some other tragedy.

Joe Kovacs is an assignments manager in Miami, and he echoes Melissa's thoughts about the importance of good bites. In South Florida, tanker truck rollovers are all too common, and it seems the more deadly the cargo, the more likely the truck is to crash during rush hour. On many occasions, Joe has had to drop all preparations for other stories (including some for which he had ordered satellite time) to get a crew to the scene of a rollover. These stories are often covered as a live reporter toss to a VO/SOT, because the crew doesn't have time to produce a package before hitting the air live. However, it's important to get a sound bite into a breaking news piece such as this, whether the sound is from a highway patrol trooper who explains what the agency thinks happened or from a motorist who narrowly missed being caught up in the flaming accident. Such a bite can enhance a story tremendously.

One word of caution from Joe Kovacs though. He says just because you do an interview, don't think you *have* to use a portion of it on the air. If the bite isn't compelling, it's just taking up air time. Sound is good, when the sound *is good*.

Scripting a VO/SOT

When we decide to make a story a VO/SOT, there are a few more steps in the scripting process than when we're working with a VO. Because a VO/SOT begins as a VO, everything that applies to scripting and marking a VO applies to the first part of a VO/SOT. It's still very important to write to the video and to follow all the other guidelines listed in earlier chapters. But with the VO/SOT story form we incorporate an SOT, and we need to do a couple of extra things with the script. As noted in Chapter 1, we believe that it isn't enough to place a super over the bite to identify the speaker. Many people are doing other things while the news is on and aren't paying close attention to the screen. If we don't verbally identify the speaker, many viewers won't know who the person is or why what that person is saying is relevant to the story. However, some writers and instructors will tell you this breaks the flow of the story, so this isn't a practice followed in every newsroom, though we think it should be for the reasons stated above.

The VO portion of the script needs to accomplish several things relevant to the SOT that the viewers are about to hear. The writer should identify the person who's about to speak by name and give the person's title, which usually is enough to explain why what the person has to say is relevant. The writer should then set up the bite by giving the viewers an idea of what the speaker is about to say. A super is a supplement to this spoken information, not a replacement for it.

Setting Up the Bite

The key to an effective setup of an upcoming bite is to give the viewers a sense of what to expect the speaker to say without parroting what we're about to hear. Let's say we've selected a bite from the mayor of a small town in our market. In the bite, the mayor talks about the give-and-take that occurred during an all-night bargaining session she's just wrapped up with the police union. We wouldn't lead to a bite like that by saying something about the mayor's being glad the impasse is over, because that leads the viewer to expect the mayor's comment to have something to do with her relief rather than the bargaining session itself. Equally bad is to lead into the mayor by saying something like "Hooverville Mayor Jane Smith says the deal involved concessions from both sides" if that's followed by the mayor saying "the deal involved concessions from both sides" or even "both sides made concessions." When the bite repeats what the anchor has just said, that sounds foolish indeed.

Another common mistake is to lead into a bite by writing something along the lines of "and Mayor Smith had this to say" or "we asked Mayor Smith about that" or "Mayor Smith commented on the issue." These are very weak ways to lead to a bite. We need to write something specific that sets the stage for the specific bite we're about to hear.

How do we know what to write to set up bites? Our interviewees often provide the words we need, and there's no shame in borrowing liberally from your sources to flesh out your scripts. After all, it's *their* story we're telling. Using our example with Mayor Smith, let's look at a typical question and answer from an interview about this subject.

> **Reporter:**   "How would you characterize last night's bargaining session?"
>
> **Mayor:**   (in typical politi-speak) "We are indeed gratified that an amicable solution has been reached and that a new contract seems imminent. We believe the union negotiators to be tough, but fair. Neither side got everything it wanted, but the deal we have arrived at proves that when people work toward a common goal and consider the ramifications of various scenarios, agreement is possible." (At this point the mayor slips up and begins to talk like a real person.) "The bottom line is, the city wanted to come to terms before the deadline and so did the union. The officers didn't want to go without paychecks and we didn't want to face the possibility of having no police on the streets. That would have brought the city to a standstill."

Because you're a sharp reporter, your sound-bite antennae immediately send a message screaming to your brain. Sound bite! The final part of the mayor's 45-second answer to the question is a nice succinct 12-second sound bite. In general, you look for bites in the 8- to 12-second range. They can be shorter, but need to be at least 5 or 6 seconds long to give the people in the control room time to get the super in and out. Bites can also be longer than 12 seconds, but it has to be truly compelling information to warrant going beyond 15 seconds or so.

The mayor has provided us with what we were after—a good bite of the sought-after length in the language of real people. But what about all that stuff she said before the bite? It isn't totally useless. She gave us a good phrase to use to lead to her bite when she said the agreement involved concessions from both sides. Based on the bite we've chosen and the additional information we've decided to incorporate in the VO portion of the script, we can write the story. But even after we write, we're not finished with this story.

Marking a VO/SOT Script

Just as we have to take a few more things into consideration when writing a VO/SOT script, we also have to add some information for the director and his control room crew that we don't include on VO scripts. With a VO, all we have to do is indicate when the tape is supposed to start and how much time is on the tape so that the director knows how much tape remains as the anchor nears the end of the script. But with a VO/SOT, we have to indicate when the tape is supposed to begin, when the audio on the tape switches from natural sound under the anchor's voice to stand-alone sound from a bite, and when the bite ends. You might wonder about the pad video that goes at the end of a VO. It's still necessary to add video pad when editing the tape, but we don't indicate the pad on the script for a VO/SOT when both the VO and the SOT are edited on the same tape. Here's why.

Let's say that we write a script that includes 25 seconds of voice-over and a 15-second bite. That tape is supposed to end at 40 seconds, regardless of when the tape was rolled or what the anchor's read rate is, because the end of the SOT determines the end of the tape. We don't want to see the interviewee just sitting there after the bite ends. We delete the audio and let the video of the interviewee continue to avoid going to black or snow just in case there are problems in the control room, but we definitely want the director to punch out of the tape right after the interviewee finishes her comment. Just in case, though, there's that silent shot (continuation of the shot of the interviewee's face) to cover us.

Reading Up to the SOT

Editing an SOT on the end of a VO creates an additional problem, because the anchor has to stop speaking at a specific time, so as not to talk over the top of the SOT or leave a long pause before the SOT begins. There are two ways to keep this from happening. Someone in the control room can count down in the anchor's ear and tell her to slow down or speed up so that the VO read comes out the right length. As an alternative, many news operations place the VO and the SOT on separate tapes. That gives the director a little more latitude for dealing with discrepancies in how long it takes to read the VO. By putting the SOT on a separate tape, we can wait until the anchor is finished reading the VO (with no one distracting her by talking into her ear while she's trying to read) and then transition to the other tape. The same guideline about including pad video is true if the SOT is on a separate tape. The first tape has no definitive out point, but the second tape does, so we indicate the pad on the VO script but not on the SOT script. We put pad on both tapes, and on both it's a continuation of the shot with which we ended. Again, we put pad on the end of the SOT *just in case,* but the plan is for the director to punch out as soon as the bite ends, and that's the time we give the director.

Let's return to our friend Mayor Smith and look at a couple of examples of marking a VO/SOT script, followed by explanations of how we arrived at the times indicated and what the new markings mean.

New Contract

	(Dave)
ON CAM	HOW DOES HOOVERVILLE MAYOR JANE SMITH SPELL RELIEF? C-O-N-T-R-A-C-T.
	(vo)
:00 take cass vid and snd under (VO)	AFTER AN ALL-NIGHT BARGAINING SESSION AT CITY HALL, THE MAYOR AND POLICE UNION REPRESENTATIVES HAVE COME TO TERMS ON A NEW CONTRACT FOR HOOVERVILLE'S FINEST. NEGOTIATIONS HAD STALLED IN PAST WEEKS AND THE JULY 1ST DEADLINE WAS LOOMING. THE 25 COPS REPRESENTED BY THE UNION THREATENED TO WALK OFF THE JOB IF THEY DIDN'T GET A 10 PERCENT PAY RAISE AND TAKE-HOME USE OF THEIR PATROL CARS. THE MAYOR SAYS THE AGREEMENT INVOLVES CONCESSIONS FROM BOTH SIDES.
:25 cass cont. vid and snd full (SOT) :26 Super: Jane Smith/Hooverville Mayor	(sot)
:40 cass out ON CAM	outcue: "the city to a standstill."
	IF THE CONTRACT IS APPROVED BY UNION MEMBERS, OFFICERS WILL GET A FIVE PERCENT RAISE AND WILL BE ALLOWED TO TAKE THEIR SQUAD CARS HOME EACH NIGHT.

The first few directions on the left-hand side of the script are familiar. But at some point we transition from the anchor's voice to sound on tape, which is new for us. We have to let the director, the audio person and other control room personnel know when to make those adjustments. How do we determine that 25 seconds is the time? Simply by reading and timing the portion of the VO from the time the tape starts until the anchor stops talking. In this example, that goes from "After an all-night bargaining session" to "concessions from both sides." So at 25 seconds the anchor stops reading and someone else starts speaking on tape. As soon as possible after that transition has occurred, we put up a super identifying the speaker. Then the director waits to see :40 on his control room timer and to hear the final few words of the mayor's comment, called the outcue. How do we figure 40 seconds? When the videotape editor was given the script, she was told to put down 25 seconds' worth of pictures to go along with the VO portion of the script. The writer would then indicate the bite that had been selected, and the editor would add that to the tape. In this case let's assume the bite was 15 seconds long as indicated by the editing machine timer, making the whole piece 40 seconds long. The editor would end the mayor's audio at the appointed time but allow the video to continue for an extra 10 seconds to give the director some pad, but the intent is to have him get out of the tape right at 40 seconds. When the director sees :40 and hears the outcue, he goes back to a studio camera shot of the anchor, who wraps up the story by relaying one final piece of information.

It's important that the story end with the anchor and not with someone else speaking. The anchor comes back on camera (or we could choose to add more VO after the outcue, making the piece a VO/SOT/VO) to wrap up that story and transition to something else. The stories wouldn't flow together very well if an SOT ended and the anchor started immediately reading a different story. The anchor's role is to end one story and transition the viewers to the next one.

Here's one final note on the script markings on our example. You'll notice that there's a big gap on the right side of the page. When the anchor sees nothing, that means stop reading. You'll also notice that the outcue is listed on the right side of the page. That's so the anchor can also listen for it and be ready for the next on-camera portion of the script. We also add a blank line or two after the outcue, leaving the outcue "floating out in space," to lessen the chance that the anchor might read it as part of his next line. Now, we'll set up the same story using two videotapes rather than one. Again, this is done so that the anchor's read of the VO portion doesn't have to come out at exactly a certain time.

New Contract

	(Dave)
ON CAM	HOW DOES HOOVERVILLE MAYOR JANE SMITH SPELL RELIEF? C-O-N-T-R-A-C-T.
	(vo)
:00 take cass vid and snd under (VO)	AFTER AN ALL-NIGHT BARGAINING SESSION AT CITY HALL, THE MAYOR AND POLICE UNION REPRESENTATIVES HAVE COME TO TERMS ON A NEW CONTRACT FOR HOOVERVILLE'S FINEST. NEGOTIATIONS HAD STALLED IN PAST WEEKS AND THE JULY 1ST DEADLINE FOR A NEW AGREEMENT WAS LOOMING. THE 25 COPS REPRESENTED BY THE UNION THREATENED TO WALK OFF THE JOB IF THEY DIDN'T GET A 10 PERCENT RAISE AND TAKE-HOME USE OF THEIR PATROL CARS. THE MAYOR SAYS THE AGREEMENT INVOLVES CONCESSIONS FROM BOTH SIDES.
:35 cass out (the remaining part of this script would go on a separate page) :00 wipe to cass 2 snd full (SOT) :01 Super: Jane Smith/Hooverville Mayor	(sot)
:15 cass out	outcue: "the city to a standstill."
ON CAM	IF THE CONTRACT IS APPROVED BY UNION MEMBERS, OFFICERS WILL GET A FIVE PERCENT RAISE AND WILL BE ALLOWED TO TAKE THEIR SQUAD CARS HOME EACH NIGHT.

The difference between this example and the first one is that we end one cassette and transition to another within the same story. Our VO should take 25 seconds to read, but if the anchor's read is a little short or a little long, it's not a problem because we have 35 seconds' worth of tape. Whenever the anchor reaches the end of the VO, the director rolls and transitions to the next tape, which is now only 15 seconds long because it contains the SOT only. The time for the super is different because it's now based on the start time of the second tape, not the first one. Also, the two parts of this story appear on separate script pages.

Stand-Alone SOTs

Let's assume that for some reason, we don't have any video to use with the VO portion of a story. We could set up the story as a straight SOT and use the same markings that we used in the second half of our second example of the contract story. However, straight SOTs are pretty rare. Because this is a visual medium and head shots aren't all that compelling, the preference is to use some sort of video to get into the bite—video from the meeting, a photo opportunity with the mayor and union officials, file video of cops on the beat or something else that goes along with our script. Still, on occasion we might script an SOT with no VO—simply an on-camera introduction from the anchor that leads directly into the bite. The same guidelines apply to that type of lead to a sound bite as to a sound bite lead accompanied by video. We still need to introduce the speaker, tell why his or her comments are important and set up the bite.

The Need for Good Communication

As you can tell, television news writers have a lot more to worry about than just the words they put on the page. It might seem that we've placed too much emphasis on the directions you add to television news scripts, but the most beautifully written piece can quickly turn into a nightmare on the air without the correct markings. Now that we've added SOTs to the mix, the directions take on added significance. Communication with all the other people who will have something to do with how that story appears on the air is critical. Many news workers have noted that the biggest problem in the communication business is a lack of communication. Never assume that others in the news operation know how you want a story to play. You have to tell them by marking the script appropriately.

Be aware that just as we might write a straight SOT story, there are variations on the VO/SOT setup to a story. We might have an SOT/VO or a VO/SOT/VO—starting with the bite and then going to voice-over or adding some more voice-over after the bite ends. The order of the elements doesn't matter, as long as everyone involved clearly understands what's going on.

Now let's look at a few more examples of how to script VO/SOTs. The first is actually a VO/SOT/VO.

Duck Folo

	(—- Colleen—-)
SS: Adoption	HAVING DUCKS AS PETS IS CATCHING ON IN TUCSON.
ENG NATVO	(—- vo—-)
	THE HUMANE SOCIETY HAS ADOPTED-OUT 160 DUCKS SO FAR. WE BROUGHT YOU THIS STORY EARLIER IN THE WEEK. BIOLOGISTS ROUNDED UP THE DUCKS FROM THEIR HOME IN KENNEDY PARK. WE WERE THERE WHEN DONNA AVERY PICKED UP HER NEW FINE, FEATHERED FRIEND.
DISSOLVE ENG SOT	
	(—- sot—-)
ENG SOT 12 sec.	"I would take as many ducks,
CG: Donna Avery\Animal lover	turkeys, geese, anything . . . chickens. They just run wild at my house, they love it. They come to the door and beg for food and they have food outside (laugh)."
ENG NATVO	(—- vo—-)
	CITY OFFICIALS SAY THERE WERE JUST TOO MANY DUCKS AT KENNEDY PARK. THEIR WASTE WAS CAUSING A VIRTUAL TOXIC SOUP FOR THE FISH . . . AND WAS ALSO HARMING OTHER BIRDS.
ENG OUT	

In this example, we start with the anchor on camera with a graphic from the still store machine over her shoulder. Notice that she's on camera for only a few seconds before we go to the video. The anchor then reads over video for about 15 seconds before reaching the (sot) marking. She knows that this notation means that a source is about to speak on tape, so she remains silent during the SOT.

On the left side of the page, we've told the director to dissolve (a different transition than a wipe) from the VO tape to the SOT tape at that point and have indicated that the sound bite lasts for 12 seconds. We've also indicated "CG," which means character generator and is another way of saying "super": at this point the written name of the person speaking is supered (superimposed) on the lower third of the screen. The sound bite is written on the right-hand side so that both the director and the anchor can follow it and listen for the outcue. Many news operations write out the bite like this for closed-captioning and also so that the anchor can summarize the comment if something goes wrong with the tape. The anchor knows not to read this part of the script because it's in quotes and *isn't* uppercase.

When we reach the outcue, the second tape continues with more VO video following the SOT. The director cues the anchor, who then reads the remaining script over the video. She knows that she won't have to look at the camera during the VO and will probably choose to read from the hard copy rather than from the prompter. This will allow her to pay closer attention to how her read rate is matching what we're seeing on tape.

Be aware that most of the time, the two parts of a story like this are on separate pages and occupy two lines on the show rundown (see Chapter 10 on producing). So in this example, everything from "ENG SOT 12 sec." would be on a second script page. This helps the director grasp that the VO and SOT are edited on separate tapes and that the producer is calling for some type of transition between the two. The second bit of VO video is on the same tape as the SOT, so no dissolve or wipe is indicated: we merely continue with the second tape.

Blood Testing

	(—- Colleen—-)
SS: BLOOD TESTING	A TUCSON HOSPITAL IS PIONEERING
	NEW BLOOD TESTING TECHNOLOGY.
ENG NATVO	(—- vo—-)
	KINO COMMUNITY HOSPITAL'S BLOOD
	BANK IS THE FIRST IN THE U-S TO HAVE
	THIS NEW TECHNIQUE, CALLED GAMMA
	REACT SYSTEM. NORMALLY, BLOOD
	TESTING TAKES UP TO AN HOUR AND A
	HALF . . . BUT THIS TECHNIQUE TAKES
	ONLY ABOUT 25 MINUTES. HOSPITAL
	SPOKESWOMAN BRENDA PARKER SAYS
	THE HOSPITAL CAN NOW CHECK FOR
	INCOMPATIBLE BLOOD MORE QUICKLY.
DISSOLVE ENG SOT	(—- sot—-)
ENG SOT 15 sec.	

CG: Brenda Parker\Kino Hospital	"In a crisis situation when you need blood in a hurry you've got to be able to find compatible blood fast . . . and this method enables us to identify the antibody fast and get compatible blood much, much faster than the previous method."
ENG OUT	(—- out—-)
LIVE	OFFICIALS WITH THE UNIVERSITY OF ARIZONA MEDICAL TECHNOLOGY PROGRAM PLAN TO VIDEOTAPE KINO TECHNICIANS DEMONSTRATING THE NEW TECHNIQUE FOR CLASSROOM USE.

This example is very similar to the duck folo story, except that we've set this one up to have the director punch back to the studio camera at the end of the SOT rather than having the anchor read over more VO tape. The (out) tells the anchor that the tape has ended and she should be ready to go back on camera. As with the previous example, everything from "ENG SOT 15 sec." will be on a separate page. Any time there are two tapes, there are two script pages.

In the following example, we'll look at a story designed to follow a related piece about reputed drug kingpin Charles Miller. The first story details charges that Miller has threatened to harm U.S. students at a veterinary school in the Caribbean if the U.S. government continues to crack down on what it terms his illegal drug operation. That story leads us to this one:

Miller Details

	(**BOB**)
2SHOT	(**2SHOT**)
	TONIGHT, WE'RE LEARNING A LOT MORE ABOUT CHARLES MILLER . . . THE MAN WHO'S MAKING THE THREATS.
GAYLE	(**GAYLE**)
	HE HAS A LONG HISTORY OF VIOLENCE BUT HAS BEEN ABLE TO AVOID ARREST ON THE ISLAND OF SAINT KITTS.
SS/CG	(**SS/CG**)
SUPER: CHARLES MILLER	AN ARTICLE IN THE WASHINGTON POST GIVES A LOT OF DETAIL ON MILLER.
add: smuggled drugs from Miami	(**add**)

to New York	AT ONE POINT, MILLER WAS SMUGGLING MORE THAN A TON OF COCAINE AND MARIJUANA A MONTH FROM MIAMI TO NEW YORK.
add: immunity, witness protection program	(**add**)
	DESPITE THAT, HE WAS GIVEN FULL IMMUNITY AND A PLACE IN THE U-S GOVERNMENT'S WITNESS PROTECTION PROGRAM IN EXCHANGE FOR INFORMATION ABOUT A DRUG SMUGGLING RING.
add: admitted to participating in murders	(**add**)
	MILLER ADMITTED IN COURT TO TAKING PART IN THE MURDERS OF FIVE PEOPLE IN A MIAMI CRACK HOUSE IN THE 19-80s.
add: State Department: still dangerous	(**add**)
	STATE DEPARTMENT OFFICIALS SAY MILLER IS STILL DANGEROUS . . . THEY WANT HIM TO FACE SMUGGLING CHARGES . . .
add: Warning U-S citizens	(**add**)
	AND THEY'RE ALERTING PEOPLE ON SAINT KITTS TO BE CAREFUL.
M2/SOT UP FULL	(**SOT**)
SUPER: James Rubin/State Department Spokesman	
	((we know of this individual and consider this threat, this person sufficiently violent to justify taking these steps))
RUNS: 08	
TAG	(**TAG**)
	THE STATE DEPARTMENT IS HINTING THAT U-S AUTHORITIES WILL RETALIATE AGAINST MILLER IF HE HARMS U-S CITIZENS. THERE ARE 250 AMERICAN STUDENTS AND 50 AMERICAN FACULTY MEMBERS AT ROSS VETERINARY UNIVERSITY.

In this example, we start with a 2shot to let the anchors play off one another as they lead to this story. The news operation has no video on Miller and certainly has no video that supports the particular points to be made in this story. So the producer calls for a picture of Miller from still store (SS) and information to be superimposed over that image. That information comes from the character generator (CG). We've indicated to the director the specific places at which new information is to be added. The anchor has this information as well, so that she can pace herself to read something as it's being added to the screen. The entire VO portion of this script is read over a graphic rather than over video.

When we reach the end of that section of the story, we go to a sound bite on M2 (a particular type of videotape) from a State Department spokesperson, and the director adds a super (name and title of the person speaking) on the lower third of the screen. The SOT lasts for eight seconds; then the director punches back to the studio camera for the anchor to read the tag. "Tag" is the term used for the final bit of information that the anchor reads to wrap up a story before moving on to something else.

Conclusion

As we noted in Chapter 7 on VOs, the wording of the directions provided to the director often varies slightly from one news operation to another. But, again, the basic information provided on VO/SOTs is the same: Do we start on camera? Where does the VO begin? Where do we transition to SOT? How long is the bite? Does the anchor finish the story on camera or by reading more VO copy? We reiterate a point made several other times in this book. The markings are important. Television news is very team-oriented, and everyone on the team has to know what's coming next for the script and the visual elements to work together as we intend.

⌐⫿ Do's and Don'ts for VO/SOTs

Do
- Write specific leads to bites.
- Put VO and SOT on separate tapes.
- Leave room for error (pad) in case of control room mayhem.
- Pick compelling bites.

Don't
- Parrot what the interviewee will say.
- End a VO/SOT without reestablishing the anchor.
- Assume other people know what's supposed to happen unless you tell them.

TELEVISION STORY FORMS— THE PACKAGE

K elli Durand wanted to be a reporter badly enough to leave a pretty good engineering operator's job in a large market television station to go to one of the nation's smaller markets in an on-air position. After being in a small Ohio market for a while, Kelli was assigned to cover a show at the county fairgrounds featuring entertainer Bill Cosby. Sounds like an interesting (and relatively easy) assignment. It didn't turn out that way.

As is often the case with big-name celebrities, the news crew wasn't granted a one-on-one interview with Cosby and was limited to a total of three minutes of video and natural sound of the show. No more than 15 seconds of continuous show video could be used during Kelli's package. She figured out a way around these two minor hurdles: just get interviews with the people enjoying Cosby's performance and use her script to start the joke and let Cosby deliver the punch line, easily within the 15-second time limit.

But then the problems started. A major rainstorm hit the fairgrounds, quickly turning the area into a massive mud pit and delaying the start of the show. It was after 9 o'clock when Cosby came on. The people in the floor seats (the more expensive tickets) were drenched and weren't very interested in being interviewed. The rain was causing the microphone to short out. The cameraperson had to wipe off the lens continually to get a usable image. Kelli and her cameraperson were dripping, and their clothes were clinging to them. It was cold.

Still, Kelli had time to get the package ready, if that was all she had to do. It wasn't. She's also the 11 p.m. weathercaster. She and the cameraperson arrived at the station about 10:15. She quickly wrote the story (she started writing it in the car) and went into an edit booth. She recorded her audio track. It was difficult to get whole sentences out, because she was still shivering uncontrollably and her heart was beating so fast she could hardly catch her breath. At her station, the reporter is responsible for editing the voice track and the bites, and she finished that at about 10:45—leaving the cameraperson 15 minutes to edit in the video from the performance. Her boyfriend had dashed to her apartment to get her a dry suit, so she changed, created her new weather maps, set up the sequence for the weather segment, and was ready to go when weather came on at 11:12. The Cosby story was the lead story, and it was ready on time.

Viewers got to see a hairstyle they'd never seen on Kelli before that night, and she has no idea what she said during the weather. She says she was so unprepared to go on live that she felt as though she was going to be sick right there on the weather set. She wanted to make the Cosby story memorable, and many viewers probably do remember it, but not for the reasons she had in mind. This is the reality of television news reporting. It isn't all glamour. It involves long hours, hard work, sometimes miserable conditions, intense deadline pressure and, in many markets, less pay than you'd earn in most other professions. But it's fun (sometimes), you get to do a lot of interesting things and meet a lot of interesting or important people, and beating a deadline can be a real adrenaline rush. Kelli Durand can certainly attest to that.

Kelli was able to get her story ready in such a short time because she has a real command of the mechanics of putting a package together. Now that we've gained some experience writing VOs and VO/SOTs, *we* can move into reporter packages. As the name implies, packages involve reporters and are "packaged," meaning that they're fully self-contained pieces. You'll recall that VOs and VO/SOTs are read by the anchor. Their involvement in a package is to set up the story in general terms and introduce the reporter. The anchor should also wrap up the story at the end with some additional fact that the reporter was unable to fit into the package itself. This is called the tag. As is the case coming out of VO/SOTs, the flow from one story to another isn't what it could be if the anchor doesn't come back on camera and wrap up a package before going on to another story. Additionally, it's important to have an anchor say something more than "Thank you, John" at the end of the package. If that's all the anchor says, he or she has no "ownership" of the story. We suggest giving anchors active roles in packages, and that would come in the package lead and the tag.

Other than the introduction and the tag, however, an anchor doesn't have anything to do with the presentation of a package. Once an anchor has introduced the reporter, the reporter takes over and relays the information relevant to the story. So, a package is the first story form we've discussed that involves a reporter's voice. A reporter might gather information for a VO and conduct the interview for an SOT, but neither of those story forms involves the reporter putting his or her voice on tape. A package does.

Stand-ups

In most cases, a package also involves a stand-up. A stand-up is when the reporter appears on camera in the field. A stand-up can appear anywhere in the package—either at the beginning or end or somewhere in the middle. When it's placed somewhere in the middle, it's referred to as a "stand-up bridge." Bridges are more common than opening or closing stand-ups. That's because we want the beginning and end of packages to be visually compelling, and the stand-up usually isn't the most compelling video we have to work with.

When a reporter does a stand-up, he or she has to have written a portion of the story so that what's said in the stand-up flows with what comes before it and what comes after it. Usually that doesn't involve actually putting a portion of the story on paper; reporters quickly develop the ability to write in their heads, coming up with good 8- to 12-second stand-ups that will flow with the rest of the script that will be written later.

Logging

One of the most helpful things a reporter can do to make writing a package easier and quicker is to log the tape once he or she is back at the station or in an edit bay in a remote vehicle at the story site. Even if the reporter has been on the scene with a videographer the whole time, the reporter still doesn't know exactly what the shots show or exactly what all the possible sound bites are. The reporter's sound bite antennae might have alerted him or her to several potential sound bites during the interview, but most people can't memorize things well enough to allow them to write a good package without reviewing the tape. You can start to get an idea of the bites you have if you use a mini–audio recorder and listen to the interview in the car on the way back to the station (assuming someone else is driving).

During logging, the reporter looks at the tape to pick out specific shots to write to, specific sound bites to use in the story, and snippets of natural sound to incorporate. Natural sound is what the microphone picks up when you're not in an interview situation. It could be bells ringing, parts of a conversation or any other naturally occurring sound. It's important for the reporter to have specific shots, bites and natural sound in mind when writing the package. We have to write words that are supported by the video we have, and the sound bites are the backbone around which any package is built. The natural sound clips that are incorporated give body to the story. So, a reporter has to note all three elements on the story log and use that material to craft an informative and interesting story. You can write a story without going through the logging process, but chances are it won't be nearly as strong as it could have been had you taken a few minutes to familiarize yourself with what's on the tape.

Leading into and out of Bites

In Chapter 8 on writing VO/SOTs, we talked about the importance of setting up the SOT by telling who the bite is coming from, why the speaker is important to the story, and by giving the viewer an idea of what will be said. We need to do the same thing in a package every time a new speaker is introduced. If we use the same speaker more than once, all we need to do to introduce the second or third bite from the same person is give the viewers an idea of what will be said. It's not necessary to give the person's name or title again. So getting into the SOTs is the same in a package as in a VO/SOT, but because the SOT in a package is followed by more narration from the reporter, we now have to be concerned about how we get out of the sound bite as well as how we get into it.

Let's say that several of the bites we're considering using are listed on the log sheet as follows:

Bob Jones-Concerned Citizen
25:30 "I think it's strange"
25:40 "no public input"

27:14 "any elected official"
27:28 "disservice to the constituents"

28:12 "what the city is trying to do is an outrage"
28:24 "we'll speak at the polls"

28:50 "in this day and time"
29:05 "government of, by, and for the people"

Note that during the logging process, we don't write down every word in the bites. Transposing an entire interview takes a lot more time than news reporters typically have. Later, after we've selected specific bites to use, we'd go back and get the verbatim of those bites for closed-captioning. But no need to write down every word of a bite until we know we're going to use it. Also note that we've indicated the time on the tape at which Jones says the first few words of each comment, called the incue, and the time at which the bite concludes along with the last few words he says, called the outcue. We do this for two reasons. First, when we time the narration parts of the package and add in the times for the SOTs and the stand-up, we know if we've hit the overall time allotted for the piece by the producer. Second, adding the times helps the videotape editor find things quickly. Whenever we can save ourselves or someone else some time, we need to do so. In this example, let's say we choose to use the third bite listed. The log shows we're dealing with a 12-second bite, and the videotape editor knows exactly where to find it—28 minutes and 12 seconds from the beginning of the tape. The portion of the script that would include this bite would look something like this:

> . . . To say that Bob Jones and his neighbors are concerned would be an understatement.
>
> Jones incue: "what the city is trying to do is an outrage"
>
> Jones outcue: "we'll speak at the polls"
>
> But city elections won't be held until 18 months from now. In the meantime, the citizens' group has other plans . . .

We've set up the bite by letting the viewers know to expect Jones to say something about being upset, and we've led out of the bite by picking up on the voting theme. In other words, our narration is a continuation of the thought that Jones started in his bite. As with all other tips we'll pass along, don't overdo this one, but these types of transitions, called tie-writing, can be very effective in keeping the flow of the story going. Let's look at a sample package script, and see how we can work for flow into and out of bites and how we can incorporate natural sound.

JURASSIC PARK

nat snd from film: "Can I touch it?"

In the make-believe world of Jurassic Park, scientists used D-N-A to recreate living dinosaurs. In real life, much of the work done by the Jurassic Park scientists is possible, and in some cases, commonplace.

nat snd bridge: "Take a look at this strand."

Gene sequencing takes place at this lab and other sites around the country every day. Project director Rob Ferl says what happened in Jurassic Park might be possible one day.

Ferl incue: in terms of basic

Ferl outcue: very rapid rate

But not quite as fast as the fictional scientists do it. In reality, scientists can extract D-N-A . . . even that of extinct animals.

Stand-up: Reproductive biologist Tim Gross is learning a lot about the diets and reproductive systems of mastodons by analyzing ancient, well-preserved mastodon droppings. Getting D-N-A is one thing, but it's the next step that science hasn't reached yet.

Gross incue: once you have DNA

Gross outcue: form an embryo

Scientists agree that it's just a matter of time before they gain that knowledge and something like Jurassic Park is a reality.

Ferl incue: certainly, once you have

Ferl outcue: reconstructing an animal

Gross incue: 20 years ago

Gross outcue: a reality today

Still, it's easier to re-create dinosaurs in Hollywood than it is in the halls of science . . . for now. In Hooverville, I'm Joe Reporter, Newswatch One.

Working with Available Video and Natural Sound

There are several things to note about how the script above is put together. First, think about the video we have to work with. If we didn't have clips from the movie, all we'd have would be shots inside a lab filled with beakers and test tubes and other shots of scientists huddled over petrified mastodon dung. Not exactly compelling stuff. But our friends in Hollywood often send out clips (they call them "trailers") of movies that are about to be released. It's good publicity for the moviemakers and good video for us to use if we have a story that lends itself to using clips from a particular movie. In this case, that's exactly what we have. After looking through the trailers, we're struck by a line from the movie as a very good way to immediately capture the viewers' attention. The two kids and their scientist friend are stuck in a tree, and the little girl asks if she can pet the friendly dinosaur that's eating some of the leaves. So, that brief clip becomes the beginning of our news story. We can then get into the facts about what real-life scientists are doing in terms of gene sequencing and the like. Notice that we also use a piece of natural sound that we captured in the lab as a way to break up the first section of narration.

Tie-Writing

Now let's look at some of the transitions. We know from the preceding narration that the project director is going to talk about how his work parallels what happened in the movie "Jurassic Park." He finishes the bite by talking about how rapidly gene sequencing takes place, and we follow that up with another comparison with the movie scientists. Moving on to the second bite, we know that Gross will talk about some "second step" in the re-creation process, and we follow that up with a note about the inevitability of reaching that second step. That leads us into what needs to happen for scientists to reach the point of being able to re-create an animal. Notice that Ferl's bite about that subject is followed immediately by one from Gross with no narration between the two. It isn't needed because one comment leads naturally into the next one. That's called "butting sound bites." We finish the story by following up on Gross' comment about things that would have been unthought of 20 years ago being commonplace today, by noting that the real scientists can't do everything the movie scientists can—at least not yet. So, the goal is to have the parts of the story flow together as seamlessly as possible to support the central theme of the package.

Two Scripts for Packages

Now this part of our script is ready to go to a videotape editor, who puts the pieces of narration and the SOTs together and places the appropriate video over the top of the sound track. The first script we provided gives the editor the order of things and is called the editing script. The next step for the reporter is to put together what's called the show script (at some stations it's called the producer's script). That script includes what the anchor is supposed to say to get into and out of the piece (the lead and the tag) and the directions for the director and other control room personnel. That script would look like this.

Jurassic Park

	(Anne)
on cam	IT TAKES A HEALTHY DOSE OF SCIENCE FACT TO MAKE A GOOD WORK OF SCIENCE FICTION. AS JOE REPORTER TELLS US, THE BOOK AND MOVIE JURASSIC PARK MIGHT CONTAIN MORE SCIENCE FACT THAN WE REALIZE.
:00 Take cass vid & snd full (PKG) Supers:	(pkg)
:01 Courtesy: Universal Pictures	
:25 Rob Ferl, geneticist	
:42 Joe Reporter, Newswatch One	
1:00 Tim Gross, biologist	
1:31 cass out	Outcue: standard
on cam	THE SCIENTISTS SAY THAT AS WE GET CLOSER TO UNDERSTANDING LIFE AND MAYBE ONE DAY RECREATING IT, THERE WILL BE MANY ETHICAL QUESTIONS TO BE ANSWERED ALONG THE WAY.

You can see that the producer's script contains none of what the reporter will say, only what the anchor will say to get us to the reporter's taped piece. The director really doesn't need to know anything about the content of the piece. She just needs to know when to transition to the tape, when to put in supers, and when the tape ends so that she can come back to an on-camera shot of the anchor.

You might be wondering how we arrive at the times listed on the producer's script. Once the videotape editor has finished assembling the piece, the reporter looks back at it and notes when each person first appears and, in this case, when a clip from the movie appears so that we can give credit to our Hollywood friends. Those are the times given to the director for insertion of the supers. The reporter also notes the time at which he finishes his final piece of narration and lists the final few words that he says or, in most cases, simply writes the word "standard" (or "SOQ" for standard outcue). In this case, we've told the director to be looking for 1:31 on the control room clock and to be listening for the reporter to say the line that's standard at the end of packages. In that line the reporter gives the name of the city or location where the story was shot, his name and the name of the news organization. That's called the signature outcue, or sig-out for short. We place the outcue on the right side of the page so that the anchor can also be listening for it. As you can see, in the sig-out we say "I'm Joe Reporter" rather than "This is Joe Reporter." "I'm" is more conversational and helps convey the personal relationship we try to build with viewers.

So, in essence, a reporter is responsible for two scripts for a package. One of those goes to a videotape editor, who assembles the story (in many small markets and even some larger markets, the reporter *is* the tape editor), and the other goes to the producer and director. The editor puts together the self-contained part of the story, the package itself, and the producer and director deal with the live elements of the story—the lead and tag and the supers.

The Diamond Approach

In Chapter 1 we mentioned that broadcasters don't use inverted pyramid style. For packages, we sometimes use the diamond style. The diamond style is especially useful when writing packages in which we're dealing with something that affects a large number of people. Some examples might be the marriage penalty tax, changes in one of the city's zoning ordinances or a promising cancer treatment. In each case, the tendency is to hit the viewers with a bunch of numbers and statistics: married couples pay 10 percent more in taxes than unmarried people living together, the zoning change would result in the closing of 20 local businesses, the new treatment would help the 400,000 Americans suffering with a particular type of cancer.

Don't misunderstand. Using some supporting numbers and statistics is important. But we want to "peopleize" stories—to tell them in human terms through the eyes of an individual, a family or a small group. We can then use the experiences of the people who are our examples to make the stories more interesting. The three stories we just mentioned might start something like this:

> Being married costs Mike and Jan Parker an extra 500 dollars in taxes each year.

> This hardware store has been in Keith Rollyson's family for 60 years. But a change in a Hooverville zoning ordinance might force the family to close the store for good.

> Sam Smith played college tennis . . . but now he can barely walk. He hopes a new cancer drug helps him get back on the court some day.

Remember, we have to catch the viewers' attention right away. Peopleizing the lead sentence helps us do that, and the example of how the issue affects a person, family or small group forms the top part of the diamond. The middle (and bigger) part of the diamond is for numbers, statistics, comments from experts on the subject and the like. The bottom of the diamond is where we come back to the person/people we're using as an illustration. Using the three stories we've been talking about, that approach would allow us to close by mentioning what the Parkers hope the tax code changes would mean for them, what the future holds for the Rollyson family hardware business, or what the prognosis for Sam Smith might be and whether he'll be hitting backhands any time soon.

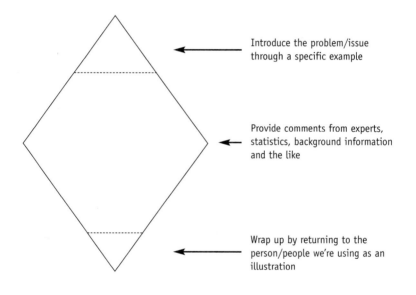

Introduce the problem/issue through a specific example

Provide comments from experts, statistics, background information and the like

Wrap up by returning to the person/people we're using as an illustration

Donuts

In local television news today, lots of stories include the reporter live on the scene. Sometimes, the reporter appears on camera for a minute or more to update the viewers on a breaking story that has just occurred, and there's been no time to shoot and edit video. More often, however, the reporter has had time to put together a taped piece, which she introduces live from the field. This type of report is called a "donut" in some newsrooms and a "sandwich" in others. So a donut is a special type of package and is a bit more involved than a regular package.

With a donut, the anchor still sets up the story in general terms and introduces the reporter. But rather than introducing the reporter's taped package, the anchor "pitches" to the reporter in the field, who is live on camera. The tone of the introduction changes a bit, and of course the script markings change some as well. The reporter further sets up the story and introduces the taped portion.

The way the package part of a donut is structured is a lot like a regular package, but there are a few differences. First, because of the extra time it takes for the live reporter segments before and after the package, the tape will have to be a little shorter for a donut than it might be if no live elements were incorporated. Second, because we see the reporter before and after the package, there's no reason to use a stand-up within the piece. That would mean seeing the reporter three times in one story. Some large-market stations take that approach, but we think that's too much reporter and not enough other video. Third, because the reporter is going to come back on camera after the package, there's no need to include a sig-out at the end of the tape. It would sound silly to hear "In Hooverville, I'm Joe Reporter, Newswatch One" and then switch to a shot of Joe saying something else. Let's take our Jurassic Park story and set it up as a donut. We'll assume that we're airing the story to coincide with the big opening of the movie at the Hooverville Metroplex. The first showing is at 7 p.m., and by the time we go on the air with this story at 6:11, the ticket line already stretches out the door and halfway around the block. Here's how we set the story up to incorporate live reporter presence at the scene.

Jurassic Park

	(Bill)
On cam	IT TAKES A HEALTHY DOSE OF SCIENCE FACT TO MAKE A GOOD WORK OF SCIENCE FICTION. JOE REPORTER IS STANDING BY LIVE OUTSIDE THE HOOVERVILLE METRO-PLEX WHERE A LOT OF PEOPLE ARE WAITING TO SEE THE NEW MOVIE JURASSIC PARK. JOE, WE UNDERSTAND THIS MOVIE MIGHT CONTAIN MORE SCIENCE FACT THAN WE REALIZE.
Take LIVE	(Joe ad lib)
	roll cue: "dinosaurs running loose"
:00 Take cass vid & snd full (donut)	(pkg)
Supers:	
:01 Courtesy: Universal Pictures	
:25 Rob Ferl, geneticist	
1:00 Tim Gross, biologist	

1:21 cass out	Outcue: "halls of science . . . for now."
Take LIVE	(Joe ad lib)
On cam	THANKS, JOE. SCIENTISTS SAY THAT AS WE GET CLOSER TO UNDERSTANDING LIFE AND MAYBE ONE DAY RECREATING IT, THERE WILL BE MANY ETHICAL QUESTIONS TO BE ANSWERED ALONG THE WAY.

The story is essentially the same as in the previous example, except that Joe is now live on camera outside the movie theater before and after the package runs. Also, we don't write down what Joe says in the field, except for his final few words leading to the tape. The roll cue lets the director know when to roll the tape.

Conclusion

As is the case with all the other television story forms we've discussed, marking scripts so that everyone is "on the same page" is very important. Packages give the control room staff a bit of a breather, because the reporter and editor have done much of the work already and we're working with a piece that's very close to being fully self-contained. That gives the folks in the control room a little time to think ahead to the next few stories and "gear up" for what's ahead.

📁 Package Do's and Dont's

Do
- Give the anchor an active role.
- Work for flow from track to bites and back to track.
- Incorporate natural sound breaks.
- "Peopleize" stories.

Don't
- Stand stick-straight on stand-ups.
- Leave out *any* cues on the producer's script.
- Become the focus of the story.
- Forget that reporting can be hard work.

PRODUCING TV NEWS

If you're reading this chapter, then chances are either (1) you've decided to pursue a career in TV newscast producing, (2) you're thinking about it, or (3) you're reading this as a classroom assignment. If the first two reasons apply, this chapter will give you a good understanding of what the job entails and how to carry out the basics. If, on the other hand, you have no intention of becoming a producer, then this chapter will still be of value. No matter what you do in broadcast news, if you aren't a producer, you'll be dealing with them. This chapter will give you a good understanding of what drives them, what their needs are, and why they act in the sometimes mysterious ways they do.

What Is a Producer?

Simply put, news producing is the art and science of filling a broadcast with news content. There's not much glamour in it, and as a consequence, most of the public at large has only a vague idea, if any, of what a producer does or even that producers exist. Yet the producer is one of the most important people, if not *the* most important person, involved with the newscast. While newsroom managers hover about trying to look important, the producer is the point person, responsible for getting the broadcast onto the air. One good way to judge the importance of a producer is to watch what happens when one falls ill and has to call in sick: instant panic! It's guaranteed that someone will have to be called in as a replacement; just as a plane can't take off without the pilot, the newscast won't air without a producer.

Though the viewer doesn't know it, few people in the newsroom are more critical to the viewer than the producer. The producer, through the decisions he or she makes, is the viewer's window to the world. It's up to the producer to decide which stories are important to the viewer, and to choose those stories and present them in a newscast in such a way as to showcase context, meaning, perspective and, above all, relevance. This requires news judgment and a sense of mission. It also requires technical expertise. Often producers don't get much training in the latter, and it's not unusual for producers to find themselves "thrown in, sink or swim." Therefore we'll go into a great deal of technical detail in this chapter.

The producer has an alter ego and partner in crime: the director. While the producer is in charge of the content and timing of the newscast, the director leads a production crew that's responsible for executing most of the technical and some of the aesthetic aspects of the plan.

Why Be a Producer?

In the course of interviewing intern candidates through the years, I've spoken with many prospective television newspeople. When I ask them what they want to be in life, all too often I hear, "I want to be an anchor." There's certainly nothing wrong with this goal. But obviously, there are only so many high-paying anchor jobs. Competition for them, and for on-air jobs of any kind, is fierce.

On the other hand, competition for producer jobs isn't nearly as intense. The typical reporter opening might attract anywhere from 50 to 150 tapes. The typical producer opening might attract 10 to 15 tapes. Do the math. If you're a good producer, you can write your own ticket. These days in many shops, an experienced producer of a major newscast often makes as much as, if not more than, most reporters.

If you're a good writer, have excellent people skills and excellent news judgment, enjoy leading teams of people and prefer to be involved in the "big picture" rather than just a piece of it, then producing may be for you. But producing isn't for everybody. Most people either really like it or really hate it. There's little middle ground.

Producer Duties

The producer's shift normally begins with an editorial meeting. The editorial team consists of the newscast producers, the assignments editor, the executive producer and other senior managers. In many (if not most) shops, reporters and photographers sit in on the editorial meetings as well. The group discusses the stories available for coverage and then assigns coverage resources. Afterward, the producer goes back to his or her desk, sorts through the local and regional news feeds, wire material and the like, and decides which stories will go into the day's broadcast, in what form and in what order. Producers write some or all of their own copy and also supervise other copy writers who may be assigned to the newscast. Producers edit reporter copy (at least, they're supposed to). They order or supervise the ordering of all graphics for the newscast. They sit in the control booth to time the show and deal with breaking news.

In carrying out those duties the producer must accomplish the following tasks, roughly arranged here in descending order of priority:

- *Precisely time the broadcast.* The newscast must end at the appointed time. It can't run long, and it can't run short. Some kind of content must separate the commercial breaks; they can't "bump together!"

- *Choose the right mix of stories.* The producer, working in concert with the assignments editor and newsroom managers, must make sure that coverage and newscast resources are devoted to the right stories. "Right stories" has a broad range of definitions, but normally it means those stories that are most newsworthy on the given day, in light of the community needs and the station's coverage philosophy.

- *Place the stories in the correct order.* This is an activity also known as "filling the rundown" or "completing the lineup." The "rundown" or "lineup" (different shops use different terminology) is a spreadsheet-like form listing the stories in the chronological order in which they'll air. This information typically includes, for each story, the page number, the slug (title) of the story, the anchor who'll be reading it, the type of camera shot or shots to be used, the form of the story, basic production elements that will be needed, the running time and so on. We'll discuss story placement in greater detail later.

- *Work with the director and production crew to get the newscast on the air.* A good producer never loses sight of the fact that the director is an equal partner in the newscast. Good communication and cooperation between the producer and director is absolutely essential!

- *Write copy.* Most producers write at least some copy, and some producers write *all* the copy, with the exception of reporter packages. This function varies from market size to market size, depending on whether writing assistance is available to the producer. Simply put, good producers must write well according to the principles outlined elsewhere in this book.
- *Edit the copy.* Good producers always carefully read any and all copy written for their newscasts. They work with the reporters to assist and help direct the development of their stories. They edit copy for accuracy, fairness, balance, comprehension and storytelling, as well as for libel and privacy concerns.
- *Order the graphics.* Generally, the more sophisticated the product, the more sophisticated the graphics. Many shops have good art departments and place a high priority on graphics. The producer orders graphics for his or her show and works with the reporters to ensure they make good use of graphics within their packages.
- *Scan the wires and feeds.* Good producers continually scan the incoming wires and feed services to ensure that the best, freshest and most updated material is included in the broadcast.
- *Work with the desk.* Good producers work closely with the assignments desk to be on top of and react appropriately to breaking news.
- *Show leadership.* The producer is a "big picture" person. He or she sees how all the individual parts fit together and, like a symphony conductor, must orchestrate everyone's efforts to achieve a satisfactory, high-quality product. In doing so, the producer works with many people whose primary responsibilities pertain to a much smaller part of the picture. In order for all of this to come together, the producer must have excellent leadership skills and must contribute to a positive and productive work environment.

Despite the "descending order" nature of this list, none of these tasks and responsibilities is unimportant. Failure to properly time a show will get you in trouble with your news director very fast. Failure to show good leadership will get you in trouble more slowly. For a producer to be truly excellent and successful, he or she must earn an "A" in each of these categories.

The Rundown

Anchors generally read their copy from scripts, which are available to them in a printed set of scripts on the news set and on electronic prompter. If the scripts are a book, then the rundown is the table of contents. But it's more than that, because it also gives the director and production crew much of the information needed to execute the newscast from a technical standpoint.

Rundown design, use and implementation vary widely from shop to shop. These days, most shops are computerized. But whether the rundown is contained on a computer screen or on a printed form, its use is the same: to list the stories, story formats, running times and other information needed to get each newscast element produced and on the air. Below is a sample of the most important columns contained in a typical rundown, followed by detailed explanation of each.

PAGE #	SHOT	RUNS
SLUG	TYPE	BACKTIME
ANC	WR	

PAGE

Most shops make use of page numbers to assist in the process of keeping the scripts in their proper order. The page number is similar to, but not exactly the same as, a page number in a textbook. Most shops label individual blocks of stories with letters of the alphabet. A "block" is usually defined as a segment of the newscast terminated by a commercial break. Thus the first segment of the newscast, containing all the stories preceding the first commercial break, is often referred to as the "A" block. The second segment up to the second commercial break is the "B" block and so on. Page numbers frequently begin with the block number. So, the first story in the newscast is generally given a page number of A1. The second story is A2. However, many shops number their stories in increments of 10; this allows producers to insert new stories into the middle of the rundown later without having to renumber every story.

Some stories take up more than one line on the rundown in order to accommodate production information. In such cases the page number usually is subdivided with decimals or trailing letters, depending on the capabilities of the newsroom computer system. Example 1: A10, A10A, A10B and so on. Example 2: A10.1, A10.2, A10.4 and so on.

SLUG

The slug is a short one- or two-word description, which serves as a daily title for the story. Different shops have different conventions for slugging stories. Some have no convention. The purpose of the slug is to make sure all scripts, graphics, tapes, live remotes and other production elements associated with the story are labeled properly and consistently. This is a critically important function. For instance, a wrong or mislabeled slug on a videocassette can often lead to someone losing a tape or miscuing it, causing major problems on the air. (Anchor: "Apparently we don't have that story. We'll try to come back to it in a moment. In other news . . .")

As mentioned, sometimes stories have more than one element, causing them to take up more than one line on the rundown. Often these different lines require slugs. Again, different shops have different conventions, but normally the sub-lines contain similar slugs along with a differentiating character or words. For instance, a typical package might require three scripts: the lead-in or intro, the package verbatim and the package tag. Typical slugs for the three package elements associated with a murder trial might be:

SMITH TRIAL (lead)

P-SMITH TRIAL (package verbatim)

T-SMITH TRIAL (tag)

Depending on the limitations of the computer system or rundown form, some shops simply use the whole term, as follows:

SMITH INTRO

SMITH PACKAGE

SMITH TAG

ANC

This column would simply contain the name or initials of the anchor reading the story.

SHOT

The shot column generally contains information about how many people will be framed in the camera shot for a given story, and whether a graphic will be electronically inserted into the camera shot. Typical basic choices might include:

- *1shot.* One anchor on camera, centered, no graphic. Sometimes known as the "head and shoulders" or "H&S" shot
- *2shot.* Two anchors on camera, centered, no graphic
- *OTS.* One anchor on camera, framed to accommodate a corner or side graphic positioned "over the shoulder"
- *3shot.* Three anchors on camera
- *Wide.* All anchors on camera
- *CK.* One anchor at the chroma key board
- *Dblbox.* "Double box" shot, typically with an anchor framed in one box and a reporter framed opposite, for Q&A
- *3box.* Same as above, with three boxes—typically, an anchor and two reporters or interview guests
- *Wipe.* Not a shot at all, but rather an indication that we'll go to the next story without coming back to an anchor, by use of a production technique during which video of the preceding story will "wipe" off the screen, to be replaced by video of the next story

There are many other possibilities, depending on the capabilities of the shop and set design. In addition, terminology tends to vary from shop to shop. For instance, a graphic shot known as an over-the-shoulder or "OTS" in one shop might be a "1box" in another. There is no universal list of terms, and producers must relearn some of these terms every time they change jobs. However, the principles are usually the same.

TYPE

A number of different terms might go here to help describe the type and format of the story. Again, specific terms used vary widely from shop to shop. The basic possibilities might include:

- *Intro.* Anchor- or reporter-read copy preceding a package.
- *Tag.* Anchor- or reporter-read copy following a package.
- *Tossback.* Similar to a tag, but usually includes two or more people with a question-and-answer opportunity.
- *Reader.* An anchor on camera reading copy without video support or full screen graphics. Normally, this implies a stand-alone story, not a package or live shot intro.
- *VO.* For voice-over. This indicates the anchor will read copy and for portions of the narrative the audience will see video while hearing the anchor's narration.
- *VOB (also VO/SOT or VOBITE).* For "voice-over with sound bite" or "voice-over with sound on tape." This indicates that the anchor will read copy, that for portions of it the audience will see pictures, and that the anchor narrative will pause while the audience hears a portion of an interview with "sound up full."
- *BITE or SOT.* Same as above, except no pictures will precede the interview.
- *VONATS.* Same as a VOB, except the anchor will pause for "natural sound"—something recorded in the field other than an interview (the crack of a bat, the roar of the crowd, a space shuttle countdown and the like).
- *PKG.* For "package." Indicates a preproduced tape element that typically includes interviews, pictures and reporter narrative in one contained unit.
- *LIVE.* Indicates the use of a live remote by microwave, satellite, fiber optic line and so forth. Some shops specify here which mode will be used: "LIVE/SAT" for a satellite shot, "LIVE/REM" for a local microwave shot.
- *SS/CG.* "Still store with character generator." Indicates the use of a full screen graphic with text to be inserted electronically live on the air. Almost all SS/CGs are voiced-over live by an anchor.

- *SS/FULL.* Same as above, but the text is prepasted on the graphic rather than inserted live on the air.
- *ENG.* For "electronic news gathering." Some shops use this as a designation for whatever standard format they're using to record and play back news video. For example: eng/pkg. Some shops prefer to list the specific format, such as "beta" or "svhs" and the like. Still others omit a tape or server designation for news stories, with the assumption that all such elements will be played from a standard news video machine unless otherwise designated. In our examples we'll also omit the use of this term.
- *VTR.* Similar to ENG, but usually denotes a production department video device other than one normally used to play back news video, such as an open-reel 1-inch tape machine used for newscast opens, teases and other standard elements.

WR

This column would contain the name or initials of the writer assigned to the story.

RUNS

This column contains a running time for the story or story segment. (An example of a story segment, as opposed to a single story, would be "weather." Weather may contain many elements, but on most rundowns it is listed with a single slug and running time.) Ideal running times for various story formats vary from shop to shop, but the following examples are typical:

Reader:	:10–:15	Pkg:	1:20–1:30
VO:	:15–:25	Tag:	:05–:10
VOB:	:35–:45	Tossback:	:05–:10, or longer if
Intro:	:10–:15		there's a Q&A session

BACKTIME

The backtiming column is crucially important. Prior to the newscast, it tells the producer whether the show *appears* to be properly filled. During the newscast, a constant check on this column tells the producer whether the show is light (not enough material to stretch to the off-time) or heavy (some material may have to be dropped to conclude on time). In some shops this is also described as being "short" or "long."

In the old days it was said that "all good producers could tell, add and subtract time backward." These days most modern newsroom computer systems automatically figure the backtimes based on the information the producer enters into the "RUNS" column. If not, the producer will have to figure this information by hand (oh, joy).

Building a Newscast

Now that you have a good understanding of what kinds of story elements are available, we're ready to learn the basics of designing a newscast.

Newscast Formats

There are as many varieties of newscast as there are news organizations. The basic principles we'll discuss here apply to all formats and newscast lengths. But for the purposes of this lesson we'll build a newscast based on a typical half-hour news format.

All newscasts are defined in part by the number of commercial breaks they contain. Our sample newscast will have four commercial breaks of two minutes' duration each. It will contain news, sports and weather in the traditional order. It will end with an external commercial break, usually known as a "terminal break." For the purpose of this exercise, this will be a 6 p.m. newscast, and we'll title it "Rumor Has It News at Six."

Here's the format: *"Rumor Has It News at Six" with Fred Feelgood and Jane Jabberon—Basic Format*

> A Block—Hard News
> Break One 2:00
> B Block—Softer News
> Break Two 2:00
> C Block—Weather
> Break Three 2:00
> D Block—Sports
> Break Four 2:00
> E Block (Kicker Block)
> Terminal Break 1:10

News Hole

Before we can fill our newscast, we must first determine how much time is at our disposal. The basic amount of time available for news generally doesn't vary much from night to night. The total amount of time required every night to run all the commercials, teases, sports, weather and chitchat is sometimes called the "skeleton time" or "filler time." When you subtract this from the total available time, you're left with what is usually known, with a certain lack of elegance, as the "news hole."

Let's figure out the news hole for our sample newscast. First, let's add in *all* the standard features that will appear every night. Typically, this will include the open, the close, the teases, the tosses and so on. *"Rumor Has It News at Six" with Fred Feelgood and Jane Jabberon—Skeleton Rundown on scratchpad*

Element	Running Time
Newscast Open	0:20
A Block—Hard News	
Tease One	0:20
Break One	2:00
B Block—Softer News	
Tease Two	0:15
Break Two	2:00
C Block—Weather	
Toss to WX:	0:10
WX:	3:20
Tossback from WX:	0:15
Tease Three	0:15
Break Three	2:00
D Block—Sports	
Toss to Sports:	0:10
Sports	3:20
Tossback from Sports:	0:15
Tease Four	0:10
Break Four	2:00
E Block—Kicker	
Tease for 11 PM	0:25
Close	0:30
Terminal Break	1:10
Total Running Time:	**18:55**

This is the "newscast skeleton"—so called because it's the bare bones that we must flesh out with news content. Adding up all of these times, we come to 18:55. Wise producers may wish to add in another :30 of time for miscellaneous slippage due to package overruns, unscheduled chitchat and the like.

Total Running Time:	18:55	
+ Pad Time:	:30	
= Skeleton Time:	19:25	

Thus the skeleton time of 19:25 is the time that's already prefilled in this particular newscast before the producer even sits down to begin work. The obvious next question is, So how much work will the producer have to do? How much time must he or she fill?

Our sample newscast begins at 6:00 p.m. and ends at 6:30, giving us one half hour's time. We must now subtract the skeleton time from the available time to get the news hole, as follows:

Total Available Time:	30:00	
– Skeleton Time:	19:25	
= News Hole:	10:35	

That's our news hole: 10 minutes and 35 seconds. It ain't much, is it? Nevertheless, your job for the day is to fill it. Note, the news hole *is* adjustable. It may expand or contract depending on the length of the commercial breaks. It can also expand or contract depending on the amount of time devoted to sports and weather. For that reason, producers are known to frequently ask sports and weathercasters to "donate time," which anchors really hate to do. Wise producers don't abuse the privilege.

These days it's a rare newsroom indeed that's not computerized to some extent. With most if not all newsroom computers, the producer has to enter and save the skeleton rundown just once. On each subsequent day, the computer prefills the daily rundown based on this skeleton information.

An "empty" computerized rundown prefilled with the skeleton information we just derived might look something like this: *"Rumor Has It News at Six" with Fred Feelgood and Jane Jabberon—Skeleton Rundown on Computer*

Page#	Slug	Anchor	Shot	Type	WR Runs	Backtime
A00	Newscast Open			vtr/sot	:20	11:05
Alast	1-tz		2shot	vo	:20	11:25
Break One					2:00	11:45
B10						
Blast	2-tz		2shot	vo	:15	13:45
Break Two					2:00	14:00
C10	WX toss		3shot		:10	16:00
C10A	Weather				3:20	16:10
C10B	Tossback		3shot		:15	19:30
C20						
Clast	3-tz		2shot		:15	19:45
Break Three					2:00	20:00
D10	Toss to Sports		3shot		:10	22:00
D10A	Sports				3:20	22:10
D10B	Tossback		3shot		:15	25:30
Dlast	4-tz		2shot	vo	:10	25:45
Break Four					2:00	25:55
E10	11 Teaze			ss/cg	:25	27:55
E20						
E30	C ya/Close			wide	:30	28:20
Terminal Break					1:10	28:50
	Totals:				18:55	6:30:00
	Over/Under				−11:05	

Most modern computerized rundowns will automatically total the story times and figure a backtime. For the moment, take a look at the total running time for all the stories together. Ideally, it should read "29:30"—which would leave us with 30 seconds of pad time. But the total in this case is 18:55. This is our skeleton time, the amount of news content time prefilled with weather, sports, teases, commercial breaks and so on. Add in :30 for pad and the total is 19:25—exactly the amount we earlier figured by hand.

Take a look at the over/under clock. We're under by 11:05. This is the amount of time we must fill with news. Subtract that 30 seconds of pad time we talked about, and the total is 10:35. That's the "news hole" for the day.

Now look at the backtiming figure at the top of the right-hand column. It reads "11:05." The computer is telling you that if you don't add any more content to the newscast, but you wish for the newscast to end at 6:30:00, then you must *start* the newscast at 6:11:05. Obviously, we *are* going to add some content. We'll discuss backtiming in much greater detail later.

A note about computerized rundowns: they're only as good as the people configuring them. It's in your best interests not to always blindly trust the computer, especially if you're producing a newscast with which you aren't familiar. In such cases you're well advised to sit down and figure out your news hole by hand as a way of verifying what the computer is telling you.

Ordering Stories—The Three Factors

Now comes the fun part, the part you're paid the humongous, hairy bucks to do. You must choose the stories you want to put in your newscast and the order in which you'd like them to run.

The first thing you'll do is to come out of the morning meeting and write down the stories that have been assigned to your newscast. Make at least tentative decisions on the format you might like for those stories—which will be "straight packages," which will be live remotes, newsroom-anchored pieces and the like. This will leave you a certain amount of time to fill from other sources. You'll want to spend the next hour or so scanning the wires, looking at the feeds and feed rundowns, and working with the desk for updates and follow-ups in order to develop a list of potential stories for your newscast.

At some point you'll want to begin sketching out a rundown. How does one decide the order in which the stories should run? This is one of the most difficult tasks a producer faces. The answer will vary from individual to individual and from shop to shop. But every producer should have a rhyme and a reason for the order of the show. In the trade magazines you'll occasionally see job ads for producers that say "Show stackers need not apply." A "show stacker" is an epithet for a producer who either stacks stories seemingly at random or stacks them simply in the order of priority without any flow from one story to the next. A good producer doesn't just stack stories, but instead takes three major factors into account when ordering them: *priority (newsworthiness), flow* and *pace.*

Priority

Though you won't order stories strictly in order of their importance, generally you'll *begin* with the top priority story. Choosing the lead may well be the most important decision you make during the day. Why? News research suggests that news consumers base their viewing decisions on the lead, which they know should be the "most important story." If this most important story isn't important to them, they may switch in search of another story, and often, they don't come back. So the ratings battle for the day is often won or lost on the strength of the lead story.

It sounds simple, right? Your lead should be the most important story of the day. That shouldn't be too hard to determine, should it? Actually, sometimes it can be maddeningly difficult. You may have several stories of more or less equal importance, none of which stands out as the clear lead. Your newscast may be competing with another newscast airing on your station an hour later or earlier, leaving you to duke it out with your fellow producer over the choice of a lead. In addition, there are other factors to consider besides the basic news value of the story. In many shops, producers are required to take the station's mission statement and coverage philosophy into account when choosing leads and stories. The process can get complicated. That's why in many shops this decision isn't left to the producer alone, but rather becomes a team decision.

Flow

Once you've chosen the lead, the next step is to choose story number two. This seems logical enough. You may be tempted at this point to place the *second* most important story of the day in that slot. But stop and think a moment. This isn't always the right choice. Good producers usually group stories somewhat according to theme, then group the themes in logical order, taking newsworthiness into account. Thus, if you're leading with a story about city council raising taxes, your second story might be a VO or VOBITE about an action some other governmental body took today. Your third story should be some subject that flows logically out of the second story. It may or may not be the third most newsworthy story of the day.

This sounds difficult, but it's easy to get the hang of it. Suppose your first story is about city council raising property taxes and the second story is about the county commission taking action to fix a problem-plagued intersection. You have a story you haven't yet placed about a bad accident. Where should it go? Chances are it will "flow" best out of the story about the intersection, flowing with the "traffic" theme. Then if you have other police- and fire-related matters, these would flow well out of the accident story and so on.

Pacing

The third critically important factor is pacing. Many inexperienced producers make the mistake of cramming all their packages into the top of the news block, then running the "less important" VOs and VOBITEs at the end of the block. This is terrible for pacing.

Remember, your greatest enemy is the remote control. If your viewer loses interest, zap, you're the history channel. One way to keep your viewer's attention is to keep a fast pace. Ideally, something should be changing every few seconds: reveal a new fact, change the camera shot, change the video, put in a new edit, change the graphic and so on. Back-to-back packages tend to slow the pace. Break up the pace by inserting tags, VOs, VOBITEs, readers.

A good, cheap and easy way to keep the pace going is to tag every package on camera, and to tag every VO or VOBITE on camera prior to changing anchors. The latter has other benefits as well. If the anchor begins every reading sequence on camera and ends it on camera before the second anchor speaks, it brings a sense of closure to the sequence and also boosts the anchor's image as being in control of the sequence. This enhances the authority, professionalism and teamwork of your anchor team, which will make your news director and news consultant happy—and in the process make your newscast better and more competitive. We'll discuss tags later.

Filling the Rundown—The Scratchpad Method

There are two methods for drafting out a rundown, and we're going to look at both. Some producers like to begin by immediately sketching out their first draft in the computer rundown. We'll see how that process works in a moment. But some find it more useful to order stories by hand on a piece of scratch paper first. This method has two advantages compared to entering the draft directly into the computer rundown. One, computers will sometimes lie to you; hand calculations give you a way to verify what the computer is telling you. Second, you can tinker with a handwritten rundown, moving the elements around fairly quickly and conveniently. Once you've found a draft rundown that appears to make sense in terms of story order and total running time, you can then enter it into the computerized rundown.

For the scratchpad method, you need only write down the slug of the story, a note about its type and the proposed running time. We'll add up these times and get a quick estimate of the total running time of the stories, then compare it to our available news hole.

So, with a list of available stories on my desk and the above principles of story ordering firmly in mind, I'm ready to scratch out a proposed plan of action. Here's a draft one of my proposed rundown. Note, by this method we write down only those stories that are *not* part of the skeleton time of the newscast. This means we are temporarily omitting opens, teases, the running time for sports and weather, and other elements that appear in the same place with the same running time every day. We'll draw a short line to separate blocks. *"Rumor Has It News at Six" with Fred Feelgood and Jane Jabberon—Rundown Draft #1 on Scratchpad*

Council Taxes	live/pkg	2:10
Intersection Repair	vo	:25
4-Car Pileup	vobite	:40
Apartment Fire	live/pkg	2:10
Fire History	ss/cg	:25
Housefire Update	vo	:25
Robbery Attempt	vo	:25
Suspect Caught	vo	:25
Robbery Trial	pkg	1:40
Murder Trial	vo	:25
Legislature/Crackdown	vo	:25
————————		
Truck Recall	pkg	1:40
Recall Info	ss/cg	:25
Toaster Lawsuit	vo	:25
Stock Market	ss/cg	:20
————————		
Weather		
Waterpark Opens	vobite	:45
————————		
Sports		
————————		
Skiing Squirrel	vonats	:35

This rundown looks great, and I'm happy as a clam. So I add up all my times and get—13:45. But wait; didn't we say our available news hole was only 10:35? We're over by 3:10!

Now you begin to understand the heartbreak of producing. You can rarely, if ever, produce your ideal newscast. We're going to have to cut some content.

First I go back and re-examine my rundown. OK, I guess I don't need that housefire update I had planned to run updating a fire from the day before. It's a shame, too, because I was going to run a "follow-up" over-the-shoulder graphic with it, and my news director loves those. Oh, well. It's toast.

Do I really need to run a bite on the waterpark opening? Nah. That gives me another :15 back. I'll write tight; another :25 saved.

The stock market is slow today. I'll only need :15 to give the results. There's another :05. But I'm still 2:15 too long.

My VO's are going to have to be more tightly written. I think I'm going to need the full :25 to explain the intersection story, but the rest of the VO's can be cut by at least :05. That gives me back :35. I'm still 1:40 long.

That apartment fire story has good visuals but isn't a complicated story. I'll ask the reporter to keep her lead, tag and tape time tight and give me back :10.

I'm still long by 1:30.

Now, I go to sports, hat in hand, and find out how heavy a sports day this has been. The sports anchor, because he's a heck of a guy, admits that there have been busier sports days, and he agrees to donate :30 to the cause. So sports will run 2:50 today, instead of the normal 3:20. I'm still 1:00 long.

Second, I head to the weather office. But wait a minute. I know the weathercaster really hates giving up time even on a slow weather day, and that she always checks my rundown to verify that the time is really needed. The first thing her eye is going to land on is that "Skiing Squirrel" kicker. So I change the slug to "Kicker" and knock the time down to :20 instead of the :35 I had hoped to run. This will cost me the ability to take natural sound up full within the story, but what the heck. I take those steps, walk into the weather office and make my pitch. She's unhappy about giving up a full :30 because there's a severe weather system in the Midwest she wants to talk about. But she owes me because I gave her 15 extra seconds on Wednesday and Thursday. She gives in and donates 30 seconds. So, weather will run 2:50 today instead of 3:20.

That still leaves me :15 long. But with a 30-second close and 30 seconds of pad time, I still have a safety margin left of :45. That should still be enough to give me a "loose" show, which my bosses like. (Anchors always complain if they have to rush through their tosses.)

So, the final rundown on scratchpad might look something like this: *"Rumor Has It News at Six" with Fred Feelgood and Jane Jabberon— Rundown Draft #2 on Scratchpad*

Council Taxes	live/pkg	2:10
Intersection Repair	vo	:25
4-Car Pileup	vobite	:40
Apartment Fire	live/pkg	2:00 (was 2:10)
Fire History	ss/cg	:20 (was :25)
(Housefire Update deleted)		(was :25)
Robbery Attempt	vo	:20 (was :25)
Suspect Caught	vo	:20 (was :25)
Robbery Trial	pkg	1:40
Murder Trial	vo	:20 (was :25)
Legislature/Crackdown	vo	:20 (was :25)
————		
Truck Recall	pkg	1:40
Recall Info	ss/cg	:20 (was :25)
Toaster Lawsuit	vo	:20 (was :25)
Stock Market	ss/cg	:15 (was :20)
————		
Weather		(minus :30)
Waterpark Opens	vo (was vobite)	:20 (was :45)
————		
Sports		(minus :30)
————		
Kicker	vo	:20 (was :35)
	Total:	10:50
	News Hole:	10:35
	Over:	:15

Filling the Rundown—The Computer Method

Rather than draft out a rundown on paper, some producers prefer to begin entering a draft directly into the computer. Using that method, the first draft we came up with earlier might look something like this when entered into a typical computer rundown: *"Rumor Has It News at Six" with Fred Feelgood and Jane Jabberon—Rundown Draft #1 by Computer*

Page#	Slug	Anchor	Shot	Type	WR	Runs	Backtime
A00	Newscast Open			vtr/sot		:20	57:20
A10	Council Taxes			live/pkg		2:10	57:40
A20	Intersection Repair			vo		:25	59:50
A30	4-Car Pileup			vobite		:40	0:15
A40	Apartment Fire			live/pkg		2:10	0:55
A50	Fire History			ss/cg		:25	3:05
A60	Housefire Update			vo		:25	3:30
A70	Robbery Attempt			vo		:25	3:55
A80	Suspect Caught			vo		:25	4:20
A90	Robbery Trial			pkg		1:40	4:45
A100	Murder Trial			vo		:25	6:25
A110	Legislature/ Crackdown			vo		:25	6:50
Alast	1-tz		2shot	vo		:20	7:15
Break One						2:00	7:35
B10	Truck Recall			pkg		1:40	9:35
B20	Recall Info			ss/cg		:25	11:15
B30	Toaster Lawsuit			vo		:25	11:40
B40	Stock Market			ss/cg		:20	12:05
Blast	2-tz		2shot	vo		:15	12:25
Break Two						2:00	12:40
C10	WX Toss		3shot			:10	14:40
C10A	Weather					3:20	14:50
C10B	Tossback		3shot			:15	18:10
C20	Waterpark Opens			vobite		:45	18:25
Clast	3-tz		2shot			:15	19:10
Break Three						2:00	19:25
D10	Toss to Sports		3shot			:10	21:25
D10A	Sports					3:20	21:35
D10B	Tossback		3shot			:15	24:55
Dlast	4-tz		2shot	vo		:10	25:10
Break Four						2:00	25:20
E10	11 Teaze			ss/cg		:25	27:20
E20	Skiing Squirrel			vonats		:35	27:45
E30	C ya/Close			wide		:30	28:20
Terminal Break						1:10	28:50
				Totals:		32:40	6:30:00
				Over/Under		+ 2:40	

Note the total running time is 32:40. The over/under clock confirms it: we're over by 2:40. Because the computer doesn't automatically add in the pad time, we're actually over by 3:10.

Now, let's repeat the horse trading we did earlier. To recap, we shortened all but one of those VO's by five seconds; we deleted the Housefire Update; we shortened the Apartment Fire story by :10; we stole :30 apiece from Sports and Weather; we shortened the Stock Market story by :05; we took the sound bite out of the Waterpark story and shortened it by :25; and finally, we took the nat sot break out of the Skiing Squirrel story and shortened it by :15. With those changes, draft #2 now looks like this: *"Rumor Has It News at Six" with Fred Feelgood and Jane Jabberon—Rundown Draft #2 by Computer*

Page#	Slug	Anchor	Shot	Type	WR	Runs	Backtime
A00	Newscast Open			vtr/sot		:20	0:15
A10	Council Taxes			live/pkg		2:10	0:35
A20	Intersection Repair			vo		:25	2:45
A30	4-Car Pileup			vobite		:40	3:10
A40	Apartment Fire			live/pkg		2:00	3:50
A50	Fire History			ss/cg		:20	5:50
A70	Robbery Attempt			vo		:20	6:10
A80	Suspect Caught			vo		:20	6:30
A90	Robbery Trial			pkg		1:40	6:50
A100	Murder Trial			vo		:20	8:30
A110	Legislature/ Crackdown			vo		:20	8:50
Alast	1-tz		2shot	vo		:20	9:10
Break One						2:00	9:30
B10	Truck Recall			pkg		1:40	11:30
B20	Recall Info			ss/cg		:20	13:10
B30	Toaster Lawsuit			vo		:20	13:30
B40	Stock Market			ss/cg		:15	13:50
Blast	2-tz		2shot	vo		:15	14:05
Break Two						2:00	14:20
C10	WX toss		3shot			:10	16:20
C10A	Weather					2:50	16:30
C10B	Tossback		3shot			:15	19:20

(continued)

Page#	Slug	Anchor	Shot	Type	WR	Runs	Backtime
C20	Waterpark Opens			vo		:20	19:35
Clast	3-tz		2shot			:15	19:55
Break Three						2:00	20:10
D10	Toss to Sports		3shot			:10	22:10
D10A	Sports					2:50	22:20
D10B	Tossback		3shot			:15	25:10
Dlast	4-tz		2shot	vo		:10	25:25
Break Four						2:00	25:35
E10	11 Teaze			ss/cg		:25	27:35
E20	Kicker			vonats		:20	28:00
E30	C ya/Close			wide		:30	28:20
Terminal Break						1:10	28:50
			Totals:			29:45	6:30:00
			Over/Under			− :15	

This will work. Now that we have the basic newscast down, it's just a matter of filling out the details.

Newscast Production: Sweating the Details— Graphics, Artwork and Visual Pacing

We've decided how to fill our newscast. Now it's time to make decisions about the production of the stories. Sets, production techniques and available artwork vary widely from shop to shop. But in every shop, producers have to ask themselves questions such as:

- Where will I use wide shots?
- Where will I use 2shots?
- Where will I use 1shots?
- Which anchor intros will make use of artwork?
- How will I get into and out of live shots?
- Will I have a reporter on the set? At the chroma key? In a debriefing area?

The answers to these questions will depend on the resources available, on your philosophy and on the philosophy of the managers to whom you report. Resources and philosophies vary widely from shop to shop, but one factor is nearly universal: when changing from one story to another, producers should almost always make a visual change as well. For instance, if an anchor is on camera reading a story on a 1shot, don't have her begin a second story on that same 1shot! That's one of the most common mistakes inexperienced or untalented producers make. You must keep up a good visual pace.

Examples of techniques that can be used to make a visual change between two stories include, but are not limited to, the following:

- Changing from a 2shot to a 1shot
- Any change of anchors
- Changing from a 1shot "H&S" (head and shoulders) to an "OTS" (over-the-shoulder graphic shot) with the same anchor, or vice versa
- While on an OTS shot, changing from one OTS graphic to a different graphic
- Changing from an on-camera shot to a tape or graphic, or vice versa
- Wiping or dissolving from one tape to another
- Wiping or dissolving from a tape to a graphic, or vice versa

How Do I Know When to Use an OTS Graphic?

Generally speaking, in any newscast, artwork and graphics are desirable. Lots of bland 1shots are not. A newscast filled with artwork tends to look sharper and more sophisticated. Good, aggressive producers seek ways to use plenty of artwork. OTS graphics work best at the beginning of stories, during the anchor leads. Tags generally are best done on a 1shot without graphics.

That said, the artwork should have a purpose. It should add to the meaning of the story in some specific way, containing a picture or piece of art and a slug line specifically related to the story at hand. Otherwise the graphic simply tends to distract from the anchor's presentation. One mistake you often see in television is the use of completely generic graphics. Thus, you'll find an anchor reading a story about a robbery and murder while sharing the camera shot with a graphic of a generic pistol and a slug that reads "Murder." It's probably the exact same graphic the audience saw in the past 57 murder stories the station aired. To add insult to injury, the pistol's probably pointing at the anchor's head. Drop the graphic. It's worse than useless; it's distracting. If, however, the graphic includes some kind of image specific to this particular case and a specific slug ("1st St. Murder"), it has more use.

When Should I Use a 1shot? When Should I Use a 2shot?

Another mistake inexperienced producers often make is to produce the entire newscast on a 2shot. In some cases this stems from a lack of resources—not enough cameras or camera operators on the floor. Just as often, it stems from a misguided effort to show the anchors as a "team." There are more effective ways to showcase teamwork than by always showing them on a 2shot for every single story. Remember: *the most powerful shot in television is the head and shoulders 1shot.* Why? Because it provides the best opportunity for eye contact. (This is another reason why you should choose your graphics judiciously; OTS shots provide less eye contact because the anchor is, in essence, competing with the graphic for the viewer's attention.) 2shots are good as establishing shots at the beginning of the newscast, as tease shots at the end of news blocks and as transition shots.

The 2shot Transition

The 2shot transition, when used properly (and quickly), is a good tool for showcasing teamwork. The basic idea is to use the 2shot to change anchors between *related* stories.

In our sample newscast above, the Robbery Attempt story and the Suspect Caught story provide such an opportunity. Suppose we had originally planned to change anchors here, and anchor "A" is tagging the final line of Robbery Attempt on a 1shot. Make it a 2shot, and write the copy for the two stories with the transition in mind, in such a way as to enhance teamwork. The first anchor will "hand off" to the second one.

Robbery attempt tag	
2shot	(Fred reads/Jane is looking at him)
	THE ROBBER LEFT EMPTY HANDED
	BUT HE DID GET AWAY.
Suspect caught intro	
	(Jane reads, addressing Fred)
	NO SUCH LUCK FOR THE MAN
	WANTED IN YESTERDAY'S HOLDUP.
	(Jane addresses camera)
Push to 1shot	JUST A LITTLE WHILE AGO POLICE
	SLAPPED CUFFS ON A SUSPECT.

When Should I Use Tags?

Tags serve two purposes. One of the primary purposes is pacing. Every time you change a visual element, you add to the pacing. Tags are one more visual element you can change.

Tags also serve to bring "closure" to a story or, just as importantly, to a story pod. For our purposes a "pod" is a set of consecutive stories read by the same anchor. In a sense the person reading that story pod "owns" it. Usually, he or she will begin the pod on camera, making eye contact with the viewer, and end the pod the same way: on camera, making eye contact with the viewer. This brings a sense of closure to the pod and underscores the anchor's ownership of it. This, in turn, serves to enhance the anchor's image and authority. Because the viewer relates to your product primarily through your anchors, anything that helps their image helps you. This is known in some circles as the "anchor in command" theory of producing. It works.

How Often Should I Alternate Anchors?

There's no hard-and-fast rule, but you should avoid anchor "ping-ponging," that's a technique wherein we see a different anchor every 20 seconds. Inexperienced producers use it for the purpose of driving an audience nuts. Generally, you should *not* always alternate anchors between every story, and certainly not between every 20-second VO. A pace of alternating every 45 to 70 seconds, or between reporter pieces, is about right.

Not every newscast has the luxury of dual anchors. In a solo newscast, you shouldn't alternate anchors at all. (Just checking to see if you're paying attention.)

How Do I Know When to Wipe between Tapes?

Another mistake inexperienced producers often make is to throw in wipes between VOs apparently at random, thinking they "look cool." Generally, they just look confusing. Wiping from one VO to a different, completely unrelated VO can throw off the audience. To be effective, wipes should take place only between related stories. For example:

- Wiping from one crime story to another
- Wiping from one fire to another
- Wiping from one consumer story to another
- Wiping from one environmental story to another
- Wiping from one weather damage scene to another
- Wipes between "thematically" related stories (back-to-back stories in state, national, or newsreels or mini-blocks)

Putting It on the Air

So. You've chosen your stories, filled out the rundown, written all the copy for which you're responsible and edited all the reporter copy to your satisfaction. You're done, right? Wrong. Now you have to get your show on the air and, equally as important, *off* the air *at the appropriate time*. To do so requires a skill set that's different from the one you've used so far to build your show.

Backtiming

As you'll learn, unexpected, terrible and traumatic things can happen in the course of producing live TV. Live shots crash; tape machines eat stories; editors don't finish stories in time; reporters ad-lib information in their tags you weren't expecting; anchors throw in ad-libbed questions you don't have time for; weathercasters go short or long; sportscasters go short or long; packages go short or long; chitchat goes short or long. Don't look now, but there are about a thousand and one things that can ruin the timing of a perfectly timed show, and you must react to all of it in the control room, while the show is live on the air. So it's crucial that you always know precisely how your show is timing out at any given moment. This is done through backtiming.

The concept is simple. Given the length of each story remaining in the newscast, at what clock time must each story begin for the newscast to end on time? In order to keep your newscast on track you must backtime every single story. Most modern news computers will take care of this function for you. If not, you'll need to do it by hand.

In backtiming a show, you begin at the end, with the off-time to the newscast. In our sample newscast the program following news begins at 6:30:00. Therefore, the off-time for news is 6:30:00. Next, look at the last element in the newscast. It's a terminal break, which runs 1:10. Subtract the running time of the terminal break from the off-time to get the backtime for the terminal break, as follows:

6:30:00 − 1:10 = 6:28:50

6:28:50 is the *backtime* for the terminal break. In other words, for the newscast to end exactly on time, the terminal break must begin at *exactly* 6:28:50. I say "exactly" because the running time of the terminal break is a "hard" time; it will run exactly 1:10, no more, no less. Now repeat this for the story element preceding the terminal break, the close, which is scheduled to run :30:

6:28:50 − :30 = 6:28:20

For your newscast to end on time, the close must roll at exactly 6:28:20. This assumes your taped close music runs exactly :30 and ends with some kind of music "stinger" or recognizable ending. However, note that just because you *roll* the close at 6:28:20 doesn't mean you have to *air* the close at that time. Chances are you don't really intend to run the full :30 of available music while sitting on a wide shot of the set. Being up to 25 seconds "late" taking that wide shot with music up full is no problem; in fact, it might be desirable, given that you're paid to put news on the air, not music.

Now repeat the process for the kicker. The kicker runs exactly :20 seconds:

6:28:20 − :20 = 6:28:00

The kicker must hit at approximately 6:28:00 for you to be on time. Don't forget, though, that being :15 late won't kill you because, as we discussed, the running time for the close is negotiable.

Repeat this process for every element in the newscast, and you will find that your backtiming calls for your newscast open to roll at 6:00:15. Of course, it will actually roll at 6:00:00, a difference of 15 seconds. This is another way of saying that you are going into the newscast :15 light or short. However, remember that the computer doesn't figure in any "pad" time for you. To be perfectly on time with a desired "pad" time of :30, we'd need to go into the newscast :30 light.

By this point in our day we've "fleshed out" the rundown, using the principles outlined above to number all the pages, insert the shots, assign anchors to the stories, add in the tags and 2shots and so on. Here's how the final rundown appears, with backtiming. *"Rumor Has It News at Six" with Fred Feelgood and Jane Jabberon—Final Rundown*

Page#	Slug	Anchor	Shot	Type	WR	Runs	Backtime
A00	Newscast Open			vtr/sot		:20	0:15
A00A		f/j		2shot			
A10	Council Taxes	j	OTS	intro		2:10	0:35
A10A	p-Council Taxes			live/pkg			
A10B	t-Council Taxes	j/f	2shot	tag			
A0	Intersection Repair	f	OTS	vo		:25	2:45
A30	4-Car Pileup	f	wipe	vobite		:40	3:10
A30A	4-Car Pileup tag	f	1shot				
A40	Apartment Fire	j	OTS	intro		2:00	3:50
A40B	p-Apartment Fire		dblbox	live/pkg			
A40B	Tossback		dblbox				
A40C	t-Apartment Fire	j/f	2shot	tag			
A50	Fire History	f	OTS	ss/cg		:20	5:50
A70	Robbery Attempt	f	OTS	vo		:20	6:10
A80	Suspect Caught	f	wipe	vo		:20	6:30
A80A	t-Suspect Caught	f	1shot	tag			
A90	Robbery Trial	j	OTS	intro		1:40	6:50
A90A	p-Robbery Trial	j		pkg			
A90B	t-Robbery Trial	j	2shot	tag			
A100	Murder Trial	f	1shot	vo		:20	8:30
A110	Legislature	f	OTS	vo		:20	8:50
A110A	t-Legislature	f	1shot	tag			
Alast	1-tz	j/f	2shot	vtr/vo		:20	9:10
Break One						2:00	9:30
B10	Truck Recall	f	OTS	intro		1:40	11:30
B10A	p-Truck Recall	f		pkg			
B10B	t-Truck Recall	f	2shot	tag			

(continued)

B20	Recall Info	j	OTS	ss/cg		:20	13:10
B30	Toaster Lawsuit	j	OTS	vo		:20	13:30
B30A	t-Toaster Lawsuit	j	1shot	tag			
B40	Stock Market	f	OTS	ss/cg		:15	13:50
Blast	2-tz	j/f	2shot	vtr/vo		:15	14:05
Break Two						2:00	14:20
C10	WX toss		3shot			:10	16:20
C10A	Weather					2:50	16:30
C10B	Tossback		3shot			:15	19:20
C20	Waterpark Opens	j	1shot	vo		:20	19:35
C20A	t-Waterpark Opens	j	1shot				
Clast	3-tz	f/j	2shot	vtr/vo		:15	19:55
Break Three						2:00	20:10
D10	Toss to Sports		3shot			:10	22:10
D10A	Sports					2:50	22:20
D10B	Tossback		3shot			:15	25:10
Dlast	4-tz	j/f	2shot	vtr/vo		:10	25:25
Break Four						2:00	25:35
E10	11 Teaze	f	OTS	ss/cg		:25	27:35
E10A	t-11 Teaze	f	1shot				
E20	Kicker	j	1shot	vonats		:20	28:00
E30	C ya/Close		wide	vtr/sot		:30	28:20
Terminal Break						1:10	28:50
			Totals:			29:45	6:30:00
			Over/Under			− :15	

In the example above, we've listed the running time of each story in one lump sum. For instance, story A10, the Council Taxes live shot, should run 2:10 including lead, package and tossback. Some producers prefer instead to time each individual story element, for example listing :15 for the lead, 1:20 for the package, :35 for the tossback and so on. Either method is valid.

The important thing to remember about backtiming is that it's a constantly shifting target. With the exception of the newscast open and the commercial breaks, the running times of newscast elements are *estimates*. They're soft times, not hard. It's extremely doubtful that every element in the newscast will run the exact amount of time you've budgeted for it. While the newscast is on the air, you must keep a constant vigil on the clock and on your backtiming, adjusting your newscast where necessary as stories go short or long.

Here's an example of how this newscast might actually play out. The perfectly timed rundown is finished, all the stories are written and the tapes are ready. The open rolls, and we're on the air. Your first two live shots take more time than you allotted, and your anchors talk longer than anticipated on the 2shot at the end of the first block. Your backtiming tells you that you're supposed to be hitting the first break at 9:25, but you actually hit it at 10:10. What does this mean? It means your newscast is now in a bit of trouble. The commercial break began 45 seconds later than planned, meaning that you're :45 heavy. You've blown your safety margin and then some. Even if you don't roll *any* close music, at this rate you'll be :15 late hitting the terminal break, which means your show will be upcutting (running over the top of) the next program by 15 seconds. This is simply not allowed. You *must* get the show off on time, which means you're going to have to make up some time. The only course of action at this point is to begin looking for stories to drop or segments to shorten.

What if you're supposed to hit the break at 9:25, but actually hit it at 9:00? The break began 25 seconds early, meaning that you are 25 seconds light or short. You'll need to add 25 seconds' worth of content to your newscast to end on time. The single easiest way to add content is to ask the sports and/or weathercaster to use it. The second easiest way is to ask all the anchors to burn up a little extra time as chitchat. For really serious shortfalls, a wise producer always has a backup package in mind, such as a piece off one of the daily feeds that an associate producer can grab for you quickly. I once knew a producer who kept three "evergreen" feature tapes squirreled away in her desk for such eventualities.

Forward Timing

Forward timing is the opposite of backtiming. It's useful for newscasts in which certain stories *must* air at a certain time. It asks the question, If a particular story must air at a given desired time, at what time must each preceding story hit for the newscast to be on time?

To figure forward times, begin with the start time of the newscast, then add the running time of the first element to get the desired start time of the next element.

As an example, let's pretend the Apartment Fire story contains a live shot we'll receive by satellite, and that the satellite window (the time you've leased from a satellite broker) opens at 6:05 and not a second sooner. Let's see if we'll hit it.

The calculation for the forward time of the newscast open is quite simple: it begins when the newscast starts, at 6:00:00. Now let's figure the forward time of our lead story. To get it, we simply add the running time of the newscast open to its forward time, as follows:

6:00:00 + :20 = 6:00:20

So our lead story will hit at exactly 6:00:20. We know this time is exact because the running time of the open is in stone; it runs exactly 20 seconds, no more, no less.

Now let's figure the forward time of the following story, Intersection Repair. To do so we'll add the running time of the lead story to the lead story's forward time:

6:00:20 + 2:10 = 6:02:30

This tells us the Intersection Repair story will hit at approximately 6:02:30. This time is "approximate" because the 2:10 running time is the producer's estimate. The actual live shot and package could go long or short when it actually hits the air.

Repeating this process for each story preceding the Apartment Fire story, we find that Apartment Fire will hit at about 6:03:35. This is too soon; we'll miss our window. Either we must lengthen the running times of the content elements, or we'll have to move the story down in the newscast.

Here's what the first block of the newscast looks like, with forward timing: *"Rumor Has It News at Six" with Fred Feelgood and Jane Jabberon— First Block with Forward Time*

Page#	Slug	Anchor	Shot	Type	WR	Runs	Forward Time
A00	Newscast Open			vtr/sot		:20	0:00
A00A		f/j	2shot				
A10	Council Taxes	j	OTS	intro		2:10	:20
A10A	p-Council Taxes			live/pkg			
A10B	t-Council Taxes	j/f	2shot	tag			
A0	Intersection Repair	f	OTS	vo		:25	2:30
A30	4-Car Pileup	f	wipe	vobite		:40	2:55
A30A	4-Car Pileup Tag	f	1shot				
A40	Apartment Fire	j	OTS	intro		2:00	3:35
A40B	p-Apartment Fire		dblbox	live/pkg			
A40B	tossback		dblbox				
A40C	t-Apartment Fire	j/f	2shot	tag			
A50	Fire History	f	OTS	ss/cg		:20	5:35
A70	Robbery Attempt	f	OTS	vo		:20	5:55
A80	Suspect Caught	f	wipe	vo		:20	6:15
A80A	t-Suspect Caught	f	1shot	tag			
A90	Robbery Trial	j	OTS	intro		1:40	6:35
A90A	p-Robbery Trial	j		pkg			
A90B	t-Robbery Trial	j	2shot	tag			
A100	Murder Trial	f	1shot	vo		:20	8:15
A110	Legislature	f	OTS	vo		:20	8:35
A110A	t-Legislature	f	1shot	tag			
Alast	1-tz	j/f	2shot	vtr/vo		:20	8:55

Writing Notes—"The Cheap Tie"

Copy writing issues are well covered elsewhere in this book, but two issues bear further exploration here: story ties and teases.

Having had it drilled into their heads that all good newscasts have good story flow, many producers try to create flow artificially with really bad plays on words. Thus you might see a producer lead with a story about a protest at city hall, then follow with a story about a house fire. What's the tie? There is none, but the producer vainly attempts to create one by using cute copy like this:

> WHILE HARSH WORDS ENFLAMED THE DEBATE AT CITY HALL TODAY, FLAMES
> QUITE LITERALLY ERUPTED AT ONE LOCAL APARTMENT COMPLEX.

Don't do that, please, else that strange rustling noise you hear in the distance will be the clicking of thousands of tuners. You should almost always avoid the temptation of tying events together that weren't tied together in real life.

Another heinous producer practice involves the use of the words "while" or "meanwhile" to link unlinkable stories, *without* wordplay. Thus you might hear an anchor read the following script.

OTS=Tax Vote	THE CITY COUNCIL WILL VOTE ON THE TAX INCREASE NEXT WEEK.
OTS=Pileup	MEANWHILE IN SOUTH WHADDADUMP TONIGHT, PARAMEDICS ARE STILL ON THE SCENE OF A FOUR CAR PILEUP.

Unless that pileup was caused by a reckless motorist madly rushing to escape the city council meeting, there's no tie and therefore no "meanwhile."

The only difference between these two forms of cheap tie is that the former is an amateurish mistake, while the latter is an artless amateurish mistake. Story flow is important. However, the fact is that stories don't always flow together. In such instances it's perfectly permissible to use an audible change of gears such as, "In other news." It's not creative, but it serves the purpose. Think of it as verbal punctuation for the viewer (but don't overuse it).

Conversely, if two stories *do* flow together perfectly, this might be a good place for a 2shot transition from one anchor to another, as discussed earlier.

Teases

Teases are some of the most important pieces of copy you can write for your newscast. Research proves people *do* base their viewing decisions on the teases. So you must make those teases compelling.

It's important to remember that teases are *not* news stories. You can't write them the same way. They're sales pitches, and you must treat them as such. In writing them you have a lot in common with any salesperson: you must try to convince the potential customer that the benefits of consuming your product are worth the price. The key word here is *benefit:* your tease must showcase the viewer benefit *without* revealing exactly what it is! Remember, you're trying to "make a sale" here, and the price you're asking is that the viewer devote his or her personal time to the story, which won't happen if you give your product away for free in the tease.

What is a viewer benefit? It's anything of value to the viewer. If you go to Fred's Taco Stand and shell out your hard-earned cash for a taco, you expect to get a tasty treat in return. You're trading value in the form of cash (the price) *for* value in the form of something nutritious, or at least enjoyable, to eat (the benefit). A similar transaction takes place between a newsroom and the news consumer. The consumer pays a price by giving us his or her time and attention, an *extremely* valuable commodity for which advertisers are willing to pay top dollar. In exchange, the viewer expects to receive something of value. You'd better deliver if you plan to keep that viewer as a consumer. No excuses: just cough up the viewer benefit.

Generally, for a viewer to obtain a benefit from a story that story must affect him or her in some way the viewer finds valuable. This includes a wide range of possibilities, including stories that provide:

- Information of any kind that is useful or that addresses a viewer need or desire
- Reassurance, or resolution of a fear
- Entertainment
- A surprise
- Affirmation of personal values
- Confirmation of personal beliefs
- An emotional connection or stimulus
- Anything interesting, enjoyable or diverting

Stories without viewer benefit are, by definition, a waste of the viewers' time. If you air enough of them, the viewers will say goodbye to you and your product and, as it were, go elsewhere for their tacos. You shouldn't run stories devoid of benefit, and you *certainly* shouldn't *tease* them. A tease for a story that doesn't provide viewer benefit is less than worthless; it is in fact *harmful* because it draws the viewers' attention to and might even cause them to stick around for a bad story. You've probably seen it yourself: a TV station teases a story about a basketball-shooting chimp once or twice in prime-time teases, then twice more within the newscast. When we get to the story itself, we find it's a 15-second VO showing some chimp from some roadside attraction in Dogs Barking, Mississippi, sinking one lousy basket. Viewers have been known to get quite angry about this kind of thing; it's a common complaint in viewer calls and letters and often comes up in research and focus groups.

It's easy to see how this kind of thing happens. Producers have a certain amount of tease-time to fill, and they have to fill it with something. But teasing a story devoid of viewer benefit is the equivalent of the aforementioned Fred's Taco Stand putting on a commercial that says, "Our tacos are dry as dust and may even make you barf, but, hey, we had to fill this commercial with something!"

Don't abuse the viewers' trust. It helps to think of it this way. Your newscast presents an array of products of varying worth. Your job, as product manager, is to set the appropriate price for each one. In TV terms, the price is the time we're asking a viewer to devote to a story. For instance, a good lead story for a 10 p.m. newscast should be worth asking the viewer to stick with us through prime time and tune in just to see the story; therefore, it's a good candidate for inclusion in prime-time teases. A good third-block medical package might be worth the same price. Or maybe it's at least good enough to ask the viewer to sit through two commercial breaks to see it, and therefore would be a good candidate for inclusion in tease #1, preceding the first commercial break. We'll assess our basketball chimp story the same way. Is it worth asking the viewer to tune in at 10 o'clock just to see it? Absolutely not. Is it worth asking the viewer to sit through four commercial breaks to see it? No. Is it worth asking the viewer to sit through *one* commercial break to see it? We hope it's at least worth that, or we shouldn't run it at all. Therefore, it's a good candidate for a quick mention at the end of the preceding block. The bottom line is this: viewers are keenly aware of the value of their time. The "price" we set for each story must accurately reflect its value. When the price and value don't match, viewers feel cheated and tend to call news directors and give them a piece of their mind, as well they should.

In planning teases, first identify the stories still to come that have the most viewer benefit. (One important producing technique is to make *sure* you save stories for the lower news blocks that *do* provide benefit—otherwise known as "teasable" stories.) Identify that benefit. Then write to it, making the viewers understand that if they don't change the channel during the commercial break, we'll reward them with a benefit—*without revealing the benefit in the tease!*

Please don't make the mistake of beginning your tease copy with the words, "Coming up next." This is an instant turn-off. "Coming up next" is a TV-speak phrase that, roughly translated, means "It's time for a commercial now." Start that way, and the viewer will zone out and probably leave the room to go to the john or whatever. Instead, begin your tease as if it were a story. Instead of giving the full story, however, you'll hook the viewer by promising viewer benefit, thereby motivating the viewer to stay for the rest. Make use of the "you" connection wherever possible. Use narrative storytelling and/or the rhetorical question whenever possible. Use the imperative voice when appropriate to literally command attention. And it can't be said enough: clearly focus on the viewer benefit!

Example 1—How Not to Do It

COMING UP: THE LATEST INFORMATION ON DIABETES FROM THE U-S GOVERNMENT.

[VO video showing doctor examining patient]

THE STATS SHOW 25 PERCENT OF ALL PEOPLE DON'T KNOW THE SYMPTOMS. DETAILS WHEN WE RETURN.

The tease practically gives the story away but still manages to leave the viewer benefit unclear. Video is generic. How am I affected? Plus, the final line isn't a strong suggestion that the viewer return. Click, see ya.

How to Do It

DID YOU KNOW YOU COULD HAVE DIABETES . . . AND NOT KNOW IT?

[Video of patient with very concerned expression listening to doctor]

THE LATEST STATS SHOW YOU OR SOMEONE YOU LOVE COULD BE IN FOR A FRIGHTENING SURPRISE. FIND OUT HOW TO TELL FOR SURE AND WHAT TO DO ABOUT IT . . . NEXT.

The benefit is very clear: watching this report could improve my health. In fact, I can't afford *not* to watch it. Video and copy make the "you" connection. The imperative voice in the final line *commands* me to return in terms that show it's in my own best interests to do so. You can bet I'll hang with you.

Example 2—How Not to Do It

STILL AHEAD: BRUSH FIRES CONTINUE TO RAGE OUT OF CONTROL IN MEXICO.

[VO video of dramatic fires]

DRAMATIC FOOTAGE WHEN THE NEWSHOUR CONTINUES.

The benefit is weak, though I may stick around to see the pictures. But the fire is a long way away. Frankly, you don't sound like you're that interested in me watching this, anyway. Gotta go.

How to Do It
_____

                                BRUSH FIRES CONTINUE TO RAGE
                                OUT OF CONTROL IN MEXICO.

[VO video of dramatic fires]

                                AND NOW THERE'S A DISTURBING
                                NEW DEVELOPMENT TO THE
                                DISASTER . . .

[Cut to VO video of asthma patient
coughing or using inhaler]

                                . . . ONE THAT COULD AFFECT OUR
                                HEALTH HERE IN THE BAY AREA.
                                LEARN HOW . . . AND WHAT
                                YOU CAN DO ABOUT IT . . . NEXT.

Benefit is clear: brush fires in Mexico might affect me. You're asking me to find out how and what kind of action I might need to take. I'd better listen up.

Example 3—How Not to Do It
_____

                                COMING UP NEXT ON THE
                                NEWSHOUR:

[VO video of washing machine
in operation]

                                NO ONE LIKES TO DO LAUNDRY . . .
                                RIGHT?

[Cut to VO video of unhappy
looking reporter sorting clothes]

                                WE MADE REPORTER JANE DOE DO IT
                                EVERY DAY FOR A WEEK!
                                BUT SHE MADE A SURPRISING
                                DISCOVERY.
                                WE'LL TELL YOU ABOUT IT . . .
                                NEXT.

Copy is semi-cute and somewhat creative—but there's no real viewer benefit other than the hint of some possible entertainment value. Yawn.

How to Do It

DIRTY LAUNDRY. NO ONE TALKS
ABOUT IT. NO ONE WANTS TO DEAL
WITH IT.

[VO video of laundry going into
washing machine]

BUT AT LEAST YOU KNOW WHAT
GOES IN DIRTY . . .

[Cut to VO video of clean laundry
coming out of dryer]

COMES OUT CLEAN . . . RIGHT?
WRONG!

[Cut to VO video of germs under
microscope]

NEW LAB TESTS PROVIDE A NASTY
AND DANGEROUS SURPRISE. LEARN
WHY AND WHAT TO DO ABOUT IT IN A
REPORT YOU WON'T WANT TO MISS . . .
NEXT.

OK, you got me. My laundry comes out dirty? This I gotta see!

A common question producers often ask about writing teases is, "Should I use my best video?" Photographers and reporters sometimes pressure producers not to "give away" the best pictures in a tease. This is a mistake. Remember, you're *selling* the story to your audience. Your best pictures normally will assist in that effort. Use them! Note, this doesn't mean the package itself has to begin with those pictures; sometimes narrative storytelling concerns will lead the reporter and photographer team *not* to lead off with the most dramatic pictures. This has nothing to do with the *tease*, however.

The Care and Feeding of Television Live Shots and Breaking News

Timing a newscast by way of a rundown isn't the only technical aspect of a producer's job. One of the most demanding is the art of coordinating and juggling remotes, otherwise known as "live shots." In this section we'll discuss some of the technical aspects of getting live shots on the air, what makes a good live shot and how to handle breaking news.

There's a lot of disagreement in the industry about how frequently stations should go live and with what types of stories. We'll save that philosophical discussion for another time. But because you can be guaranteed you'll be doing live coverage to one degree or another, you need to know how to do it well.

So what makes a good live shot? The rule of thumb for any good live shot is similar to the standards for a good stand-up. It's not just about face time, though that's important too. Rather, all good live shots are interactive in nature. The audience can't be at the scene, so the reporter goes there for us, taking us by the hand and giving us a guided tour. He or she demonstrates something, touches something, picks something up, kicks something, opens or closes something. Walk-throughs often are effective, but not if they're "walks to nowhere." If the reporter is going to move through the scene, then there should be a point to the trip; it can't simply be a journey down 5 feet of sidewalk. Often the reporter can give this trip purpose by simply gesturing to the surroundings and explaining what we're seeing.

Immediacy is also a factor: is this story late-breaking, or was it done and over with before noon? In most shops, there won' t be enough live units for every reporter, so the producers have the luxury of deciding which stories are most suited for a live shot on that particular day.

Another factor for producers to consider is the *time* required to air live shots. A live remote probably will add 30 seconds to the running time of the story, maybe more. Producers have been known to cram in more live remotes by deleting the question-and-answer opportunity at the end of the remote. Usually this is a mistake. The Q&A provides a much-needed opportunity to provide context, perspective and meaning to the story. It also provides an opportunity to showcase the expertise of both the anchor and the reporter, which is important from a competitive standpoint. However, to get a meaningful answer, the question itself has to be meaningful.

Here is an example of a nonmeaningful, wasted Q&A opportunity:

[Rip N. Reed]	THAT'S THE SCENE FROM THE COURTHOUSE. BACK TO YOU, FRED.
[Fred Feelgood]	RIP . . . HAS THE DATE BEEN SET FOR THE NEXT HEARING?
[Rip N. Reed]	YES . . . FRED . . . IT WILL BE HELD TWO WEEKS FROM NOW ON THE TENTH OF OCTOBER.

Now, here's an example of a more meaningful Q&A:

[Rip N. Reed]	THE NEXT HEARING IS SCHEDULED FOR OCTOBER TENTH. FRED?
[Fred Feelgood]	RIP . . . IS THE DELAY NORMAL FOR A CASE OF THIS NATURE?
[Rip N. Reed]	NO . . . IT'S NOT. THE PROSECUTOR ISN'T TALKING. BUT THE DEFENSE

> ATTORNEY TELLS ME IT'S MORE PROOF
> THE CASE IS WEAK.
>
> HE BELIEVES THE PROSECUTOR IS
> STALLING . . . HOPING TO FIND NEW
> EVIDENCE IN THE WAKE OF TODAY'S
> SETBACK.

Command and Control

Some shops assign an associate producer, tape editor or desk assistant as a *live coordinator,* also sometimes called an *ENG coordinator* (ENG being an abbreviation for electronic news gathering). Other shops don't have an extra person to spare just to coordinate live shots; in such cases, usually it becomes the producer's responsibility. The live coordinator has three primary duties.

- Facilitate communication between the crew in the field, the producer and the engineers tuning in the live shot.
- Supervise to make sure that each live remote is ready at the appropriate time.
- Make sure the producer is fully apprised of the status of all live remotes and especially is informed if a live remote is in trouble.

Of those three points, the last is the most important. *The absolute number one most important task of any live coordinator is to ensure that bad live remotes don't get on the air!*

Here's an extreme example of what can happen if this doctrine isn't followed. It's election night. Reporter Jane Sittenfijit notices that the incumbent mayoral candidate she's covering is coming to the podium to declare victory. Jane needs to get this on the air *right this very second!* First, she tries shouting into the microphone, hoping that someone back at the station is listening to the live feed. Nothing happens. Next, she disconnects her cell phone, which she was using to monitor the station's off-air signal, and dials the producer's direct line. As the seventh caller, she wins a free ticket to Voice Mail Hell, where a recorded voice invites her to leave a message. With mounting panic, she calls the assignment desk, where a polite but clueless intern promptly puts her on hold and leaves in search of someone who can make a decision. Now completely desperate, Jane writes the words "PLEASE TALK TO US" in huge block letters on her reporter's notebook and begins waving it at the camera. As the mayor begins speaking, she finds herself resorting to "the jumping jacks," waving frantically and springing and bouncing in front of the camera like a poodle begging for table scraps in a desperate attempt to get someone's attention.

Meanwhile back at the ranch, the intern talks to the assignments editor, who talks to an associate producer, who talks to the executive producer. The executive producer reads between the lines and realizes the urgency in Jane's message. He orders the associate producer to run to the control booth and tell the producer that the mayor is declaring victory and he wants Jane live on the air right this very second.

In the control booth, producer Terry Timex gets the message. He presses the IFB button, which pipes his voice into the anchor's ear, and orders, "Fred, toss out to Jane in the field; the mayor's at the podium."

On air, viewers see Fred put his finger to his ear and say, "I'm told Jane Sittenfijit has some breaking news for us. Let's go live to her now." Viewers are then treated to a picture of Jane jumping up and down in front of the camera, waving and shouting, "Hey! Can you hear me? You guys need to come out to me now! Can you hear me? Hey! Those idiots, they're not listening to me!"

This goes on for what seems like an eternity but really lasts only 10 seconds. The program cuts back to Fred, who says, "Sorry about that folks, we're having some problems. In other news tonight. . ."

This kind of thing happens all the time in the course of live TV news. Chances are you've seen many similar on-air train wrecks as a viewer yourself. Ninety percent of such incidents never have to happen and don't happen if someone at the station is doing a good job of live coordination.

In a well-run shop the producer never, ever attempts to air a live shot unless the coordinator has specifically pronounced the live shot ready. For a live shot to be ready, five elements must be established and verified. They are:

1 *Signal.* Is the microwave, satellite or fiber signal strong and airworthy?
2 *Video.* Obviously, we have to see a camera picture.
3 *Audio.* The same is true of audio; we must be able to hear.
4 *IFB.* The reporter must be able to hear audio from the television studio.
5 *Readiness.* The reporter and photographer must be standing by and ready for the live shot!

The concept of IFB merits further discussion. In some shops "IFB" has become a generic term used to describe all methods by which a reporter in the field can hear some or all of the television station's off-air signal. IFB is an abbreviation for "interruptible feedback." True IFB is indeed "interruptible," meaning that the producer or live coordinator can open a mic, interrupt the program audio going to the reporter and speak to the reporter. Stations have various ways of delivering IFB. A common method is to route all or a portion of the station's program audio to a phone line, then have the reporter dial into that line by telephone (usually a mobile phone). IFB can also be delivered by way of a subcarrier on the station's broadcast signal, which is monitored in the field by way of a special receiver. Some stations deliver IFB through a two-way radio system. IFB can also be delivered by satellite signal.

In the absence of IFB, a producer can still salvage a live remote *if* it's caught in time. Talent in the field sometimes can receive cues by various other methods. For instance, a field producer or photographer who's on the telephone or radio with someone back at the station can relay cues by hand signal. Or talent in the field can monitor the station's on-air signal by way of a portable television receiver. None of these methods is ideal because the producer isn't able to communicate directly with the talent, but these methods will do in a pinch. In fact, the use of a TV monitor *in addition* to IFB is often necessary for sports or weather remotes, during which the talent needs to see the program in addition to hearing it.

However IFB is received, no live shot can air without it or a substitute method of communicating cues to the talent in the field. Otherwise, the reporter has no way of knowing when or whether he or she is on the air. Lack of IFB is one of the most common causes of live shot failures. In our example above, the live shot crashed primarily because the reporter had disconnected her IFB line, and no one at the station noticed. It's easy to see how this can happen. If a live picture goes to snow, it's fairly obvious; the producer and director normally won't deliberately put that on the air. The same is true of audio; if it cuts out, normally that will be very obvious to an alert live coordinator or audio director. But if IFB suddenly disconnects, it's not always immediately apparent and the live coordinator won't immediately realize the shot has gone south.

Live shots can also fail through *improper* IFB. Satellite remotes present a particular challenge. In the typical satellite remote, the signal travels thousands of miles into space, bounces off a satellite, then returns to earth. The round trip, even at the speed of light, can take a large fraction of a second or more depending on the position of the satellite in relation to the uplink. So when the reporter speaks, his or her words travel into space, come down again, are received at the home television station, then retransmitted *back* to the reporter on an IFB phone line. Thus the talent hears his or her words *repeated* a second or more after having said them. This echo effect can throw the reporter off balance and even cause slurred speech.

Typically, the way to correct this is with a form of IFB known as "mixed-minus." Using the mixed-minus method, the reporter's home station sends a special feed down the IFB line that consists of some or all of the station's program audio *minus* the reporter's own satellite signal. Through this method, the reporter hears what's going on back at the TV station without hearing a distracting echo of his or her own words.

It's the job of the live coordinator—or, in lieu of a coordinator, the producer—to verify all five elements of a live shot, as follows:

- *Signal readiness.* Typically, a station engineer will tune in the signal and clear it for airworthiness.

- *Video readiness.* The live coordinator, usually in cooperation with an engineer, will visually check the camera picture, noting stability, lighting, white balance, framing and the like.

- *Audio readiness.* The live coordinator will listen to the audio. Usually an engineer will check it through a VU meter to make sure it's within acceptable limits.

- *IFB.* This is a simple but important task. The live coordinator merely has to open the microphone and ask, "Can you hear me?" and then listen for the reporter's response on the live feed from the reporter's microphone. A wise live coordinator asks the reporter for a *visual* confirmation, such as a "thumbs up." Otherwise, the live coordinator can't always be sure the reporter didn't nod and say yes in response to a question someone *else* asked on the scene of the story. (For satellite remotes, the coordinator should verify with the audio director that the talent is receiving mixed-minus IFB. If not, the problem won't be apparent until the reporter starts speaking.)

- *Readiness.* The coordinator verifies this by giving time cues to the talent. Most shops give the field talent time warnings at 5 minutes, 2 minutes, 1 minute, 30 seconds and 15 seconds. Some shops and talent like more cues, some like fewer. The practice in some shops is also to alert reporters when they're live in a double box, when they're in a VO, and to give time cues for the running times of packages or sound bites within the live shot. Most crews like to be told when the live shot has ended and they're clear to tear down.

Special Live Coverage

On certain big coverage days, live coordination can become very complicated. For instance, on a major election night even a small-to-medium-market television station might have four or five live shots, including some from other cities. More than one live coordinator may be needed to keep track of all of them.

A very good rule of thumb is to set up a system whereby the remote crews can be assured that when they call the station for coordination or IFB, they never get a busy signal! One solution is to surround the live coordinator with a bank of telephones, with each phone line assigned to one given crew. Or the live coordinator may choose to have just two phones—one to be used to accept calls, the other used for a "rolling conference call." The way this system works is that a crew calls in on Line A and then is immediately transferred to the ongoing conference call with the coordinator on Line B. The live coordinator gives all of the live cues to the various people in the field using Line B.

In either scenario, ideally the live crews all have a preassigned number to call for IFB. This helps sort out confusion, because crews won't have to call in frantically at the last minute to learn their IFB assignments. Plus, lines can be labeled in the control room and IFB coordination stations with the names of the crew members who'll be using the lines, thus making it unnecessary for the producer to punch six buttons to discover which one is connected to Jane at the mayor's headquarters. In major coverage situations, even large-market TV stations may not have enough IFB lines to go around. Some crews will have to double up. This will require close coordination so that crews dial the right line at the appropriate time, and no one gets a busy signal.

Now let's go back to Jane Sittenfijit, covering our hypothetical mayoral race. If our system works as it should, when Jane frantically needs to get onto the air, all her photographer or field producer has to do is pick up the phone, talk with the live coordinator and remain on the line. The live coordinator calls the newscast producer in the control room. The producer gets the message, quickly finds a spot for Jane's report, tells the live coordinator to have Jane stand by, and within seconds, Jane is on the air—calm, collected and kicking the competition's rear.

Contingency Plans

Count on it: if your station does live shots, it *will* experience live shot failures. The main idea behind live coordination is to make sure bad live shots never get on the air and the audience never knows about your technical difficulties. Even with the best live coordination, however, occasionally a live shot will go bad before your very eyes, live during your newscast: the microwave transmitter will blow a fuse, the camera will die, a short will suddenly develop in a microphone, the IFB line will disconnect without warning, a drunken bystander will stumble and kick a cable loose. A thousand and one things can go wrong with live television, and the broadcast corollary of Murphy's Law states that you'll experience each and every variety of live shot failure during the course of your career, probably multiple times.

There are three major steps you can take to prepare yourself. First, at all times be prepared to have your anchor apologize for technical difficulties and move on. Second, *always know* what your next step will be! Never go to the control booth without a viable "Plan B" you can execute quickly in case of live shot failure. Make sure that your director and everyone else who needs to know about the plan is informed. Third, see to it that all taped elements that can be fed back in advance *are* fed back in advance. That way, if the live shot fails, it won't take every coverage element with it. (For instance, you can always roll the reporter's package even if the reporter's live signal dies at the last minute—but only if you have the package already in hand.)

While working in Florida I heard a legendary story about what can happen if the above rules aren't followed. One station decided to send most of its newsroom to cover an approaching hurricane. The satellite truck rolled and just about everyone rolled with it—anchors, reporters, photographers, everyone except the producer and a couple of editors. All day the crew worked to cover the hurricane. The tapes were to be played on the air live from the satellite truck: nothing was fed back in advance. Can you guess what happened? The truck croaked. The poor producer back at the station was left with 30 minutes to fill, and no way to fill it. Now, having heard this story thirdhand, I can't vouch for its veracity; it may be one of those Urban Myths you sometimes hear about. But it's certainly plausible; I've personally witnessed similar television disasters myself on a smaller scale.

Now here's an example of a backup plan that worked. One day on the job in Texas, my station sent a crew to cover a major spot news story in a nearby city. Not long before airtime, we learned our satellite truck was having problems. We hadn't been able to feed back tape, but another affiliate of our network had managed to uplink about two minutes of rough-cut video. So, moments before the open rolled to our newscast, we ran out a stack of Associated Press wire copy and asked the anchors to ad-lib over the rough-cut video and narrate what they saw on the tape. The open rolled, and they proceeded to do exactly that. While this was going on, we managed to get in contact with our reporter and put her on the air by phone for a Q&A with the anchors. Shortly after that, the satellite truck operator resolved the technical problems, and the reporter went live. It wasn't elegant, but it worked. When all was said and done, we actually had more and better coverage than our competitors.

What other options might we have employed as a backup to that live shot? What if we had *no* video at all? If you have *information,* you can do television. In an absolutely worst case scenario, in an emergency, you can have your anchors sit and read wire copy right off the wires. With a little prep time, you can prepare graphics support in the form of a map and full-screen bullet points. You can usually arrange a live phone interview with officials on the scene or at a command post. While you're doing that, you can have a producer or reporter put together a backgrounder/perspective piece using file video of similar stories from the past.

One option you definitely do *not* have: when a big story erupts, you can't hold it and push it lower down into your newscast while you get your act together. When the newscast open rolls, you *must* be there with the lead story. Period. It's your job to make sure it gets on the air with as much information as you have, in the best format you can prepare.

In the event of live, breaking news, your audience will forgive you for all kinds of technical glitches, provided you handle them smoothly, fully explain what's going on and step quickly to your next coverage element. The audience will *not* forgive you for looking confused or unprofessional, which is likely to happen in the absence of contingency plans. Wise producers have a backup for everything.

A Final Word about Breaking News

Compared with any other medium, local television news has two major strengths: pictures and immediacy. Combine them, and you have a live shot. The station that's the most versatile and quick on its feet in breaking news situations will be the one that wins. The successful television station will be prepared to go live with breaking news at the snap of a finger.

Are you prepared to win in this game? Let's find out. Consider the following scenario. You're sitting in the control booth a few minutes into your newscast when you get a frantic call from the assignments desk: one of your live weather cams has caught a tornado on the ground! You punch up the remote on your router and sure enough, there it is—no audio, but spectacular live pictures of a huge black tornado now looming over the downtown skyline. You check the program monitor and find that your anchor is now reading the lead to a long medical report, which your station has been promoting heavily all day.

Which of the following would you do?

1 Climb under the control desk and whimper.
2 Get on the IFB and tell the anchor to stop reading and listen. When she stops reading, tell her to toss to live pictures of a tornado on the weather cam and ad-lib over it.
3 Allow the anchor to continue reading the lead to the taped medical report. Once the report is on the air, use the time to find out more information about exactly where the tornado is and where it is going, and to get the weathercaster to the set.
4 Do nothing; wait for the National Weather Service to issue an official tornado bulletin.
5 Run outside and roll up your car window.

If you answered 3, your heart's probably in the right place but your posterior would be kicked. If you answered 2, you're the one who will be doing the posterior kicking.

"But wait a minute," you object. "I can't talk to my anchor while she's on the air. She can't handle it. She'll choke on-air, then hunt me down and harm me!"

If it's true your anchor can't handle breaking news, then it's probably not her fault. Anchors can handle breaking news situations such as the one described above if they're trained for it and, more importantly, if they understand they'll be asked to do it this way. It's up to the news managers to set the tone and direction. Stations that can handle such situations are ready to do battle in the TV news wars of the 21st century.

One Final Note: What If It All Goes to Hell, or "Why Are We in This Handbasket, and Where Are We Going So Fast?"

If there's one universal factor about live television, it's that occasionally it will crash and burn. Count on it. Murphy's Law has several television corollaries, including:

- If a live shot can crash, it will.
- If an editing machine can jam, it will.
- If this is the worst possible day for one more spot news story to erupt, it will.
- If a tape might not make it, it won't.
- If the president of your company's broadcast division is in town, all of the above will occur simultaneously.

Your only defense is to remember the Boy Scout motto. Assume the worst and be prepared for it. If the lead story is in jeopardy of not being finished in time because the reporter was late with the copy, you'd better have a Plan B that's better than "I'm going to kill the reporter." Know in advance what you'll say to the director and anchors if the story doesn't make it. Don't get caught not knowing where to go or what to do in an emergency! Have a plan and don't hesitate to execute it. Don't wait too late, either; remember, you need time to get word of any changes to the director, anchors, tape rollers and everyone else affected! Many newscasts have crashed and burned with anchors looking lost and confused on camera, while a producer was still trying to issue instructions. Always think *two steps ahead*.

Even with all those preparations, the worst will sometimes happen even to the best of producers. When that happens, don't lose sleep because of it. Simply learn from the experience, and come fighting back the next day. Don't let the occasional TV production tragedy get you down. No matter how bad it was, tomorrow is another day. And the same can be said in the aftermath of excellent newscasts as well! An often-heard truism in this business is that "you're only as good as your most recent newscast," and there's a great deal of truth to that. The best way to cope with that reality is to try bringing a fresh sense of energy, enthusiasm and determination to the beginning of every day.

We've talked a great deal about how to produce a newscast, but we haven't addressed the question of *why* you should produce one. Only you can answer that. Every producer has a different set of drives and motivations. Some produce because they love writing. Others like the excitement of calling the shots, especially in control room environments. Still others enjoy being newsroom leaders and having the ability to shape the "big picture." One thing is for certain: to do well as a producer, you must have passion. Whatever passion brings you here, don't lose sight of it. Nurture it. Cherish it. Never let it go. You'll need it to keep you going during the tough times.

As we discuss in other chapters, our medium is incredibly powerful. On the best days, producing television news can be very fulfilling. Enjoy yourself. But don't squander the opportunity to do some good.

WRITING SPORTS COPY

S ports is the only "beat" to which several news person-nel are assigned on a daily basis. No other subject except weather receives as much airtime on local newscasts every day. Therefore, it's important to make the sportscast as watchable as it can be—and not just for die-hard sports fans. How the stories are written is a big part of that. As is the case with covering any beat, it's important to under-stand the subject and to know what you're talking about, but it's even more important to be able to impart informa-tion in understandable terms. Science and medical reporters have to "boil down" information and specialized terminol-ogy for viewers. Sports reporters should do the same.

How Writing Sports Differs

As for writing guidelines, many things about writing sports copy are the same as writing news copy. The story types are the same: VOs, VO/SOTs, packages and all the little variations of those basic TV story types and their radio counterparts. The keys to good writing are the same as well, and sportswriters should follow the guidelines that news writers are supposed to adhere to. There are a few differences between writing sports and writing news, and there are some guidelines that broadcast journalists covering sports should pay particular attention to.

In TV, especially with VOs, writing sports is even more driven by the available video than is news, particularly when it comes to highlights. Because it's important to identify particular players and what they did to help win (or lose) the game, highlights can almost become play-by-play in miniature. Because the pictures often speak for themselves, other than the name of the player in question and a brief description of the play, sports writers don't need to provide a whole lot of information. They can get away with dropping verbs and doing other things that would be taboo when writing a news story. For example, consider this description of a basketball play: "Jordan . . . from long range . . . good!" That's not much of a sentence in grammatical terms, but it gives the viewer everything he or she needs to know about that particular play. So when writing sports, you can get away with incomplete sentences—but never incomplete thoughts.

In addition to having some latitude with sentence construction, sportswriters also enjoy some freedom when it comes to numbers and statistics. News writers are cautioned about trying to cram too many numbers and statistics into a story, but stats and numbers are a big part of sports, so television sports journalists use numerical information more freely. Of course, this can still be overdone. Stories containing sentences such as these actually go on the air: "Meet Joe Hoopster. The six-foot-nine-inch, 210-pound junior at Local High School averages 22 points per game, shooting a sizzling 72 percent from the floor. He pulls down an average of 11 rebounds, and blocks six shots while playing only 27 minutes per contest." Only the most avid sports fan can sit through that. The problem is that people covering sports for local television or radio news sometimes get caught up in a sports culture and fail to remember that many potential viewers aren't so enamored with numbers. By falling into that trap, sports producers, reporters and anchors might actually be alienating potential viewers.

People covering sports enjoy more freedom when it comes to openly criticizing the teams they cover. Newscasters are supposed to be unbiased observers, but sportscasters are sometimes *expected* to be judges of the effectiveness of a new strategy or of a decision by team management. Opinion and commentary are part of a sportscaster's repertoire, but as we have cautioned about many things, this can certainly be overdone.

Things about Which to Be Cautious

Although some commentary and criticism are acceptable in sports, sportscasters and writers should be cautious about being critical all the time. That just leads to charges of cynicism. But those covering sports should also avoid the other extreme—becoming shameless boosters of a team. If a team does well, it's certainly OK to say so, but anybody putting sports stories together should be careful not to let a personal affinity for a team affect how that team is covered. Although writers of sports scripts do enjoy some latitude compared with their news writer counterparts, there are some liberties that are taken on a regular basis that make the people in the newsroom think that the sports department could never cover serious news. Part of that comes from a marked overdependence on clichés in sports copy.

"Sports Speak"

A look at sportscasters from stations in markets of all sizes across the country would show that many sportscasters and the people who write some of their scripts for them tend to use terms that might be difficult for anyone but the most avid fans to follow. Some news directors and consultants are fond of saying "only 25 percent of the audience is interested in sports." There is some evidence to back up that claim,[1] but the question is asked, Then why are the ratings so good for the Super Bowl, the Olympics, the World Cup? Might it be that many of our potential viewers have some interest in sports, but local sportscasters don't do a very good job of taking advantage of that interest? If so, what can aspiring television sports journalists do about it? One solution would be to write stories that don't require the viewers to have a sports dictionary handy. Currently, "sports speak" abounds on local sportscasts in all parts of the country, and it doesn't come just from the new folks in small markets trying to break into the business. Here are just a few of the terms and phrases that sportscasters overuse and the interpretations of those phrases.

> "He was hacked in the act." (A basketball player was fouled while shooting.)

> "He has all the tools." (Then maybe he should guest star on a home improvement show.)

---

1. See, for example, T. Atwater (1984), "Product Differentiation in Local TV News," *Journalism Quarterly, 61*, pp. 757–762; T. Wulfemeyer (1983), "The Audience for Local Television News: Getting to Know Interests and Preferences," *Journalism Quarterly, 60*, pp. 323–328.

"He's a team player." (He's not the star.)

"The team is taking things one game at a time." (It would be difficult to play two games at once, now wouldn't it?)

"They have their work cut out." (These guys don't stand a chance.)

"The team can't take anything for granted." (The team should win this game by 40 points.)

"They need to turn it up a notch." (The normal halfhearted effort won't be enough against this opponent.)

The list could go on and on and fill up several pages. In addition to using tired phrases, sportscasters also slip into sports lingo frequently. Here are some of those examples and what they really mean.

dinger, tater, round tripper—home run

ribbie—run batted in

he went yard—he hit a home run

frozen rope—an accurate football pass

laser beam—a solid base hit

reaching paydirt—scoring a touchdown

a kiss off the glass—a soft shot off the backboard

between the pipes—where a hockey goalie plays

Again, the list could go on and on, but you get the picture. The problem is that sportscasters and writers have to come up with interesting ways to say essentially the same thing night after night. Recognizing that, we still suggest that using terminology that requires viewers to figure out what's being said does sportscasters and producers more harm than good. It's more important to be clear than clever, and speaking in code certainly doesn't encourage those outside the culture to become a part of it. The goal is to attract viewers: it isn't to send 75 percent of the viewers scrambling for their remotes or to their computers to check scores there.

Getting Good Bites

No reporter can control what an interviewee says, but we have ultimate control of whether a certain comment makes it on the air. A large-market news director once told the people on his sports staff that they wouldn't be allowed to use bites from coaches or athletes any more if they couldn't come up with some people to interview who didn't speak using clichés only. On one occasion, a sportscaster even made fun of the coach he had just quoted for saying that his team could "take nothing for granted" against an opponent that the better team crushed on a regular basis. The sportscaster made fun of the coach, but he used the bite. Here are some proclamations from coaches and athletes that indicate almost no thought on the part of the speaker and even less thought on the part of the person who let these comments go on the air. Again, interpretations are provided.

"We have to put that game behind us." (We really stunk up the place, and I sure hope we don't play so poorly again this week.)

"I'm more interested in team goals than in personal accomplishments." (Yeah, right.)

"I do what I can to help the team." (If it weren't for me, these bozos would have lost.)

"We have to stay focused and give it 110 percent." (In terms of deep-thinking competition, Plato has nothing to worry about from jocks who use this line all the time.)

"We'll do our best and hopefully we'll come out on top." (Don't most sports figures hope their teams come out on top?)

If those conducting interviews would do some homework and come up with good questions, coaches and athletes might not use such tired, banal phrases all the time. Good questions frequently lead to good answers. But if you come up with really outstanding questions and still find yourself interviewing someone who is stuck in the sports-speak rut, go interview someone else. You'll be doing the viewers and the person in question a favor.

Locker-Room Interviews

Often, sports reporters interview sports figures in controlled settings. Sometimes, however, that isn't the case, such as after a big game covered by a lot of television stations, newspapers, magazines and radio stations. Semicontrolled mayhem is a fairly accurate description of what you'll find. In the locker room, it's fairly common to see an athlete surrounded by 20 or more members of the media, all trying to get a nice cogent bite for use that night or a quote for the next morning's newspaper.

There are a few "rules of the trade" to remember in these settings. First, you're not doing a documentary on the athlete in question, and he or she probably isn't in the mood (especially after a loss) to expound on the meaning of life. You're there to get a comment or two about the game that just ended and about the athlete's or the team's performance in it. Everything else can wait until another time. Asking a dozen questions tends to upset the athlete and your media colleagues. They all see it as a waste of their time.

Second, every one of your colleagues is on a deadline, and some deadlines are coming up more quickly than others. For example, the radio reporter who's in the locker room to get comments for a live broadcast is under greater pressure than the television reporter who needs to get a bite or two for a newscast that's two hours away. By deferring to the radio reporter for a few minutes, you might set the stage for a return favor sometime in the future. A little professional courtesy can go a long way in forging a relationship with someone you work alongside of on a regular basis.

Third, although the audience rarely hears your questions (except when you're doing a live report), your colleagues hear everything you ask. Sometimes you have to ask something that the first athlete has already addressed because you were talking to another athlete at the time and you need a particular answer from the first athlete. Asking questions that have already been asked by someone else is expected and most athletes handle it graciously, as do other media representatives. But the truly dumb questions will hound you throughout your career, so try not to ask any. Many newspaper writers tend to think of television and radio reporters as something less than journalists anyway, and when you ask a question for all to hear that makes you sound as though you don't think before you speak, you only make matters worse.

A classic example happened in the Washington Redskins' locker room after they won Super Bowl XXII. Doug Williams, a product of Grambling and the legendary coach Eddie Robinson, was asked: "Doug, how long have you been a black quarterback?" To his credit, Williams handled it beautifully, answering: "Since I left Grambling." (Grambling is a historically black institution.) The reporter who asked that question may never live it down.

Grammar

Just as we have to think about the questions we ask, we also have to think about the words we write. Grammar is something that gets too little attention in broadcast journalism in general, and particularly in sports. The sports department is often physically separated from the newsroom in television and radio stations across the country, and that can lead to a philosophical separation as well. It often seems that the sports report isn't scrutinized as carefully by news managers as are other parts of the newscast. There's almost a sense of "as long as you fill your time" (or don't offend someone in a major way), the news directors and others in news management pay little attention to what goes on the air during sports. In newsrooms in which that's the case, it's incumbent upon those working in sports to police themselves in terms of good writing, proper grammar and the like.

Two particular grammatical problems crop up all the time in sports reports. The first is the reference to "the team" as "they." The generic pronoun used in reference to a team should always be "it." For example: "The team extended *its* winning streak to 22 games," not "The team extended *their* winning streak to 22 games." There's only one team, so don't use a plural pronoun. The second problem is closely related to the first. If the team nickname is singular, then the pronoun should be singular. If you're talking about the Dolphins, the Yankees, or the Supersonics, then using "they" is correct. But if you're talking about the Heat, the Magic, or the Jazz, then the pronoun should be "it" and verbs should be singular as well.

The confusion comes because we're talking about a team that's made up of a number of players and almost all team nicknames are plural, so the tendency is to use plural pronouns in reference to all teams. But that line of reasoning doesn't follow. You wouldn't write: "Utah won their third game in a row." You'd write: "Utah won *its* third game in a row." You should also write: "The Jazz won *its* third game in a row." Likewise, you wouldn't write: "Utah are one of the best teams in the league." You'd write: "Utah *is* one of the best teams in the league." You should also write: "The Jazz *is* one of the best teams in the league." Think of the team nicknames not as references to teams but rather in terms of how the nouns are normally used, and you'll see how silly it sounds to use a plural verb with a singular noun.

> David Copperfield's magic are very impressive. (Did some hick write this?)
>
> The heat in south Florida in the summer cause electric bills to skyrocket. (English teachers cringe when they hear stuff like this from people who are supposed to know how to write.)
>
> Jazz have been one of my favorite musical forms for a long time. (Incorrect in this context, and incorrect when you're talking about Utah's pro basketball team.)

Think of team nicknames as normal nouns and you'll be OK. If the noun is plural, use plural pronouns and verbs. But if it isn't, impress the viewers with your command of the English language.

Be Proactive

The second part of trying to attract viewers to watch the sportscast even though they might not be die-hard fans is to cover events and stories that aren't about professional football, basketball, baseball or hockey. Using what seems to be the popular approach to covering sports, many 11 p.m. sportscasts could be written on Monday and replayed each night of the week simply by inserting the names of the teams and the athletes playing today.

_____ with a homer to left.

_____ reaches paydirt.

_____ with the monster slam.

_____ with the slap shot . . . he scores!!!!!

We don't want to sound cynical here, although many sportscasts almost seem to invite cynicism. Highlights and scores are a necessary part of a sportscast. After all, you can't discard that 25 percent of the viewers and listeners who are interested in how their favorite teams did while you're trying to attract the other 75 percent of the audience. But a sportscast that consists entirely of scores, highlights and material from satellite feeds is the sign of a lazy sports department and a sure way to send people to bed early or searching for some other program to watch.

So what should sports departments cover to try to broaden the viewership base? Quite simply, anything that would be of interest to a broad cross section of the audience, sports fans and nonsports fans alike. If a Little League baseball game were covered the way pro baseball games are covered, that wouldn't accomplish anything. We might have more sports bloopers to show, but other than the skill level and size of the players, Little League games are played and won or lost the same way the pro games are. People who wouldn't be interested in pro baseball highlights wouldn't be interested in Little League baseball highlights either. But let's assume that three sets of twins play for one team in the city league. A feature story about what the coach goes through trying to tell the kids apart would appeal to almost anyone in the audience because *almost anyone can relate to it*. Dan Hicken works as a sports anchor in Jacksonville, Florida. He did this very story. It won a statewide award and is still one of the most memorable sports stories I've ever seen.

There's a river of video available on satellite feeds emanating from any number of sources several times a day. But if every sports staff in the nation uses the same basic feeds and airs the same basic video, what is it that makes a local sportscast local? Even in those markets with four, five or six professional sports teams (or, perhaps, especially in those markets), the sports department has to work to find material that's of interest to people other than those who call in to sports-talk radio programs.

To wrap up, let's look at a few examples of sports scripts using the various story forms we've discussed earlier.

Devilrays

SQ/SS	(chris) WHEN THE RAYS MADE TONY SAUNDERS THEIR TOP PICK IN THE EXPANSION DRAFT . . . EVERYONE POINTED TO THE FACT THAT HE HAD BEATEN THE ATLANTA BRAVES TWICE IN HIS ROOKIE SEASON LAST YEAR. RIGHT NOW . . . I'M NOT CERTAIN SAUNDERS COULD BEAT THE ATLANTA GOLDFISH AND IT MAY BE TIME FOR HIM TO TALK TO LITTLE ANIMALS.
M2/VO	(vo) THE MARLINS JUMPED ON SAUNDERS EARLY TONIGHT. IT WAS AN UGLY FIRST INNING AND BEFORE TONY KNEW WHAT HAPPENED . . . IT WAS THREE TO NOTHING . . . FLORIDA. AND THEN IT GOT WORSE. THE MAN WHO DROVE IN THE WINNING RUN MONDAY NIGHT . . . TODD ZEILE . . . WENT OPPOSITE FIELD IN THE 5TH INNING AND SUDDENLY THE GAME WAS GETTING OUT OF CONTROL. SAUNDERS WAS ON THE WAY TO HIS 8TH LOSS IN NINE DECISIONS AND THAT . . . IS NOT GOOD. MARLINS WIN EIGHT TO FOUR.
:45 M/2 ENDS	

This is a fairly straight treatment of highlights of the local team, except for the way the anchor leads into the story. What we see isn't outright commentary in the sense of "the team ought to send this guy back to the minors," but the anchor is clearly making a judgment about the pitcher's abilities at this point in time. Again, sports people have a bit more latitude than news anchors and reporters in this area.

Strikers

M2/VO	(chris) (vo) AND IN DETROIT TONIGHT, HISTORY IS EQUALED WHEN SAMMY SOSA RIPS HIS 18TH HOME RUN OF THE MONTH . . .

THAT TIES OLD-TIMER RUDY YORK OF
THE TIGERS FOR MOST HOME RUNS IN
ONE MONTH. IT ALSO GIVES SOSA A
TOTAL OF 31 AS HE CHALLENGES MARK
MCGWIRE FOR THE MAJOR LEAGUE
HOME RUN LEAD.

:30 M/2 ENDS

Often, sports highlights are very short. This one reads only about
15 seconds. It's a common practice in sports to make highlights
short—to allow for as much visual variety in the show as possible. It's
also fairly common for the director to wipe from one piece of video to
the next, without going back to the anchor's face. So we could have a
couple of baseball highlights stories with wipes between them, then
wipe to a baseball scoreboard, then to another highlight, to another
board, to a tennis highlight, to a golf highlight, and never see the
anchor again until the end of the sportscast.

Of course, that makes it seem as though we're advocating a sportscast of nothing but highlights. Indeed, the late evening sportscast is
more highlights-driven than those earlier in the day. But even on the
10 or 11 p.m. sportscast, you should try to work in something that
would be of interest to all viewers.

Jenkins

SS: UA-STANFORD   (—- DaveS—-)
                                         U-A HEAD COACH DICK TOMEY'S NOT
                                         SAYING WHO'S GOING TO START AT
                                         QUARTERBACK FOR THE WILDCATS THIS
                                         WEEK. . . ALTHOUGH YOU'D HAVE TO
                                         THINK KEITH SMITH EARNED THE JOB
                                         IN HAWAII.

ENG NATVO :35 seconds   (—-vo—-)
                                         IT WAS *NOT* A GOOD DEBUT FOR
                                         ORTEGE JENKINS. . . WHO WON THE
                                         STARTING POSITION DURING TRAINING
                                         CAMP. . . BUT CAME OUT THROWING
                                         SOME AIR BALLS . . .AND NOT HAVING
                                         MUCH LUCK. BUT, JENKINS AND SMITH
                                         ARE BOTH EXPECTED TO PLAY THIS
                                         WEEK. O-J . . . PLAYING TEACHER . . .
                                         WASN'T IMPRESSED WITH HIS FIRST
                                         GAME.

ENG OUT
DISSOLVE ENG SOT :22 sec.

(—-sot—-)

"That game, I think I played a C level. Maybe C level as a team . . . individual I played a D level . . . haaa . . . I'm just excited to have a game . . . have to play and I think our whole team feels that way . . . we just want to play and get these road games out of the way and get a couple of wins on the road . . . we'll have a nice home stretch toward the end of the year."

ENG OUT
SS: FULL SCREEN
STANFORD/ARIZONA SERIES

(—-ess—-)

THE CATS HAVE DONE A GOOD JOB AGAINST STANFORD THROUGH THE YEARS. THIS WILL BE THE 16TH MEETING.

In this example, we have a VO/SOT about the quarterback situation for the University of Arizona football team. We begin with a VO to show some of Jenkins' miscues when he was in the game the week before, then wipe to a separate tape containing his comment about his performance. We come back at the end of that bite with a full-screen graphic out of electronic still store (ESS) for some information about how Arizona has fared against Stanford in previous meetings. Be aware, as we mentioned in Chapter 8 on VO/SOTs, the two parts of this story will be on separate script pages, just as the VO and the SOT are on separate tapes.

Conclusion

Although sports people have a bit of latitude in some areas (such as referring to a player by his initials only), it's just as important for sports producers and anchors as for anyone else to be clear and concise in what they write, and to provide clear directions to the technical part of the team. This brings us back to the most important aspect of the communications business—a need to communicate with each other. If we don't all know exactly where we're going, we can't expect the audience to follow along.

📁 Do's and Don'ts When Writing/Covering Sports

Do
- Look for features that would interest all viewers.
- Worry more about being clear than being clever.
- Find athletes who can talk, and ask them good questions.

Don't
- Cover only pro sports.
- Get caught up in a "sports culture."
- Fall into "sports speak."
- Think that because you're covering sports the writing rules don't apply.

WHY WE FIGHT

U p to this point, this book has been largely technical in nature. We've discussed the mechanics and style of broadcast copy writing, news gathering and news production at length, but we haven't delved as much into its substance or purpose. For the next few pages we'll put aside the *how* of journalism and concentrate on the *why*. It's our intention to give a broad overview and summary of the ethical process at both the newsroom and the individual levels. We'll also explore a topic not often addressed in the available literature on ethics, that is, motivational challenges, professional disappointments and on-the-job frustrations that can adversely affect a journalist's ethical focus and quality of work.

The subject of ethics in journalism deserves far more attention and study than we'll be able to devote to it in the relatively brief chapter that follows. We strongly recommend that readers pursue this topic further. There are many fine books on the market dealing with ethics in journalism. One of the best is *Doing Ethics in Journalism: A Handbook with Case Studies* (1999, Allyn and Bacon) by Jay Black, Ralph Barney and Bob Steele. Steele is director of the Ethics Program at the Poynter Institute for Media Studies, *www.poynter.org,* and we'll draw on his expertise extensively in the pages that follow.

Building the Ethical Newsroom

Let's assume for a moment that you work in an average newsroom. Most if not all the journalists within consider themselves ethical. They probably have above-average intelligence and abilities and at least average motivation. Now, imagine that an ugly episode plays out in the community, a news coverage challenge that strains emotions to the breaking point and severely strains the newsroom's decision-making processes. Would your newsroom rise to the occasion?

On Tuesday, April 20, 1999, two heavily armed students walked into Columbine High School in Littleton, Colorado, and opened fire. More than a dozen people died. With no warning, local media found themselves having to cover what turned out to be the bloodiest school rampage in U.S. history. Some stations performed better than others. Many made mistakes, some of them spectacular. Consider the following:

- While the gunmen were still presumably roaming the halls, some stations aired live cell phone interviews with students in hiding. One anchor went so far as to urge students to call the TV station instead of 911 (advice that was quickly retracted). One purported student cell phone call, which also aired live on a network news service, turned out to be a hoax.

- By contrast, at least one other local TV news producer took such a student call and handled it far differently. Realizing she wasn't trained as a crisis counselor or hostage negotiator, she didn't even consider putting the caller on the air. Instead, she urged the student to call 911 and then disconnected the call.

- Stations aired emotional interviews with extremely distraught juveniles at their most vulnerable moments, interviews that wound up being replayed again and again on the national news media.

- Almost every station showed, to at least some degree, live helicopter pictures of police positions and student escape routes, which of course might have been of extreme interest to the gunmen inside the school, who did have access to televisions.

Clearly, different ethical and decision-making processes were at work here among the various newsrooms and journalists. In the aftermath of Littleton, the local and national media endured a firestorm of criticism. But there was some praise as well for the self-restraint and balance some of the journalists showed.

Now picture this happening in your newsroom. Would your team handle it well? Even if the people in your newsroom are ethical, if your newsroom has had no training in ethical decision making, the outcome is doubtful. A newsroom filled with ethical people isn't necessarily an ethical newsroom! Bob Steele of the Poynter Institute says that our individual ethical principles "compete with each other and may compete with other people's principles. So we have to have the skills of ethical decision making, the process and tools to work through conflicting principles and colliding values."

On October 2, 1999, journalists and ethics experts gathered in Charlotte to address these and related questions in a Radio-Television News Directors' Foundation (RTNDF) *www.rtndf.org*–sponsored workshop entitled "Newsroom Ethics: Decision-Making for Quality Coverage." Workshop leaders addressed the thought processes and systems newsrooms should have in place to enable them to handle such situations well. Participants learned that ethics isn't something you *have*; it's something you *do*. Ethics isn't simply an injunction to "do right." It's a process for achieving that goal.

According to facilitators Jill Geisler and Al Tompkins of the Poynter Institute, the decision-making processes in most newsrooms come in three flavors. They are:

- Gut reaction
- Rule obedience
- Reflection and reasoning

Reliable, ethical decision making is likely to take place only on that third level.

Gut Reaction

It's probably safe to say that most journalists consider themselves ethical. If pressed to justify that claim, many of them might say they "go with their gut" or "trust their instincts." But according to Geisler and Tompkins, gut-level reactions, though important, are just the first step. The problem with your "gut" is that it's unique to you. It's shaped by an entire lifetime of personal experiences and past incidents, both pleasant and unpleasant. Your gut feelings can be emotional, prejudicial, unreasonable, strongly set, even irrational. Steele puts it this way: "Too strong of a gut reaction can prevent reflective and reasoned thinking. Too strong of a gut reaction can keep us from hearing the contrarian thoughts of others. Too strong of a gut reaction can trap us in the rigidity of rules and keep us from seeing the gray that always exists between the black and the white." Steele says you *should* listen to your gut, but don't completely trust it. Your gut reaction *will* have value, though, if it gets a conversation going—provided that conversation doesn't stop at the "gut level."

Rule Obedience

If you're talking about an ethical issue, you're already ahead of some newsrooms. What sometimes happens, however, is that conversation proceeds to the next level, rule obedience, then stops there. According to Geisler and Tompkins, at this level the participants recognize there's an issue, but they're not sure how to proceed. So, they open the station's policy manual—or, if there isn't one, they discuss the issue in light of the station's known rules, regulations and precedents. They pick the rule or regulation that seems to fit (examples: "We don't cover suicides" or "We don't show bodies") then proceed accordingly. The problem with this, of course, is that no rule book can possibly cover every situation. A blind obedience to rules precludes reflection and reasoning. At this level the best courses of action may never even come up for discussion.

Reflection and Reasoning

In healthy newsrooms most rules are really *guidelines* meant to provoke further discussion, not end it. In such a newsroom, the decision-making process will now proceed to the third level. At this stage, participants attempt to find the proper course of action in light of the given facts while taking into account the station's guidelines and policies. Such discussions are best if they include a wide range of viewpoints, especially when working through major crises. Participants must ask certain questions, and the discussion might make use of formal guidelines for ethical decision making, which we'll discuss in a moment.

What Is Ethical? A Case Study

So how does one decide whether a given course of action is ethical?

One of the best ethical codes is that adopted by the Society of Professional Journalists (SPJ) *www.spj.org*. It contains four basic points. Ethical journalists should:

- Seek the truth and report it
- Minimize harm
- Act independently
- Be accountable

When newsrooms fail to act ethically, often it's because the decision-making process either got hung up on or never got to that second point. The concept of minimizing harm suggests that the end does *not* always justify the means, and that not every fact or fact-gathering tactic is worth the collateral damage it might cause to people or organizations. Working these problems through isn't easy. It requires a *process*. Mistakes are likely to occur when the process fails or none is in place to begin with.

During the RTNDF workshop Geisler and Tompkins presented a fascinating case study that shows how this can happen. A station in Denver wanted to interview a victim who had suffered burns and other injuries in a building explosion. First the reporter tried an open front-door approach; she sought the interview through the hospital's public relations department. A spokesperson denied permission for the interview, telling the reporter the family didn't wish to talk. The reporter contacted the family directly and discovered, as she had suspected, that this wasn't true; the victim and his wife very much wanted to talk. Angered that the P.R. spokesperson had misled her, the reporter decided to sneak up to the hospital room and obtain the interview on the sly. Accordingly, the photographer stuck the camera under his coat. The two of them made it up to the hospital room unchallenged, grabbed the interview, and presented a compelling exclusive story on the next newscast.

Would you have a problem with this course of action? At this point none of the 40 or so participants in the RTNDF workshop, which included some veteran news managers, objected. Many said that if the reporter and photographer were in the hospital room at the invitation of the patient, then they had a legal right to be there.

The problem with the law is that it tells you what you can get away with, not what you *ought* to get away with. Or, as Tompkins put it, "The law tells you what you can do. Ethics tells you what you *should* do."

In this case, the television station's actions might have been different had the decision makers stopped to thoroughly discuss the proposed course of action before taking it and had asked any of the following questions during that discussion:

- Will the crew's presence in the room interfere with the patient's medical treatment?
- Will the crew's presence in the room adversely affect the patient in any way?
- Is this the type of environment where the crew would need to be capped and gowned?
- What if the crew plugs in its lights and blows a circuit?

As it turns out, burn patients require special germ-free environments. The crew's entry into the room *was* potentially dangerous for the patient. In the aftermath, the hospital raised a hue and cry. This led to a public relations problem for the TV station, which had to apologize for its actions.

The concepts of seeking the truth and minimizing harm go hand in hand. But of the two, the duty to seek the truth and report it is primary. As Steele puts it, the idea is to minimize harm while maximizing truth-telling. Decision-making processes fail if they don't include prudent steps to reduce the harm a story might cause. But they fail even worse if they minimize harm by eliminating needed truth-telling.

In the case study above, the television station would have been well served to consider other options. Among the possibilities:

- Confront the P.R. spokesperson with the truth about the family's willingness to talk and enlist her help in setting up a safe interview.
- Consider a phone interview with the hospitalized patient.
- Interview the wife separately outside the hospital.

These options might have preserved the station's ability to tell the truth of what happened while minimizing the harm the interview might have caused.

Doing Ethics: Excerpts from the Poynter Guidelines

In a healthy newsroom environment one or more people, perhaps making use of a gut reaction, will red-flag issues of truth-telling versus harm for discussion. The discussion will proceed to that third level, reflection and reasoning. Steele has a list of questions participants should ask. Among them, paraphrased below, are:

- What do we know? What more do we need to know?
- What is our journalistic purpose?
- What are our ethical concerns?
- Which organizational policies and professional guidelines must we consider?
- Which other voices, people with diverse perspectives and ideas, should we include in the decision-making process?
- Who are the stakeholders—those who will be affected by our decisions? What motivates them? How would we feel if we were in their shoes?
- What are the possible consequences of our actions?
- What are our alternatives?
- Will we be willing—and *able*—to publicly explain our actions?

One might reasonably question whether there's *time* to go through all of these steps in a crisis situation, given the deadlines a typical television or radio news operation faces. The answer is yes. A station's news operations do not have to grind to a halt during the decision-making process. The desk can still dispatch crews and begin the process of getting the news on the air. It is possible even in such situations to convene quick meetings, either in a nearby conference room or in the middle of the newsroom, to seek staff input for identifying red-flag issues and to discuss options. Nor does the process have to stop when the formal planning meeting ends. Some stations have ongoing conferences, in the news director's office or some other central location, which people can join and leave as their deadlines permit. Regardless of the method, if a news organization believes ethical decision making is important, it will find a way to do it.

Acting Independently

The SPJ's admonition to "act independently" isn't as complicated or hard to interpret as the injunction to "minimize harm." Though the code contains several bullet points of advice under this heading, the gist of it is simply this: the only item on your news gathering agenda should be an intent to gather the news. You should steer clear of any influences that might call that agenda into question. There are hordes of people out there trying to influence your reporting, both overtly and subtly, and swing you over to their point of view. Land mines and pitfalls litter the journalistic landscape. If you step in one, the best course is to simply back out of it—and, if necessary, disclose the conflict, apologize for it and take corrective action.

Accountability

That fourth ethics point—"be accountable"—is a relatively new addition to the SPJ code, having been added in 1996. Journalists are still struggling with it. Most television and radio stations do a fairly poor job with it.

The text of the code itself speaks of abiding by high standards, promptly correcting mistakes and the like. But it also urges journalists to "invite dialogue with the public over journalistic conduct." Television and radio stations are in a position to do this much better than any newspaper; after all, we're actually *capable* of the speech the word "dialogue" implies. Many television stations have viewer mailbag segments that include comments from the public received by way of telephone and e-mail. This is a good start. Segments that specifically solicit viewer feedback on the station's news coverage decisions are better. Segments that invite such feedback and respond to it sincerely are the best. Very few television or radio stations have such segments. Fewer still—as of this writing, only two or three—have viewer representatives or ombudsmen to facilitate this process.

If a television station, radio station or network news operation truly wishes to hold itself accountable to the public, it should clearly state what it stands for and provide a mechanism for soliciting, airing and, most importantly, openly and sincerely *responding* to public feedback.

It takes a bit of courage to do this. A commitment to public feedback implies a commitment to own up to mistakes. Journalism is difficult; few of us are completely without ethical sin. Mistakes are inevitable. History suggests the public can be very forgiving—*if* forgiveness is requested. On the other hand, the public has nothing but contempt for people and institutions that ignore or deny their mistakes or, even worse, defend them as if they were some kind of virtue.

Criticism of the media has long been a high art form, and lately it's become a public sport. Some publications—notably *Brill's Content*—specialize in making journalist's lives more or less miserable. If you read media responses to challenges from *Brill's* and others, an interesting pattern emerges. A few media organizations are willing to discuss the issues, but many aren't. Some respond with words such as, "Yes, we have a policy on that issue—but we can't share it with you." That's hogwash. The American people, by way of the U.S. Constitution, have given our industry protections afforded to no other. In return we owe it to our public to share and explain our methods and motivations.

An Ethics Barometer

We've seen that newsrooms can't rely on the collective gut instincts of their employees for ethical decision making. They need a process, and that process requires training, implementation and maintenance. Newsrooms with such a system in place will create a culture characterized by some or all of the following:

- Training in and frequent discussion of the ethical decision-making process within the newsroom.
- Frequent "red-flagging" of ethical issues by employees or managers for discussion.
- Management and rank-and-file attitudes that cultivate, encourage and respect "contrarian" viewpoints.

- Special in-house workshops or staff discussion groups to go over ethical questions the station may have encountered or case studies of ethical issues other stations have encountered.
- Regular staff meetings, one-on-one or in groups, to critique stories and go over the issues.
- Frequent dialogue, through formal or informal meetings, with members of the public affected by coverage decisions.
- On-air acknowledgment of viewer feedback and public discussion of major coverage decisions.

Summary

Why is all of this so important? According to Geisler and Tompkins, when faced with a crisis such as Littleton, television news can't merely be good. We owe it to our viewers to be *excellent*. Says Tompkins, "It is not possible to be ethical without being excellent."

And vice versa.

Building the Ethical Journalist

To conduct yourself ethically on a personal level, you'll need two items. The first is your bag of decision-making tools, which you'll put together and continually sharpen through training and experience. The second is that most elusive ingredient of all: a good attitude, made up of energized spirits, respect for your co-workers, a determination to make a positive difference for your viewers and community, and a passion for what you do for a living. Much has been written about the basic tools for ethical decision making, but much less is available on the subject of how to keep your personal energies properly focused. In the pages ahead we'll talk about both: how to keep a good ethical balance in the face of the tough personal and professional challenges you'll encounter, and how to influence others to do the same.

The Importance of Training

In the first part of this chapter we saw that without the proper training a newsroom filled with ethical journalists nevertheless may fail to act ethically. The same is true at the individual level.

Ethical challenges and choices big and small face individual journalists every single day. Every choice you make—ranging from the stories you elect to pursue, the people you choose to interview and the way you treat the people you encounter—has ethical implications and potential pitfalls. Sometimes the choices aren't clear. More frequently, it's not always clear there *are* choices. You may find yourself blindly pursuing a course of action without having stopped to even question whether there might be alternatives. In such cases you might traipse along blindly, not worried about anything—until you suddenly step on an ethical land mine. At that point, of course, the damage is done and the only real question is how to make repairs and clean things up.

How can you steer through the sometimes treacherous waters of journalism? Even if you have a heart of gold, it won't be enough. Even if you're kind to children and animals, pay your taxes and don't rob banks, this doesn't mean you're ethical. If you want to play the piano, you have to practice, practice, practice. The same is true of journalism. To hone your ethical sense you'll need training in the art of ethical decision making and critical thinking, and experience doing it.

The principles of ethical decision making we discussed in the first part of this chapter also apply at the individual level. Hopefully, by the time they've landed their first job, most journalists will have had some exposure to these concepts in college. If not, they'll have to learn the ethical process on the job. But even if you *have* had some training in ethics, you can't stop there. Says Bob Steele of Poynter Institute, "Journalists should be in a life-long learning mode."

It's been pointed out that journalists get less continuing education than members of any other profession. Chances are you'd be shocked if you were to discover that a surgeon who's about to perform heart surgery on you hasn't brushed up on the subject since leaving medical school 10 years ago. The same is true of journalism. According to Steele, "You should always be searching for new information. We should always be challenging our own assumptions by adding knowledge to our noggins. We should be constantly sharpening the tools in our professional bag, including the skill-based tools of writing and interviewing and reporting, but also the decision-making tool."

The single best way to learn every day is through interacting with your colleagues, asking many questions, looking for mentors and, as Steele puts it, for "models of excellence in our colleagues and in other newsrooms." You should be constantly observing and analyzing the effects of your actions and words on colleagues and on the public. Another good learning tactic is to read books and trade publications to learn about the ethical challenges others have faced and how they've dealt with them. Finally, formal ethics training is available through seminars and workshops sponsored by the RTNDF, the Poynter Institute and others.

If the process works as it should, you'll still be learning about journalism and ethics the day you retire.

The Importance of Being Earnest

When you get that first job, chances are you'll be excited, pumped, filled with good intentions and eager to get to work. You may assume your new co-workers feel the same way. If so, you're probably in for a shock. It's true that most journalists begin the same way: we're optimistic, determined, eager, idealistic. But here's a disturbing truth: something ugly often happens along the way. We start out as people not too different from our viewers and listeners. But after a few years many of us are profoundly different. Some of us become cynical, jaded, distrustful and bitter. We don't react to stories and situations the same way our public does. We develop an attitude of "We've seen it all." Stories have to be bigger, more sensational and more splashy to get our attention. We begin to think we're smarter than our viewers and listeners and have a right to decide for them what is and isn't worthy of public discourse. We're less respectful of people and of each other. Of course, this isn't true of all journalists. But you can walk into almost any newsroom in the country and see these forces in action—forces that do little to create a healthy environment for good journalism or ethical behavior.

It doesn't have to be this way. Plenty of journalists find a way to keep themselves energized, and their spirits renewed, in the face of the inevitable on-the-job frustrations, disappointments and disagreeable bosses. The probability that you will be a capable and ethical journalist rises in direct proportion to your success in keeping a healthy attitude and maintaining your ability to enjoy your work.

Let's face it, journalism isn't just a job. We hope it's not something you do because it sounded more appealing than becoming an accountant or tax attorney or meter reader. Journalism is a calling. Like most callings, the only truly successful players will be those who have a passion for it. Why else would you be willing to work holidays? Or be on call 24 hours a day, seven days a week? Or work the long hours we're often required to work? If you don't have a passion for it, not only will you not succeed, but you may be standing in the way of someone who might. As NBC anchor Brian Williams told news directors at the 1999 RTNDA convention, if you don't have a passion for this business, then please get out of the way of those who'd be willing to crawl through broken glass to get here.

So, you've arrived on the journalistic scene, fresh out of college, with a microphone in one hand, a notepad in the other, and a heart burning with enthusiasm and a passion for the business. How are you going to keep those fires burning? There's no profession that doesn't sometimes lead to burnout, but ours—with its unique combination of high ideals, grueling deadlines and profit pressure—is more susceptible than many. The most ethical journalists will also be those who've done the best job of coping with these forces and remaining true to their ideals.

How to Immunize Yourself against Disillusionment

That first disillusionment can come very quickly. Speaking personally, I'd been on the job in a television newsroom as a copywriter and fill-in reporter less than three months when I faced mine. I suddenly realized that the company I worked for cared very little about journalism and a great deal about profit. The newsroom wasn't well managed. There was a great deal of focus on the cosmetics of our presentation, but very little on substance. The news product went through what most of us considered to be some rather wild stylistic gyrations in the search for the right on-air "formula." Morale was low on a good day.

Only one thing got me through it. I latched on to the primary enjoyment my job afforded and never lost sight of it. In my case, I had a love of writing. I didn't claim to be that good at it, mind you, but I loved it. I went into journalism because I was thrilled with the idea that someone might actually pay me to write. And that's exactly how it worked out. Even on the worst days, I still enjoyed writing, and still got paid for it. That realization kept me going.

Second, I was developing a passion for the ability to make a difference. I knew that my words had an effect on people and on our community. I grew to enjoy that position of power, influence and responsibility. It was for that reason that I moved into producing full-time rather than reporting (that, plus the fact that I was lousy on the air).

Unless you're lucky enough to wind up in a very special newsroom, you're likely to face similar disillusionment sooner or later—probably sooner. You can get through it the same way. Focus on your passion for what got you into journalism in the first place. Don't lose sight of it. As long as your job continues to afford you the opportunity to express that passion, you can get through even the worst days.

Much has been written about "youthful idealism." But idealism doesn't have to be the province of the young. There's no reason that you can't hang on to your ideals and fight the disappointment and disillusionment that strike so many. But to be successful, you must not be so idealistic that you can't cope with the reality of the daily grind. More importantly, you have to cope with the fact that others have ideals, too, and they're likely to be different from your own. Says Steele, "I think we can be both idealistic and pragmatic. I believe that high ideals help us search for excellence. But I also believe that we have to search for the common ground that allows for differences, that respects and tolerates opposing ideas, that accepts that there is a great deal of gray between the black and white of ethical decisions."

You and the Stockholders

As I nearly did, you may come away from that first disillusionment disgusted at your station's profit motive. Don't. Profit is a perfectly honorable motive for any business. In fact, the profit motive, and the underlying work ethic that makes it possible, form the bedrock of our society. If you work for a commercial television or radio station, then you're in the business of providing news and information for profit. You expect to be paid for your services, do you not? So do the owners and investors who make it possible for you to do your job. It's a simple equation: resources for journalism rise in direct proportion to profit. No profit, no journalism. (Even if you work for a public broadcaster, then contributions and taxes from people and institutions who work for a profit fund your efforts.)

If your station appears to be taking inappropriate steps in the pursuit of profit, that's not necessarily an indication that something is wrong with capitalism or the profit motive. More likely it's just bad management.

Chances are you didn't get into television or radio news because you have a burning desire to make stockholders rich. Conversely, it's a good bet the stockholders didn't invest in your station because they wanted you to have a job. It's possible that many of them don't give a rat's patoot about journalism, though doubtless some of them do. Yet the two of us—journalists and stockholders—can get along just fine if we remember one key principle: we can't live without one another! The relationship will be mutually profitable if we create value for one another. Good journalism will increase shareholder value. Growing shareholder value will make more good journalism possible. Mutual benefit is the foundation of any viable business relationship. As long as your interests complement those of the stockholders, and vice versa, you can continue doing business.

Bottom line: don't let contempt for the profit motive of stockholders adversely affect your attitude, performance or ethical balance.

The Ratings and You

The popular media, especially those in Hollywood, love to portray journalists as evil, ratings-grubbing sensationalists. This tends to paint an honorable aim, the pursuit of ratings, with the brush of a dishonorable tactic, sensationalism. Too many of us journalists tend to agree with the critics that the pursuit of ratings is somehow wrong or at least distasteful, and because of that we lose respect for our industry and, in essence, for what we do for a living. To say the least, this is not a morale booster. You can see the detrimental effects of this constant criticism on the morale and attitude of journalists every day in trade magazines, on the Internet, in journalism forums and in electronic publications such as *Shoptalk.*

But as with the pursuit of profit, there's nothing wrong in and of itself with seeking to enhance ratings. For one, you want your station to be profitable, for all the reasons we've already discussed. Second, you want your journalism to be *effective*. The best story in the world will have no beneficial effect on anyone if no one sees or hears it.

It is true that the thoughtless pursuit of quick ratings sometimes leads broadcasters to take actions that are unethical or, at very least, tasteless, silly and counterproductive. This is where journalists need to be on guard. But don't sneer at the basic desire to grow ratings and profit, not unless you're willing to show you mean it by giving up your paycheck and working for free. An honest craftsman provides honest value for payment received. An honest broadcaster provides benefit for viewership or listenership received. Ratings and profit are the measures by which we're judged, and in a free market society, this is as it should be. Concentrate on providing the viewer and listener benefit, and your viewers and listeners will reward you.

Remember Why You're Doing This

No matter how discouraged you might sometimes become on the job, and no matter how much respect you might lose for your employer, there is one key factor that ought to keep you going: your viewers or listeners.

As a news director, I receive many unsolicited job inquiries. Many are from reporters who detest their current employers and are sending out "escape tapes." I recently talked to one such reporter who painted a bleak picture of his boss's news philosophy and management style. To say he detested this person in particular and his newsroom's environment in general would be an understatement. But he claimed he still did the best job he could day in and day out *despite* his feelings. I asked him why. "My viewers are counting on me," he said. "I can't let them down."

He is exactly right. Your viewers do count on you. If you can't motivate yourself to do a good job for your employer, then do it for your viewers or listeners. They won't know the difference!

In fact, you should always keep your viewers or listeners in mind whatever you do. It's a fact that most newsrooms have a thinly veiled contempt for news consumers. How many assignments desk personnel don't refer to the newsroom's published telephone number as the "nut line" or "idiot phone"? To be sure, members of the public can be quirky, cranky and sometimes downright abusive. Often they ask dumb questions. Still, we're there to serve them. If you can't embrace that concept, then you really should find something else to do in life.

A respect for members of the public and compassion for their feelings in your personal conduct should be a basic part of your ethical makeup. In an interview situation, which do you prefer: a confrontational question designed to show how aggressive and smart you are, or an even-toned question designed to elicit information? Which is better: to jump out of the bushes with microphone in hand and ambush someone on camera, or to make an attempt to schedule an appointment to interview that person? Which would you rather ask: "How do you feel?" or "Who are you?" If you picked the second answer to each of these questions, you're beginning to get the idea.

Broadcast journalism, especially at the local level, is all about serving people and serving the community. The best reporters seek out the unheard voices, listen sincerely and tell their stories. The best television and radio stations reach out to all segments of the community. They establish a dialogue with community members and may even formalize it on the air through a feedback segment or community reporting beat or both. Their reporting will address community needs and reflect community values.

You'll face many ethical challenges in your career. Sometimes the process of weighing your journalistic duty against the potential harm a story might cause is very difficult. The options can be very murky. Your ethical compass stands the best chance of remaining true and pointing you in the right direction if you energize it with the goal of providing service and value to your viewers or listeners and to the community.

When You and the Boss Disagree

It's bound to happen sooner or later, and odds are it won't be later: you and the boss will disagree. Like individuals, organizations tend to have a personality of sorts, and like people, some organizations are more skilled and likable than others. There are as many different news philosophies as there are journalists. The chances of your personal news philosophy being in perfect harmony with that of your employer aren't great. Perhaps you're a "high road" producer working for a "flash and trash" newsroom, or vice versa. Perhaps you find that you're a conservative working in a liberal environment, or vice versa. How are you going to cope while keeping your sanity, your sense of ethics and, we hope, your job?

Realize that no matter what kind of environment you find yourself in, on-the-job clashes are inevitable. Don't expect to win every battle. Do make sure your voice is heard. Never lose sight of the fact that you *do* have influence. Have the courage to present your ideas. Most importantly, work to develop the skills you need to *properly* present them. Says Steele, "A young journalist will have a much better chance of achieving her own ethical standards if she can make clear, concise principled arguments to her boss as well as to her colleagues." The good news, according to Steele, is that the best news organizations not only listen to their youthful members but value them. "The most thoughtful counter-intuitive idea may come from one of the youngest and newest members of the organization, those fresh eyes and new perspectives that may drive the decision-making process. The chance of that happening is enhanced when the young and/or new person makes a clear, concise argument that will get other people saying, 'Uh, huh, I hadn't thought of that.'"

It must be acknowledged, however, that even in the best news-rooms your voice won't be as strong and respected or have as much leverage as those of the more experienced journalists. To make your-self heard you'll need to network with people and form alliances. Says Steele, "Even if you don't have a stripe on your sleeve because of your youth or shortness of tenure, you can influence people through your intelligence, through your commitment, and through the ques-tions you ask and the knowledge you bring to the discussion." And he adds, if you want change, "you can only get the change through influence."

What if you have an urgent problem or a strong ethical objection in a given situation? First of all, do *not* be a hothead. Don't pitch a fit. Don't storm out of the room or seek some big confrontation. Steele says the proper tactics are essential. "There are a number of ways for a young journalist to raise concerns with a news director or executive producer. You can pose it in writing, raising three or four questions about a particular dilemma and how it's being handled. You can ask for a private conversation in which you raise some questions and state your beliefs." It does take a little courage to speak up. It also takes patience. It's not reasonable to expect that you'll be able to single-handedly change your newsroom's policies, ethics and values. It is reasonable to expect to be able to *influence* them, however, and have an effect on your newsroom's culture over time.

What if, despite your best, patient efforts, you find yourself in a job environment that's unethical or in some other way intolerable? According to Steele, you have three basic options. They are:

- *Survival.* A situation in which you've more or less given up, are just marking time and are pretty much miserable.
- *Coping.* A step up from survival. You haven't totally given up and are still trying to have a positive influence, but you're pessimistic and unhappy.

- *Influence.* You refuse to give up and are determined to make a difference, through the tactics we've just discussed.

Of the three, Steele much prefers the third. But he acknowledges that some situations really are intolerable. "If you are convinced it is impossible to influence things for the better, then leaving and finding a better situation is a reasonable alternative."

Even in such cases, don't be in a hurry. As satisfying as it might be to tell your boss precisely what he or she can do with the job, you'll still be dealing with the consequences of your action long after the satisfaction has faded. Don't make career decisions in anger or haste. Unless you're the target of abuse or sexual harassment, even if you feel you "just can't take it another second," you probably can. Don't let an on-the-job crisis or setback push you into taking a rash action that you might regret. Think about it long and hard. Remember what got you into the business to begin with, whatever that was. Reflect on your passions. Consider your viewers or listeners. Above all, be honest with yourself and make sure *you* aren't the problem. If that's the case, leaving isn't the solution. As the saying goes, "No matter where you go, there you are." Your personal problems always follow you. Deal with them first. Says Steele, "You don't want to leave a bad professional relationship only to have it re-created elsewhere."

That said, if after careful thought you decide that the current environment doesn't allow you to pursue the things you enjoy and doesn't allow you to serve your viewers or listeners, then it's time to vote with your feet. Do it on *your* terms. And while you're searching for a new job, continue to do your best in the one you have. Act ethically, serve your viewers and listeners, and give good value to your employer for the paycheck you're drawing. If you have a job in journalism, then regardless of what's happening between you and your employer you have an obligation to the public. Fulfill it. When it comes to your viewers and listeners, never say die, and never give up.

A Final Thought

There are several sayings TV news professionals use to console themselves when their efforts go down the toitie. My personal favorite is, "No one ever died from bad TV." Probably the most common is, "Thank God it's not brain surgery." Indeed it's not. *It's more powerful and important than that.* Television news has the ability to build reputations or destroy them, to guide society to noble or ignoble action, to calm riots or start them, to start wars or end them, to make kings or dethrone them, to inspire the heart or depress the soul, to give hope or destroy it. The power we hold is incredible. It's so incredible, people are always trying to take it away from us or limit it. The First Amendment to the

U.S. Constitution, which was designed in part to protect Americans from such attacks, isn't always up to the challenge, and protection in other countries is even more uncertain. It's therefore incumbent upon us to wield this incredible power with sensitivity, responsibility, humility, a sense of ethics and respect for the individual. As of this writing, few of our consumers believe we do that. Is that assessment justified? What do you think? And more importantly, what do you intend to do about it?

Television news is one of the few occupations available that allows you to have a wide impact on people's lives, for better or worse, while having more fun than the law allows. Do have fun. But never lose sight of the power in your hands.

THE 21ST CENTURY

Broadcast news was born in the 20th century when radio and television came into being. Stations put news on the air to inform their viewers and to build their audiences. By the end of the century, most U.S. citizens turned to radio and television for most of their news. As we enter a new century, the broadcast news business continues to change rapidly.

The 21st century will almost certainly involve changes in the technology used to gather and distribute news, changes in the business structure of media companies, and changes in what news employees are expected to contribute to those companies.

Good writing will be key to surviving and navigating the changes ahead. As the technology changes, a need for trained writers who can use the language effectively will remain constant, and such people will be in demand. By good writing, we mean simple, clear, accurate, coherent, grammatically correct sentences. This writing will increasingly become more multidimensional and will involve the layering of information. It will include writing with words and audio and video and graphics and links to sites on the Internet and World Wide Web. And as live news reporting becomes the norm, the ability to produce quality writing at the speed of spot news is increasingly important.

Changes in the Technology Used to Gather and Distribute News

The world of broadcast news is increasingly technical, and the time between gathering the news and delivering it has shrunk to seconds in some cases. Since the 1950s, the format of news-gathering equipment has changed from film to tape to digital. The digital environment is leading into a multimedia world, where radio and television programming is being delivered by way of computer terminals linked to the Internet and the World Wide Web.

Millions of Americans now use the Internet, and the number grows larger every month. The Internet is neither radio nor television; it's a whole new form of interacting that radio and television are starting to use both to expand and to promote traditional programming and news. The major broadcast companies and cable networks and many local stations have sites on the Internet. Viewers can see and hear broadcast news on their computers, and they can access archived programs there as well. Many news programs tie into the Internet with "read more about it" sites. Viewers and listeners are directed to check Internet sites for excerpts from books, speeches, court testimony and other public documents (such as the Starr Report, Miss America biographies or medical research on colon cancer).

We see examples of this on NBC's "Dateline" news magazine program wherein viewers are directed to the show's Web site for additional information about a story. Viewers can read additional in-depth material about a story or the main players involved, they can "chat" with the newscasters, they can react to the broadcast itself by sending e-mail messages in response to a particular story, they can respond to an online poll, and they can participate in the news-gathering process by suggesting ideas for other stories. This interactivity underscores the need for good writers, because all of this information, from the broadcast script itself to the Web site material, is written.

The television networks are also beginning to unveil "Web specials" that feature original content tailored to Internet audiences, thus blurring the boundary lines between television news programming and online journalism. The purpose of these specials is still to promote

network shows. But the specials themselves are increasingly sophisticated and multilayered. Getting people involved through Web sites is
expected to result in a bigger impact when specials air.

Traditional media companies are themselves evolving into multimedia groups. Gannett Company, based in Arlington, Virginia, is the
nation's largest newspaper company, but it also has TV stations and
cable TV systems in several states. A.H. Belo Corporation, based in
Dallas, Texas, began as a newspaper publishing company in the mid-
1800s, but it's now a multimedia conglomerate that owns newspapers,
network-affiliated television stations, Web sites for most of them and
a Texas regional cable news channel, which programs news 24 hours a
day, seven days a week. Newspaper reporters are increasingly
involved in that cable cast. The network news divisions are expanding
their activities into such new media as cable, online, satellite and digital services. The Associated Press, once strictly oriented to newspapers, now provides newsroom technology, audio and video to broadcast
media outlets around the world.

In such an environment it makes less sense for writers to think of
themselves as strictly television, radio or newspaper people. It seems
more practical to take a multimedia approach and to think of being a
broad-based communication practitioner. *The ability to write well is the
key skill one needs in a multimedia environment*, whether that writing is
strictly with words or also involves audio, video or a combination of
some or all of those elements. In published research and in conference
presentations, news directors and publishers repeatedly emphasize
good writing as the key skill they seek.

Changes in the Business Structure
of Media Companies

In the beginning, news wasn't expected to make money for a station
or network; it was expected to lend prestige and legitimacy to the
company and to provide useful information to the public. Now, news
is expected to make money, and unrelenting pressure to do that is
leading to changes for those who work in and write for the media.

There's new competition, from cable and from satellite and Internet
programmers. TV viewers may choose to view traditional broadcast
news programming, but they may also choose alternatives such as
cable, satellite pay-per-view and webcasts on the Internet. In the early
1950s, the new medium of television offered just three viewing options.
Today, the average cable subscriber has 53, and some have nearly twice
as many. This situation has led media companies into a ferocious competition for the "eyeball time" of information consumers/viewers.

And there's intense pressure for profits in this increasingly competitive media marketplace, which is dominated by huge corporations
such as Time Warner, Disney and Viacom.

This new corporate ownership structure followed broadcasting
deregulation in the 1990s and is making the broadcasting business
environment increasingly complex and interrelated. ABC is owned by
Disney, which also produces movies and TV shows and owns theme
parks, retail stores and interests in cable networks such as ESPN, A&E
and Lifetime. CBS is owned by Viacom, which also owns MTV, Nick-
elodeon, Country Music Television, The Nashville Network and the
Paramount Pictures film studio. NBC's parent is General Electric, a
huge company that makes everything from lightbulbs to turbine
engines. Fox is part of Rupert Murdoch's News Corp., which owns
20th Century Fox, the Los Angeles Dodgers and several newspapers.
Time Warner and the Tribune Co. back WB. In 1999, Clear Channel
Communications consolidated 955 radio stations into one radio broadcasting behemoth, which includes station Web sites. A few companies
have vertically integrated everything from bookstores to video stores,
to television and radio stations, to newspapers and Internet sites all
under one umbrella.

This situation is leading traditional news organizations to co-produce
news programming with corporate partners. For example, some CNN
news programming is now linked to the Time Warner magazines such
as *Time, Fortune* and *Entertainment Weekly.* Other television news programs are also combining with their own and related print companies
and Web sites, further blurring the traditional lines between broadcast
and print. NBC News co-produces news stories with *Newsweek* magazine, and NBC's "Dateline" co-produces news stories with *People*
magazine, The Discovery Channel and Court TV. The "PBS Newshour" works with correspondents for *The Washington Post,* and NBC
Sports promotes its MSNBC Web sites.

NBC and The Washington Post Co. have joined forces to share news
reports in print, on TV and on the Internet. Contributors to the alliance
will be NBC News, the MSNBC cable network and Internet site, along
with print and Web operations of *The Washington Post* and its sister pub-
lication, *Newsweek* magazine. Journalists from *The Washington Post* and
Newsweek will appear on NBC News programming and on MSNBC
Cable, including regular segments of its nightly program "The News
with Brian Williams." A merged Web site, *Newsweek.MSNBC.com,* is
planned. NBC's other cable network, CNBC, already has a deal with *The
Wall Street Journal* to share business news. MSNBC is itself a joint venture created in 1996 between NBC and Microsoft.

On the local level, examples include Cleveland ABC affiliate
WEWS (TV) and Akron's *Beacon Journal,* which have formed a strate-
gic partnership that will link their news services and Web sites, with

each gaining from the other's strength in its respective community. Akron is a significant part of the Cleveland television market. The station will use the newspaper's resources to beef up its Akron coverage, possibly featuring stories from the *Beacon Journal* newsroom. Also planned are collaborations on news, features and special reports. Because of limited resources and a saturation of news options, some stations can no longer afford to stand alone and expect to serve their audiences in the best way. Partly as a result of these economics, writers are expected to be able to perform in both broadcast and print environments.

Today's media executives are also being directed to "do more with less," and that means media employees will increasingly need to be flexible and versatile. Reporters for the *Dallas Morning News* also appear on the parent company's regional cable news channel. Newspapers in many other markets across the country have set up similar operations. Jim Cummins, an NBC news reporter based in Dallas, Texas, now not only reports for "NBC Nightly News," but does live interviews for MSNBC and writes articles for the MSNBC Web site. Brian Williams, who substitutes for anchorman Tom Brokaw on "NBC Nightly News," also writes for and anchors MSNBC's "The News with Brian Williams."

Changes in What News Employees Are Expected to Contribute to Those Companies

The ability to write accurately and to work swiftly in a rapidly changing environment has never been more important. Those entering the broadcast news business today feel the full impact of the 24-hour news cycle in a way previous generations of writers did not. The unrelenting pressure of the 24-hour news cycle has resulted from the growth of CNN and the more recent arrivals of MSNBC and Fox News Channel. All-news seemed like a grand concept, and it is, except it has created competitive pressures to constantly "feed the beast." Each news network has many programs, the needs of which must be filled. And each news network is locked in a continual race to attract viewers—and advertisers. Whereas we once had ABC, CBS and NBC, we now have ABC, CBS, CNN, Fox, Fox News Channel, MSNBC, NBC, C-SPAN, CNBC and Headline News competing "live" around the clock for news viewers. Viewers interested in sports and weather can turn to ESPN, ESPN2, regional sports channels, The Weather Channel and local cable systems' weather information channels. Broadcast journalists who work within this crowded, 24-hour-a-day news cycle face constant and relentless pressure from the clock.

But they also face new pressures from several other sources as well. They face economic pressure from media owners and news executives for higher ratings and profits. And they face competitive pressure from other journalists for a story.

A 1996 survey of news directors across the country asked them to define the characteristics they considered most important in new employees and to evaluate graduates seeking entry-level jobs in their organizations. The results were published in what is known as the "Jane Pauley Report." Based on the survey responses, news directors today look at four major characteristics in job applicants: writing ability, good attitude and personality, knowledge, and good work habits. The news directors are most concerned with the writing skills. News directors want applicants who can write. The news directors complain that many applicants they see for entry-level jobs don't write well, can't express themselves in writing, lack basic grammar and spelling skills, and need to develop better "people skills."[1] One of the key recommendations of the report is to emphasize strong writing skills within the university curriculum, and that's what this text is designed to help do. The news directors say the abilities to gather information and to write with style are equally important. They say students must learn to produce copy on deadline that answers the five W's and H, offers context and (in the case of television) is written to video in short, active-voice, declarative sentences. And whether you're dealing with beta, digital, satellite delivery, or writing for three different media as part of one job, writing is the one skill that cuts across technologies and media. The computer revolution has created a booming economy with plenty of communications jobs. But software hasn't been designed that can replace solid writing skills. And the first skill that employers who are looking for interns or new hires ask about is writing.

Clarity of meaning is crucial for today's writers. So are specific word choices. As we've noted on numerous occasions in earlier chapters, it's paramount that broadcast journalists be clear, be specific and use the words that best convey the meaning they're trying to convey. The audience for broadcast news is becoming increasingly diverse. This makes clear language, understandable language and inclusive language all the more important. You want to avoid all "isms" such as sexism, racism, ageism and—in many newsrooms, such as CNN's—nationalism. CNN founder Ted Turner objects to the use of the word

---

1. *Tomorrow's Broadcast Journalists: A Report and Recommendations from the Jane Pauley Task Force on Mass Communication Education* (1996), Greencastle, Indiana: The Society of Professional Journalists.

"foreign" in CNN broadcasts; it's more specific to name the country itself. Students must also learn to write with accuracy; they must get the story "right."

Broadcast journalists enter the business for a variety of reasons. Some harbor a desire to become celebrities and to make money from personal fame gained from on-camera exposure. Others burn with a desire to report the news fairly and accurately and to make a difference in people's lives. The audience in the meantime is being overwhelmed with the amount and uneven quality of news products, and the public is growing more and more skeptical about the media's trustworthiness.

In fact, the public's faith in the media may be at a new low. According to a poll conducted in the summer of 1998 for *Newsweek* magazine, 61 percent of those responding said they get most of their news about current events from television. But when asked how much they think they can believe of what they see, hear or read in the news media, 11 percent said almost all of it, 35 percent said "most of it," but 42 percent said "only some of it" and 11 percent said "very little of it." That's more than half (53 percent) of Americans who characterize news reporting today as "often inaccurate." And 76 percent say the race for ratings and profits has driven the media "too far" in the direction of entertainment rather than traditional reporting. Now there's more need than ever for broadcasters to be clear, to be truthful, to be accurate and to be fair in their news reporting and writing.

As public confidence in television news erodes, some stations are experimenting with a style of journalism called "public" or "civic" or "community" journalism. Broadly speaking, this journalism aims to reinvigorate public thinking by re-engaging people with public life. It has been described as an effort on the part of journalists to make public life work by becoming involved in the process of finding solutions to community problems rather than just reporting the problems. Those involved in the movement stress its cooperative, collaborative nature. Broadcast stations often work with newspapers in their communities. And they seek "solution" coverage rather than conflict coverage. They interview "average citizens," not just "experts" or polarized combatants.

At the October 15, 1958, meeting in Chicago of the Radio and Television News Directors Association, Edward R. Murrow, one of the founders of traditional broadcast news as we know it, said, "This instrument [television] can teach, it can illuminate; yes, and it can even inspire. But it can do so only to the extent that humans are determined to use it to those ends. Otherwise it is merely wires and lights in a box. There is a great and perhaps decisive battle to be fought against ignorance, intolerance and indifference. This weapon of television could be useful." We would expand Murrow's definition to include the multimedia environment of today. These means of information transmission can be useful, they can be helpful, they can be educational, provided we use them to those ends. Like Murrow, we also encourage all who write for the media to strive to be the "wordsmith" Murrow himself became, choosing his words thoughtfully, writing his copy carefully, rewriting as often as need be to get the story right.

In this text, our approach has been to craft good writers by laying a solid foundation and then building on that. We believe excellent writing is the essential skill in radio news, in television news, in online news. Equipment operation and HTML (HyperText Markup Language) can be learned in a couple of days. Good writing can't. It takes time. It takes effort. It takes thought, and it takes practice. We hope we've provided the tools and inspiration for you to begin.

SO YOU WANT A JOB? THE ART OF THE RÉSUMÉ

The question I'm asked most often has nothing to do with any of the gems of wisdom thus far imparted in this book. It's simply this: "How do I land a job?" Or, in its indirect form, "What do you look for in a résumé tape?" This section will provide some answers to those questions and arm you with information that, we hope, will help you land a job. The information and advice herein are based both on my own personal hiring preferences and on practices I've witnessed or heard about during my time in the industry.

What Does a News Director Look For?

Of course, every news director is different. That's a good thing, or else few people would be able to land jobs! Tastes vary. What doesn't appeal to one news director may appeal to another. However, when a news director looks at a tape or résumé, some factors are of typical, or possibly even universal, importance. These follow, in roughly descending order of priority.

Talent

Plainly speaking, is the candidate any damned good? If the candidate is applying for an on-air position, the news director will judge talent—in most cases, rather quickly, I'm afraid—from the résumé tape. News directors will judge line producer, photographer and editor candidates the same way. Assignments desk and off-line producing or writing candidates normally skip this step and are judged directly from the written résumé.

Experience

Has the applicant performed this job before, or done anything that might prepare him or her for the job? If the candidate currently holds a similar job, how long has he or she been doing it? Did he or she have any major successes, as judged by ratings, blockbuster stories, or professional awards?

Entry-level candidates with no professional experience aren't excused from this question. If the candidate is a recent graduate and is looking for an entry-level job, what kind of experience did he or she gain while in college? Internships or media-related extracurricular activities are important here. Woe betide the candidate who graduates from college and starts looking for that first job without having worked as an intern or at least gained experience some other way, such as by working at the campus newspaper, yearbook, radio or TV station.

References

What kind of references does the candidate have? Here, what's important isn't the number of references, but the type and quality. If a candidate doesn't list a single news manager as a reference, we distrusting, evil-minded news directors usually assume there's a reason why. It's usually a given that your cronies and friends will speak highly of you. What news directors really want to know is what your supervisors have to say about you.

What if you don't want your supervisors to know you're looking for a job? Speaking personally, I've never worked for a television station that didn't respect and support the efforts of its employees to better themselves. I once worked in a television newsroom where the boss would even pick up the phone and help his employees find jobs elsewhere, if that's what they wanted to do. Not only were there no hard feelings, but this particular newsroom was known to hire some of those people back from time to time (in fact, I was one of them). Alas, not every television station is like that. But even if you must be discreet, you still should work hard to provide references who aren't just friends and cronies. For instance, producers and assignments editors, who are notoriously hard to please, make good references.

If you blew something up on the job and don't have any references, believe it or not, it's not necessarily the end. You can take some solace in the fact that not every news director checks references or, at least, checks them well.

The Cover Letter and Résumé

How good should your résumé and cover letter be? In terms of spelling and grammar, it should be *absolutely perfect*. The cover letter and résumé speak volumes about the quality of the candidate. Presumably, landing a job is the single most important task on your event horizon. If your résumé and cover letter aren't important enough for you to get right, then what will be? Is your potential employer to presume that if you exhibit sloppiness, illiteracy or incompetence on the résumé and cover letter that you'll suddenly blossom into a quality performer after you get the job? Not.

An applicant for a writing job once sent me a cover letter that contained the following sentence (the locations have been changed to protect the guilty):

> I just currently moved down to Texas in June from Florida, where from time to time I worked for NBC, ABC, and ESPN from time to time in a freelance capacity from time to time.

Needless to say, the applicant didn't get the job. But I was so enamored of this particular line of prose that I framed it and hung it on the wall of my office.

Although spelling and good grammar on your cover letter and résumé count, I'm not looking for prose by Ernest Hemingway. Remember, you're proposing a business transaction here—your services in trade for a piece of my hard-won and jealously guarded news budget. Your letter should state in plain terms what's in it for me. It should provide, in order of priority, the following information:

- What job it is you're seeking (you'd be absolutely amazed how many candidates don't say).
- Why you believe you're the best candidate for the job.
- Your salary requirements. We aren't negotiating a final figure here, but I need to know if we're within shouting distance. I have a certain amount of money to shop with, and if you're

already making more than I can pay, then we're wasting each other's time. It's better to find that out sooner rather than later. Don't say "salary is negotiable" without naming a range, unless you really, really mean it—and as a test, if you aren't prepared to accept minimum wage, then you don't mean it.

- Whether you're under contract or any other legal encumbrances, how much notice you would have to give your current employer and how quickly you could relocate. Again, this is to avoid us wasting each other's time. If you're under a contract that doesn't expire until six months from now, I need to know this up front.

You don't need to provide any more information than that. I don't need to know how much you love the business; how much you'd like to live in my part of the country or in my specific city; the fact that your sister, brother, uncle, or mother-in-law lives here; or any of the other thousands of extraneous things candidates love to place on cover letters. In fact, this information could work to your detriment. For instance, if you tell me that you have "always wanted to live here" and I believe you, then I may reduce whatever salary I was going to offer you by 10 percent. Why should I give you my top-dollar offer if you're already motivated to come here? (Mean, ain't it?)

Job Stability

Another factor many news directors, including this one, look for is job stability. A certain amount of jumping from job to job is understandable, especially if you've started out in a small-market, low-paying job. But after a jump or two I'd hope you'd stop and catch your breath for a while. In addition to the rate at which you change jobs, news directors may also look at the *kinds* of moves you make. For instance, if you're a reporter and in the past 18 months you've moved from a job in the 90th market, to one in the 95th market, then to one in the 85th market, then I certainly am going to wonder what's driving you, and whether you changed jobs voluntarily or were run off. On the other hand, if you've jumped upward several market sizes each time you've moved, this fits the profile of someone whose career is tracking upward.

However, if you've changed jobs every six months for the past three years, I'm not going to be interested in you, period. I don't think I'm overly demanding, but for contracted jobs I'm going to want at least a 2-year commitment. For noncontracted jobs, I usually request a one-year verbal commitment. These days many news directors and newsrooms, especially in the larger markets, ask for more than that. Your past track record will show whether you're inclined to make and keep such commitments.

The Interview Process

If you make it through the steps above, you'll be on a "short list" of finalists, from which the news director will choose one or two candidates for personal interviews. Some news directors do hire by phone, but most will fly the candidate in for a face-to-face interview.

There's only one secret for success in getting through the interview: be yourself! Don't try to be something you're not. In some (if not most) organizations, a person's personality is an important factor in the hiring process. News directors want to know not only that you'll be good at your job but also that you'll fit well into that particular newsroom environment. The last thing you want to do is to present a false portrait of yourself and your personality. If you do and you land the job, then both you and your employer will be unhappy, if not miserable, in the long run.

It does help if you do a little homework ahead of time to find out about the market and that particular newsroom's challenges. Speaking personally, I'm almost always impressed with a candidate who knows something about my station's news philosophy and position in the market. Call ahead and speak with a few people in the newsroom. If you're feeling particularly industrious, you may even want to talk with some of the station's competitors. Doing so will allow you to talk with the news director much more intelligently about the job at hand.

During your visit, be prepared to demonstrate your skills. Many stations will give writing tests of one form or another, even for veteran candidates. I give a mean one, based on a test a former news director once gave me, which I've enhanced to provide added cruelty. Other news directors may throw wire copy at you and ask you to rewrite it. I know of one news director who takes all reporting candidates for a "test drive," asking them to actually go out into the field and turn a story. I know of chief photographers who do the same for photojournalist and editor candidates.

Remember that the interview process is as much for you as it is for the station. As much as it's checking *you* out, you must check *it* out. Ask tough questions. Talk with employees. Find out whether this particular company is one for which you'd like to work. It does go both ways, and keep in mind that there are a lot of really bad television stations out there! As the saying goes, look before you leap.

Negotiating

If all goes well, the news director will offer you a job. Now it's time to negotiate a salary, moving expenses, perks and the like. Probably by this point you've named a salary range. The news director usually will attempt to lowball you (hey, nothing personal—it's just business).

Make a counter offer. If neither you nor the news director is greedy (which is by no means a given), you should be able to reach a mutually acceptable figure without a great deal of pain and suffering.

Also keep in mind that not every news director plays this "you go high, I'll go low" game. Some will tell you that the job pays, flat out, such and such figure, nonnegotiable. If the news director is adamant that he or she has named the top dollar figure, then you may want to see if there's anything else on the table to talk about. In the case of on-air people this could include, among other things, a clothing allowance, contract "outs" and other considerations. For all employees, it could include such things as the shift to be worked, moving expenses, cell phone access and so on.

When you think you're negotiating with the news director, actually you may be negotiating with the general manager. If the news director says to you, "Gee, I don't know if I can pay that much, I'll have to check with the GM," don't assume he or she is lying. In fact, in some shops the GM negotiates directly with the talent, though it's unusual for any GM to participate in direct negotiations with producers, photojournalists and assignments editors.

The Résumé Tape

As discussed above, for many positions the résumé tape is absolutely crucial. It's so important it merits a separate discussion.

Photojournalists

For photojournalists, the news director or chief photographer wants to see what you consider to be your best work. Don't load the tape with examples: four or five stories will do for starters. Show the range of your work: include one or two live shots, a good general assignment story, a franchise or series piece, a spot news story. The people hiring you want to see the range of your talents, including:

- How you shoot
- How you edit
- How you light
- Whether you capture and use natural sound
- Good pacing
- How you shoot live shots
- How you shoot stand-ups
- Whether you know when to use a tripod, and when not to
- Your creativity
- Your visual storytelling skills
- Your industriousness

Producers

I generally ask producers to send me "last night's newscast." Producers also usually want to send their best "four alarm fire" newscast. That's fine and I'll look at it, but first I want to see what you're able to do on a slow, "normal" news day. I know of many other news directors and executive producers who hire by the same method.

In landing a job, producers face one hurdle not faced by most of their counterparts, and that's the fact that there are so many different "flavors" of newscast: conservative, middle-ground, tabloid, "big story" and so on *ad nauseam*. All that aside, when I look for a producer, I hope to see a tape that reflects the following abilities and qualities, in descending order:

- Writing ability
- High production value (as reflected through aggressive use of graphics, maps, banners and the like)
- Copy written to the pictures, and vice versa; no "wallpaper" video
- Live shots
- Team coverage (where appropriate)
- Appropriate story selection
- Stories about real people, not officials
- Good story flow
- Stories containing viewer benefit
- Teases that sell viewer benefit
- Good storytelling within packages (yes, I do hold the producer responsible for that, too)
- Stories showcasing context and perspective
- Anchor showcasing (through tags, 2shot transitions and appropriate block-ender stories)
- Good pacing
- Stories that provide "breakouts" for the anchors to read (as opposed to having all the information contained within the packages)
- Newscasts that are comfortably timed (anchors aren't rushed or stretched)

The above list is personal; not every news director looks for the same things. Some, for instance, don't care about breakouts. Some look for lots of anchor "happy talk"; others couldn't care less. Some place an extremely high premium on story count, while others (myself included) place more of an emphasis on stories that take enough time to provide the proper relevance, detail, context and a human perspective. Most news directors and executive producers I've known place a high importance on the production quality of the newscast. Speaking personally, I place a greater emphasis on writing ability, on the grounds that I can easily teach the former, but not the latter. Bottom line: your tape can't possibly appeal equally to every news director, but good writing and high production value are almost universally respected.

If you're currently producing in a small market you may not have access to such goodies as quality graphics, artsy 2shot transitions, live shots and the like. If so, explain this explicitly in your cover letter. Let the news director know what your limitations are, or else it might be held against you!

Reporters

If you're on the air or are seeking an on-air position, then you've entered a brutally competitive arena. Here's a sobering fact for you: when the news director pops your tape into the machine and presses "play," you may have only about 10 seconds to get his or her attention. Most news directors have so many tapes to go through for any given position that they can't possibly view every minute of every tape. So, the tape goes in, the reporter appears, and the news director makes a very quick decision as to whether the candidate is a keeper. Keeper tapes go into a "hold" box for further review. Many news directors quickly eject the others and toss them into the recycle bin. It's highly subjective, it's brutal, it's unfair, and it's reality. Live with it. Ten seconds. Don't waste it.

Begin your tape with a montage of live and package stand-ups—four or five of the best ones. Follow this up with four or five of your best stories, including two or three examples of live shots. These can be the same stories from which you excerpted your stand-up montage.

As mentioned, there's a chance the news director may hit the "eject" button during the montage and never get around to seeing your stories. Don't let that lead you to conclude your package samples aren't important. If your on-camera work makes the cut, your stories will get a fair viewing. It's important that you showcase your best storytelling skills. It's possible to have a decent stand-up montage and then blow your chances with poor packages. Ultimately, your writing skills will determine whether you get and keep a job, but applicants for on-air positions must clear the presentation hurdle first.

In examining your résumé tape, news directors generally look for the following talents and qualities, in roughly descending order:

- Good physical appearance
- Good voice
- Good on-camera communication skills—no hesitation or "uhs" and "ahs," no "notes-diving"
- Stand-ups and live work in which the reporter interacts with his or her surroundings, pointing something out, demonstrating something, walking us through a scene and so forth

- Good writing
- Stories presented in narrative storytelling style
- Stories centering on everyday people, not officials
- Copy written to the pictures, and vice versa; no "wallpaper" video
- Good use of maps, graphics and artwork to support the stories
- Good pacing and use of natural sound within the stories
- Stories containing viewer benefit
- Stories containing details, context and perspective

In your cover letter, make sure you explain the limitations under which your material was shot. If your shop doesn't have a live unit, or if you have to shoot your own material, make sure you say so. Otherwise the news director will be looking for live and stand-up elements your tape can't deliver.

Anchors

These days, most anchors also report. Begin your tape with a quick montage showing yourself in different environments—in the studio reading a story, in the field doing live and or taped stand-ups, in the studio on a 2shot or 3shot and so forth. Follow with some excerpts from some of your anchoring. Include some variety—examples of straight news reading, live shot introductions and tossbacks, reporter Q&A and the like. Then edit on several examples of 2shot and 3shot teases, tosses, and chitchat. Finally, include three or four examples of your best reporting.

In viewing an anchor/reporter tape, the news director generally looks for all the skills mentioned above regarding reporters, *plus* some or all of the following:

- Good eye contact when reading
- Copy delivered without hemming, hawing or stumbling
- Proper tone, inflection and emoting
- Reading with comprehension
- Intelligent Q&A in live shots
- Tasteful and appropriate clothing
- Good posture and body language
- Good teamwork and intelligent interchanges with co-anchors on teases and tosses
- The right personality

"The right personality" can be one of the most important factors, and each news director may be looking for something different. What one news director finds appealing another may find distracting or even repulsive. It's an incredibly subjective business.

Other Issues and Questions

Which Tape Format Should I Use?

Once upon a time ¾-inch U-matic was a fairly universal format. You can no longer count on that. But it's a poor news director indeed who doesn't have access to a VHS machine either at work or at home. Unless you're responding to a job advertisement that states otherwise, VHS is usually your best bet, and it also has the virtue of being the cheapest.

The format of your tape might make a difference in your prospects of landing a job. For instance, in my case I currently work in a Beta shop, but I don't have a Beta machine in my office (they're *quite* expensive). To view Beta tapes, I have to take them into an edit bay, and ours are almost always in use. So despite Beta being the standard in my shop, Beta résumé tapes are in fact the hardest for me to view. U-matic is easier to view because we have an ancient U-matic machine in our conference room. But I have a VHS machine in my office, so VHS tapes get first viewing. If I have a great deal of tapes to slog through, the U-matic and Beta tapes sometimes don't get seen at all.

Labeling and Packaging

You'll do news directors a great service if you label your tape with your name, address, phone number and *the job you are seeking*. Also, remember that if your tape does go on a "keeper" shelf, the only thing showing will be the spine. Label that with your name and the job you're seeking.

Before mailing your tape make sure you protect it properly. Placing your tape in a hard plastic case is ideal. If you don't have access to one, make sure you at least use the cardboard box the tape came in and a padded envelope. The shutters on VHS tapes are particularly easy to break in transit, and I've had to perform emergency surgery myself on more than one.

Some applicants, for reasons that aren't readily apparent, lovingly cocoon their packages in several layers of tape as if they were wrapping a mummy or protecting the czar's jewels. This isn't necessary. The tape isn't likely to break out and escape. I've never received a ruptured, empty envelope from a job hopeful. I have, however, been known to throw packages into the trash rather than go out and rent the acetylene torches and hacksaws necessary to get into them.

State Your Objective

Occasionally I receive résumés from applicants who state as a job objective that they're "seeking any job" that will make use of their "skills and abilities in the communications field." If you're willing to do anything, then my assumption is that you're not good at anything. Yes, I have an opening for you. And don't slam it on your way out.

By the time they graduate, serious students will have worked one or two internships in TV newsrooms and should have a good idea of what they'd like to do. Target a specialty and seek it aggressively. That's not to say you can't change your mind. For instance, if you spend six months seeking a reporter's job and come up dry, then you may want to begin again, targeting entry-level producing or copywriting jobs instead. But, to quote KGUN9 managing editor Craig Smith, "Before you can change your mind, you must first make a decision."

Should I Call?

If you're responding to a job ad that says "No calls," then do yourself a favor: don't call. Many news directors disqualify people who disregard that admonition. Why? Because they can. If a news director, especially one in a large market, disqualifies you for breaking that rule, then he or she may be left with only 99 other tapes from which to choose.

News directors do this not just because they're mean-spirited, cantankerous, antisocial grumps, but because they can't afford not to. Otherwise, they'll spend every waking moment talking to job hopefuls.

If the ad doesn't say "No calls," then the news director is fair game. But here again, do yourself a favor. Don't call with inane questions. Chief among them is, "Did you get my tape?" In my case, all tapes go into a set of boxes until I get the chance to go through them. I don't have the time or inclination to dig through those boxes to find your tape and verify its arrival. Believe it or not, FedEx, UPS and even the postal service don't lose packages very often. Assume your tape has arrived.

News directors are busy people, and being the egomaniacs that we are, we think we're even busier than we are. Again, speaking personally, if I get a tape from you, whether it's solicited or not, I'll look at it at some point. If I like it and it's going on the "keeper" shelf, I'll contact you—I promise. If it's not going on the "keeper" shelf but if I think you could benefit from some advice, I may send you some. If I don't like it and don't think there's much potential, you won't hear from me, but you'll get a form letter at some point from our Human Resources office letting you know you didn't get the job. This isn't the way things should be, but it's the way things are; most news directors find there simply isn't enough time in the day to give personal service to every job hopeful, especially the unsolicited ones. So, if you haven't heard from the news director after a reasonable amount of time (three to four weeks), you may assume you're not the top candidate for the job.

So what kind of calls *are* appropriate? If a news director calls you and asks you for a tape or informs you that you're on a short list of candidates, ask him or her at that time if it's OK for you to call for an update from time to time. Once a candidate is hired, many news directors will call or write their other "short list" candidates personally to inform them. Not all of them do this, however. Human Resources departments usually will get around to contacting all the candidates to inform them the position has been filled, but this process could take weeks and you can't count on it happening in every case. So a call to the news director may be the quickest way to find out if you're still in the running for a given job.

Don't abuse the privilege. If a news director doesn't return your call, this usually is a sign that he or she is very busy and you're not the highest priority item at the moment. Believe it or not, this doesn't necessarily mean you're out of the running. But one factor remains absolutely constant: if a news director is thinking about hiring you, then you will get a call eventually.

Finally, remember that on-air jobs usually aren't filled quickly. Again drawing on personal experience, once I get an opening, it takes about a week to get approval to hire a replacement; about a week to 10 days to get the job posted on the Internet and in any trade magazines in which I may care to advertise; about three weeks to get in a good selection of tapes and résumés; then about three to four weeks to cull through the tapes, select a list of finalists and negotiate a deal. This is the *fast* track. It can take much longer. If you've learned you're on a short list, don't despair just because the news director doesn't call you every week. If you're the number two or three candidate, you may not hear from the news director in weeks. Then the news director's negotiations with the top candidate fall through or go sour, and suddenly you find yourself with a job offer. This, too, is how the business works.

Should I Send a Tape Unsolicited?

The power of networking has been demonstrated again and again. You never know when an unsolicited tape might strike a chord with a news director. Some agents make a very good living sending out loads of unsolicited tapes.

The fact is, however, that in sending out unsolicited tapes you're fighting an uphill battle. To get a job, your tape must land on the desk of a news director who (1) has the time and inclination to look at it, (2) has an opening, or (3) will get an opening in the not-too-distant future. The odds of all these things coming together quickly at any given station aren't particularly good. However, if you send out a large number of unsolicited tapes, chances are some of them will wind up in the hands of interested news directors. Even if the news director doesn't have a current opening, if your tape goes into a "keeper" stack, then you'll get *first* crack at any openings that do arise. This technique does work, and it's a good choice for anyone who has an unlimited amount of time, energy and money to devote to the effort of sending out tapes. Two of my most recent hires were people who had sent me (or whose agents had sent me) unsolicited tapes not knowing whether I had an opening.

If you're not able to devote every waking moment to the job search, however, you'll find it's much more cost-effective to target stations that do have openings. Keep your eye on the trade magazines, scan the Internet and, if necessary, cold-call stations (assignments editors usually are a good choice of people to call; they know everything).

Final Points

- Some news directors get irritated at people who cold-call asking whether the station has any job openings—especially if the job hopeful then goes on to ask the mailing address of the station, to whom to address the letter and the like. You're supposed to be a journalist. Show your journalistic prowess by finding out this information some other way than by calling the insanely busy news director.

- Don't bombard the news director with calls, even if you're on the short list of candidates. Making a pest of yourself isn't a good way to begin a working relationship.

- Never, ever, ever begin a cover letter with the salutation, "To Whom It May Concern." It doesn't concern me! See ya! Again, you're supposed to be a journalist. Do a little research. *Find out* whom it concerns. In doing so, don't rely on broadcasting yearbooks, Internet job sites or mailing lists to determine the name of the news director. *Always* call the station directly to find out. If you address your letter to the news director's predecessor, you might as well sign it "Too Lazy To Care, The Loser." (Obviously, this rule doesn't apply if you're answering a blind ad.)

- If you're a recent graduate applying for an entry-level job, you need to list on your résumé only those jobs that have prepared you for the field you're attempting to enter. News directors will assume that, like most students everywhere, you have held a series of part-time or full-time jobs as you worked your way through college. We really don't need to know that you worked as a waiter or waitress at the Bonanza steak house or flipped hamburgers at McDonald's (unless you rose to management status), so there's no need to clutter up your résumé listing these types of positions. (You may, however, list supervisors from these jobs as references.) If you held no media-related jobs, it's not a deal-breaker for entry-level positions. Instead, on your résumé treat your academic career as if *it* were a job. Explain how it's prepared you for the job you're seeking. List and emphasize any and all media-related extracurricular activities and internships.

- Don't put your life on hold waiting for a station to make a decision! If you would really like to go to Station A but Station B has made you a job offer, consider Station B's job offer on its own merits. If you're on the short list of candidates for Station A, then by all means give the news director a call and let him or her know you have another offer. But don't be surprised if Station A doesn't accelerate the selection process to accommodate your schedule. If they're not ready to make a decision, *you* may have to make one.

- If you have an aunt, uncle or cousin who's a station manager or GM, don't ask him or her to pull strings to get you a job. Most news directors really, really hate this. If you can't succeed on your own merits, find something else to do in life.

- Don't send a résumé that says "references available on request." If you have them, include them.

- Don't make any errors of spelling or grammar on your cover letter or résumé—not any. Have friends and relatives proof it to be sure.

- Never, ever send out an original, irreplaceable tape! Few news directors return tapes. If you want your tape returned, include a self-addressed envelope with the correct amount of postage— and even then, don't hold your breath.

- If you're having a tough time finding a job, don't give up easily. Television news is one of the most selective and competitive industries in the world. But there's a demand for good people. If you have the skills, the talent and the desire, and you're willing to start small and go wherever the job takes you, then you'll make it eventually.

Good luck.

How to Make Your Tape Impressive— the First Time

Like most news directors, I get a lot of unsolicited reporter and anchor tapes. When I find a candidate who has potential but isn't quite there yet, sometimes I'll dispatch a letter giving a brief critique and some tips. Over time I realized I was giving out the same advice again and again. As a time-saving measure I began compiling a "master list" of tips from which I could cut and paste whatever advice might be appropriate for each individual candidate. In the hope that this might be of benefit to other job seekers, I offer a version of that list below, under the presumption that what impresses me in a tape might impress at least some other news directors as well.

Some of the points below summarize advice presented elsewhere in this book. You may find it helpful to bookmark, clip or photocopy this list and keep it at your fingertips for quick reference.

Shoot Interactive Stand-ups

The number one hallmark of the rookie reporter is the static "I'm standing here in front of city hall" stand-up. But movement alone isn't the solution, because the number *two* hallmark of the rookie reporter is the infamous "walk to nowhere." Remember the purpose of a stand-up. It's *not* to give you "face time." Rather, a stand-up provides you the opportunity to act as a personal tour guide for the audience. People relate strongly to other people through eye contact, so it *is* important that viewers see you. But *do* something *with* that eye contact. Take us by the hand and walk us through a scene. Point something out. Gesture. Demonstrate something. Touch something. Hold something. Knock on something. Kick something. In all good stand-ups, including live ones, the reporter interacts with the environment in a manner that makes the story more meaningful or relevant to the viewer. To accomplish that, you must make sure that the words coming out of your mouth directly relate to what you're doing with your hands, feet and eyes.

Maintain the Appropriate Presentation Energy

The performance skills required to communicate well on television are akin to acting. There's no shame in that; the ability to perform well on camera or tape is a highly prized skill. The key is to make sure you don't *sound* like you're acting. Rookie reporters often fail this test. When they're covering a chili cookoff, their energy, inflection and tone of voice are so bubbly you want to strangle them. But when covering unpleasant news such as a murder, they take drastic steps to sound "serious." Usually this entails adopting a lower tone of voice and removing all inflection. At best this tactic might leave you sounding dull and boring. At worst it leaves you sounding dull, boring and *fake.* Certainly you should adjust your demeanor somewhat to reflect the subject matter. However, somber matters don't necessarily require *you* to act somber. They require you to be sober and serious, but not depressed. Even with an emotionally uncomfortable story, you should be interested and *sound* interested. Vary your inflection. Show some energy. The audience wants to know you have a personal investment in the story. The best way to showcase that is through well-written copy appropriately and professionally delivered, *not* by sounding dejected.

Don't Sound "Canned"

Another common characteristic of the rookie reporter is the dramatic difference between copy delivered on camera and that delivered in a voice-over track. Stand-ups might sound fairly natural, but the reporter's voice track within the package sounds canned and stale. I've talked with many students and new reporters about this problem. A common theme is that many beginners *perform* for the camera, but when they get into the audio booth, they revert to *reading.* Copy delivery is a performance, but the key, as the song says, is to "act naturally." When doing a stand-up, address the camera as if it were a person, and picture yourself conducting one side of a conversation. When in the audio booth, it sometimes helps if you stand while tracking and address the microphone as if *it* were a camera—or, better yet, a person. Relax, and try to be yourself. At the end of the day, go back and listen to your stories. If you can detect a voice difference between your track and your stand-ups, keep working on it.

Narrative Storytelling

The single most powerful concept in communications is that of narrative storytelling. Narrative storytelling means, ideally (1) finding the most interesting character and then (2) allowing the viewer to relive the story through that character's eyes. To relive an event, you have to experience it the way it really unfolded. The storyteller must present the facts in chronological order. Tell the story *from the beginning.* In a 1:25 TV report, if you have to break the chronology, try not to break it more than once; more than that becomes confusing. As with all rules, there are exceptions. But you will see elements of narrative story-telling in every good TV story. Conversely, rookie reporter packages often present facts strung together in apparent random order.

Avoid Using Bites with Officials

I've seen so many mediocre crime scene reports on the air and on résumé tapes that I can format them in my sleep: reporter track over perp walk, blah blah blah bite with boring police officer, reporter track over crime scene, blah blah bite with boring police officer #2, motionless stand-up at scene, blah blah blah bite with police officer, closing track. Do yourself, and us, a favor: bag all of those mind-numbing police bites, shoot an interactive stand-up, put the story into chronological order, and you'll have a much better report. This con-cept frightens a lot of reporters, but it shouldn't. Yes, you should make every attempt to find and interview interesting people. But you aren't paid by the bite. What do you say to a newscast producer when, despite your most diligent efforts, the only bites you've been able to get are with boring police officers? You say, "I don't have any bites." A report with compelling narrative storytelling, a good stand-up, and no bites at all is far preferable to a report with boring bites laced through it.

Make the Human Connection

Remember the purpose of a sound bite: it's *not* to give information. That's your job! *The purpose of a sound bite is to make a human connection.* Sound bites with everyday people who express personal feelings or who can put events into a human perspective are best. Yes, despite the preceding tip, this can even include officials—*if* they are being human, not just factual. This "feelings not facts" sound bite rule applies to everyday people, too. Don't bore us with the seemingly required "It sounded like a freight train" bite from a tornado victim; after half a century of television news, we can all agree tornadoes sound like freight trains. Instead, tell us the story of that victim's life—how fright-ened he or she was during the tornado, and how thankful afterward; how long he or she has lived there; what's been lost; what's been saved; who's helping; what happens next; what his or her hopes are for the future. Remember: *the best reporters don't report.* Anybody can dig out and recite a list of facts! The best reporters *tell stories*. In TV terms, you're going to set a scene, introduce us to at least one compelling character, tell his or her story and, above all, *make us care*.

Remember the Importance of Pacing

Don't bore your viewers. Keep the pace moving. Alternate frequently between your voice track and other elements such as sound bites, natural sound, and stand-ups. Don't waste words. Cut out the lulls!

Passive Writing

Many tapes plagued by passive writing are placed in the mail by reporters. These reporters were not taught well by their instructors. A sentence that has been filled with passive writing by a reporter may be rejected by the viewer. Viewers are often bored and confused by passive writing. The meaning of a story can be easily confused by passive writing, or made harder to follow by the lack of active construction. We hope you noticed something wrong with the construction of the past five sentences; if not, we need to talk. A passive sentence presents the receiver of the action before presenting the action itself, out of chronological order, in violation of the principles of narrative storytelling. One or two passive sentences can make a story sound dull. A lot of passive writing will suffocate the story by making the action difficult or impossible to follow. If there's a universal problem appearing on almost all reporter and producer tapes, it's passive writing. It's also the easiest to correct. Just make it active. Remember, it's "Alice kissed Fred," not "Fred was kissed by Alice," and *definitely* not "Fred was kissed."

Summary

I rarely get a "flawless" résumé tape, even from veterans. With almost every tape, the candidate can benefit from at least one of the points of advice above. The average is higher. Competition for on-air jobs is fierce. The more you polish your presentation, the better you'll fare against the 25 or 30 other people seeking the same job.

Good luck!

Word Usage and Grammar Guide

Many words in the English language are frequently misused. What follows is a list of some of the more common problem words and phrases for broadcasters. This guide or any other stylebook should be supplemented with a good, recently published dictionary, but it's important to note that dictionaries list all the ways that words are used, even in slang. Writers should stick to the definitions that are most accepted, usually the first two definitions listed. Going to the sixth or seventh definition of a word in the dictionary can cause broadcast writers problems in terms of the viewers or listeners being able to follow what's being said. We stress again, television and radio news writers should make sure that what they're writing is easily understood the first time it's heard.

Some Helpful Hints

In broadcasting, you can probably have a successful career without knowing the difference between a complex and a compound-complex sentence, or the difference between a gerund and a participle. But you do have to be able to recognize what the subject of the sentence is, whether verbs and pronouns agree with it and so on. Here are three guidelines to help in troubling cases.

Using "I" or "Me"

These should be used in conjunction with other nouns and pronouns just the same as they're used when they're alone. For example, you wouldn't say "Bob went to the store with I." You also wouldn't say "Bob went to the store with Jill and I." The key is to remove the second person and the word "and" from the sentence, see if you should use *I* or *me*, and then reinsert the second person and the word "and." It would be "Bob went to the store with me," so it should be "Bob went to the store with Jill and me." Also, it would be "I went to the store," so it should be "Jill and I went to the store."

Identifying the Subject of the Sentence

This is sometimes a problem when the sentence includes a prepositional phrase. For example: "a group of students," "a herd of elephants" and "a coalition of English teachers" are all singular. The general rule is to remove the prepositional phrase, determine whether the subject is singular or plural, use an appropriate verb, then reinsert the prepositional phrase. So take out the phrases "of students," "of elephants" and "of English teachers," and you'll see that it would be "a group goes," so it should be "a group of students *goes*"; it would be "a herd charges," so it should be a "herd of elephants *charges*"; and it would be "a coalition votes," so it should be "a coalition of teachers *votes*."

There is one exception to this. If you're talking about something or someone who is one of many in a group, then the verb should agree with the group. So in situations when you're talking about one of many, don't apply the general rule of removing the prepositional phrase. For example: "She's one of the best teachers who *have* ever worked at City High." The reason you treat these differently is that if you removed the prepositional phrase, all you're left with is "She's one." One what?

Here's another way to think about it. If you lump someone or something into a group, the reference goes back to the group and is plural. However, if you pull that person or thing out of the group and consider the person or thing individually, then it's singular. For example:

"One of the boys is coming to the party."
"He's one of the boys who are coming to the party."

Subject/Verb Agreement

First, you have to determine what the subject is and whether it's singular or plural. How about "Two thousand dollars is/are enough to buy the stereo system"? That's singular, because you're talking about a quantity; so it should read "Two thousand dollars is enough . . ." If you were referring to 2,000 individual bills, that would be plural, such as with "There were two thousand dollars stacked on top of one another." But with most quantities, the subject is singular. For example: 500 dollars, a million pounds, 2,500 square feet and so on. However, with most portions and proportions, the subject isn't the amount, but the noun itself. For example, "a third of our viewers," "27 percent of the respondents," and "half of the supplies" are all plural.

Word Usage

A, the   Some writing texts advise not using "a" when referring to something that can be numbered because "a" sounds too much like "eight." However, if we write and pronounce words as we do in conversation, this isn't a problem. Pronounce the word "a" as "uh" and the word "the" as "thuh." That's how we all talk, and it sounds very stiff to say A (long "a" sound) train derailed and spilled the (as in "thee") cargo. Also, this allows us to say "a million dollars" and not "one million dollars." The latter sounds a bit stiff, and again, that's not how people talk.

Also, don't use "the" in the first reference to something. For example, don't say "police discovered the body" if the viewers don't know which body we're talking about. Say "police discovered a body"; then on subsequent references it's OK to say "the body" because we've already established which body is the subject of the story.

Abstinent   See **celibate**.

Abuse, misuse   Both words mean to use wrongly or incorrectly, but abuse often has the added connotation of physical injury or harm.

Accept, except   Accept means to receive with approval; except means to exclude. For example: The club voted to *accept* everyone *except* John.

Across, around, about   Around means encircling; therefore, it's impossible for things to be happening around a certain area. Instead, things happen across (from one side or end to the other) the state or nation. Also, things happen about a certain time, not around a certain time.

Acute, chronic   Acute is something that's sharp, sudden and of short duration. Chronic is of long duration and might or might not also be acute. So in most cases, acute pain is different than chronic pain.

Administration   See **government**.

Adopt, approve, enact, pass   Amendments, resolutions and rules are adopted or approved. Bills are passed; laws are enacted.

Adopted, adoptive   Children are adopted, making their new parents adoptive.

Adversary, opponent   An opponent is anyone on the other side. An adversary is openly hostile.

Adverse, averse   Adverse means harmful or unfavorable, such as with adverse weather. Averse means not in favor of or disposed against.

Advice, advise   Advice is a noun, and it's what you give. Some people seem to like to give it whether they're asked for it or not. Advise is a verb and means to give advice, to suggest a course of action.

Affect, effect   These words create much confusion, but that doesn't have to be the case. Both can be used as verbs or nouns, but in the most common usage affect is a verb meaning to produce a change or to influence; effect is a noun meaning the change itself, the result. For example:

How will the vote *affect* the council's stance on the proposal?
The *effect* isn't likely to be seen for some time.

Affluent, effluent   Affluent typically means wealthy; effluent means liquid waste.

Afterward, backward, downward, forward, toward, upward   Not afterwards, backwards, downwards, forwards, towards or upwards.

Aggravate, irritate   Aggravate means to make something worse, as in "He aggravated an old football injury." Irritate means to annoy. You can't aggravate someone nor can you be aggravated about something.

Agnostic, atheist   An agnostic believes there's not enough evidence to conclude that there's a God. An atheist believes there is no such thing as God.

Allude, elude   To allude is to refer to something indirectly; to elude is to escape from or avoid, often by deceitful means.

Although, while   Use although when you mean "in spite of the fact that" or "on the other hand." While means "at the same time as" or "during the time that." For example:

Although Sarah doesn't like sleeping on the floor, she agreed to do so *while* the relatives are visiting.

Alumna, alumni, alumnus   A male graduate is an alumnus, a female graduate is an alumna, and more than one graduate are alumni.

Among, between   Things take place among three or more people or objects, and between two parties or objects. However, even if there are three or more people or objects involved, if they interact two at a time, it's between.

Amoral, immoral   Someone is amoral if that person has no morals, and is immoral if he or she breaks an existing moral code.

Annual   An event isn't considered annual until it has taken place for three consecutive years. In its first year, call it the inaugural or the first. In its second year, call it the second.

Anticipate, expect   Anticipate carries the added connotation of preparing for what's expected.

Anxious, eager   If you're anxious about something, you're nervous, fearful or apprehensive. If you're eager to do something, you are excitedly anticipating it.

Anybody, anyone, everybody, everyone, nobody, no one, somebody, someone   All take singular verbs. For example:

Everybody *comes* to my house after Friday night football games.
Someone *knocks* on my door every Saturday morning at seven.
No one *jumps* when the tiny cannon is fired.
Anybody *has* the right to voice an opinion.

Apparently, evidently   Both mean appearing to be so. However, apparently implies some doubt as to the truth of the statement. For example:

Apparently, Jane is sincere this time. (It seems that way, but you're not sure.)
Evidently, the burglar left some clues at the scene. (In this sense, you don't doubt that this is true.)

Apprise, appraise   Apprise means to inform; appraise means to place a value on something. For example: The jeweler *apprised* the couple that he had *appraised* the diamond necklace at two million dollars.

Approve   See **adopt**.

Arbitrate, mediate   After hearing the sides of an argument, an arbitrator comes to a decision that the parties must adhere to. A mediator helps the parties talk through and solve their differences.

Around   See **across**.

As   See **like**.

Assassin, killer, murderer   An assassin kills by secret assault and frequently for political reasons. Someone who kills with a motive of any kind is a killer. A murderer is someone who has been convicted of murder. However, be careful calling someone a murderer even if that person has been convicted of the crime. It's preferable to say he or she was convicted of murder, because we don't know the person did the crime unless we were there to witness it. However, we know that the person has been convicted. That's a matter of record.

Assure, ensure, insure   Assure means to convince or make secure or stable. Ensure means to make certain that something happens. Use insure when referring to insurance. For example:

I want to *assure* you that I'll be there.
She *assured* him that everything would be OK.
I'll *ensure* that the package arrives on time.
Do you want to *insure* the package?

Atheist   See **agnostic**.

Athletics director   Not athletic director. The full title is Director of Athletics.

Author   Use this word as a noun only. If you want to say someone wrote something, then say the person wrote it.

Average   If you write about *the* average, it's singular. *An* average is plural. For example:

The average age of incoming students *has* risen in the past decade.
An average of 250 people *have* seen the play each night.

Averse   See **adverse**.

Backward   See **afterward**.

Bad, badly, good, well   People feel bad or they feel good. If you say someone feels well or feels badly, it means that the person's sense of touch either is or isn't well developed. However, in terms of *doing* something, people either do well or do badly. If you say someone did good, the meaning is that he or she did a good deed such as feeding the hungry or working with Habitat for Humanity. The same is true of someone who does bad. So, on a test or project you do well or do badly. Don't be confused by the difference between how you feel and how you perform. However, if asked how you feel, it's appropriate to say "I'm well." The meaning is that you're not sick. But don't say "I *feel* well."

Ban, bar   Ban means to forbid or prohibit; bar means shut or exclude. People can be banned from doing something, and things can be banned. Only people can be barred from something. For example:

My father *banned* me from seeing Jill again.
Demonstrations are *banned* on the library lawn.
I was *barred* from entering the courthouse.

Bear market, bull market   A bear market means declining stock prices; a bull market indicates rising stock prices.

Because   See **since**.

Because of   See **due to**.

Benefactor, beneficiary   A benefactor does good; a beneficiary is the one who benefits from the doing of good.

Between   See **among**.

Biennial, biannual, semiannual   Something is biennial if it occurs every two years. It is biannual or semiannual if it occurs twice a year.

Blatant, flagrant   Something is blatant if it's very noticeable, noisy or offensive. It's flagrant if it's overtly outrageous, that is, not just a little harmful. Something can be blatant (there for everybody to see) and not be flagrant.

Both, each   Both means two things collectively; each means two or more things considered individually.

Boy, girl, man, woman, gentleman, lady   Only people in their teens or younger should be called boys or girls. Some suggest only those younger than 16 years of age should be called boys or girls. Man and woman are the preferred terms used to refer to physically mature individuals. Definitely don't refer to a group of males as men and a similarly aged group of females as girls. Use gentleman or lady only with titled people or in very specific circumstances when that's definitely what you're trying to say (as in First Lady, Lady Diana, everyone considered him a true gentleman and so on). Don't use lady or gentleman in a generic sense as synonyms for woman or man, because most of the time you have no way of knowing if someone is a gentleman or is a lady. Also, don't use man as a replacement for human, human being, or person.

Boycott, embargo   A boycott involves a group agreeing not to purchase goods or services from another group or business until certain conditions are met. An embargo is a legal restriction of trade and usually involves not allowing goods into or out of a country. For example:

Southern Baptists said they'll *boycott* Disney theme parks and products until the company quits producing R-rated movies.
The United States will continue its *embargo* of Cuba.

Bring, take   You *bring* something toward the speaker or subject and *take* it away from the speaker or subject. For example:

Grandma wanted Red Riding Hood to *bring* her some cookies.
Red Riding Hood decided to *take* cookies to her grandma.

Brothers-in-law, daughters-in-law, fathers-in-law, mothers-in-law, sisters-in-law, sons-in-law   Not brother-in-laws and so forth.

Bug, tap   A bug is a concealed electronic listening device used to pick up sounds in a room. A tap is a device attached to a telephone line and is used to pick up phone conversations. Hence, offices are bugged and phone lines are tapped.

Bull market   See **bear market**.

Bullet   See **shell**.

Burglarize   See **rob**.

But, however   Both of these words indicate that what follows contrasts with what's been said or written already, but many people use them to continue a thought. For example: "Bethany went to the store but came back with groceries." One would expect that she'd come back with groceries if she went to the store, so there's no contrast. That sentence should read: "Bethany went to the store and came back with some groceries." A sentence in which "but" would be appropriate is "Bethany went to the store, but she came back without anything." There's a contrast because what happened is different than what we'd expect. Likewise, "but" doesn't work in this sentence: "He only wanted to stop crime in his neighborhood but that might have cost a Miami man his life." There's no contrast here; it's a continuation of a thought. Either replace "but" with "and" or, better yet, make it two sentences. "He only wanted to stop crime in his neighborhood. That might have cost a Miami man his life."

Can   See **may**.

Celebrant, celebrator   A celebrant conducts a religious ceremony; a celebrator is someone having a good time. So, don't refer to celebrants on Bourbon Street on New Year's eve. They're celebrators. Or, better yet, they're revelers or party-goers. Celebrators doesn't sound too conversational, does it?

Celibate, chaste, abstinent   Celibate means unmarried, so priests who take vows of celibacy have agreed to remain unmarried. Chaste means abstaining from carnal love, and chastity often goes along with a vow of celibacy, but they're not the same thing. Practicing abstinence also means deciding not to do something, at least for a time, and is often used in reference to a decision not to engage in premarital sex.

Cement, concrete   Cement is the powder that's mixed with water to make concrete. So houses are made of concrete blocks, not cement blocks. (And the Beverly Hillbillies didn't swim in a ce-ment pond.)

Censor, censure   Censor (as a verb) means to delete as unsuitable, to find fault with. A censor (as a noun) is the person who does those things. Censure (as a verb) means to officially criticize or reprove. Censure (noun) is the criticism. Representatives and senators who run afoul of their colleagues are censured.

Centers for Disease Control   Considered one entity, so use singular verbs.

Character, reputation   Your character is what kind of person you are; your reputation is what others think about you.

Chaste   See **celibate**.

Cheap, inexpensive   Both mean costing little, but cheap has the added connotation of poor quality.

Childish, childlike   People who are childlike display the positive attributes of childhood, such as being innocent, trusting, loving and the like. Childish is derogatory and means displaying negative and inappropriate traits often associated with children, such as stubbornness, selfishness and so forth.

Chronic   See **acute**.

Citizen, resident   A citizen is a person who has acquired all the civil rights afforded by a nation through birth or naturalization. So, one can be a citizen of a country, but not of a state or city. Refer to Chicago residents rather that Chicago citizens. Some of the residents of any major city, we're sure, *aren't* citizens.

Climatic, climactic   Climatic means having to do with the climate and is rarely used in broadcast. Climactic pertains to a climax. So don't write about a *climatic* event unless you're talking about the weather, and be careful with *climactic*. It isn't very conversational, anyway.

Coed   Out of date and considered sexist. Avoid it.

Cohesive, coherent   Both mean sticking together, but cohesive is used in reference to people and objects, coherent in reference to ideas or other abstractions and has the added connotation of logical flow. For example:

The army platoon was a *cohesive* unit.
He made a *coherent* argument in favor of the bill.

Collision, crash   For there to be a collision, both objects must be moving. A car can't collide with a utility pole, but it can crash into it.

Comedian, comic   Use these for both males and females. Comedienne is considered out of date.

Compare, contrast   When you compare you look at similarities and differences; when you contrast you look only at differences.

Comprise, compose   Compose means be the parts of; comprise means to include or contain. For example:

The 50 states *compose* the United States.
The United States *comprises* 50 states.

Make up or includes is preferred.

Concrete   See **cement**.

Constant, continuous, continual   Continuous means without ceasing; continual means repeatedly. If it were to rain continuously during an extended period of time, we'd all be looking for an ark in which to stay dry. It could rain continually for weeks without causing any major concern. Constant is a problem because it can mean either ceaseless or regularly recurring. Because constant is used in different ways and the viewers might not be able to figure out which way you're using the word, you're better off writing continuous or continual.

Contagious, infectious   Something that's contagious can be spread only by physical contact. Something that's infectious is communicable by the spread of germs, with or without physical contact.

Contemporary, modern   Something that's modern is recent or is happening now. Something is contemporary if it happens or happened at the same time as something else. So, something can be contemporary and not be modern.

Convince, persuade   You convince someone *of* something; you persuade someone *to do* something.

Could   See **may**.

Couple   This word causes grammatical problems because it can take either singular or plural verbs. It depends whether you're referring to the couple as a unit or as distinct individuals. For example:

The couple *has* standing dinner reservations at Bob's Steak House.
The couple *were* married at St. Vincent's Cathedral.
A couple of gang members *were* brought in for questioning.

Also, the "of" is needed. It's not a couple apples or a couple years; it's a couple of apples or a couple of years.

Crash   See **collision**.

Criteria, criterion   Criteria is plural; criterion is singular. For example:

The *criteria* for the contest have changed.
The primary *criterion* for membership in the club is a hefty bank account.

Criticism, critique   Criticism carries the connotation of a negative evaluation; critique commonly means pointing out both the good and the bad.

Cupfuls   Not cupsful.

Currently, presently   Currently means now; presently means soon. Don't use presently to mean "at this time."

Cynical, skeptical   Skeptical means inclined to doubt; cynical means contemptuous, quick to find fault. A good dose of skepticism is healthy in journalism. Cynicism can get you in trouble in a lot of ways.

Data   Correctly used, data is a plural noun and takes plural verbs. Often when you use this word, you're doing a story involving scientists, economists and the like, and they know the difference.

Daughters-in-law   As written.

Daylight-saving time   Not daylight *savings* time. When you're referring to a particular time zone, it's Central Daylight Time, for example.

Defective, deficient   Defective means having a defect; deficient means lacking something. For example:

He sent the *defective* part back to the manufacturer.
He was *deficient* in the number of credit hours needed to graduate.

Definite, definitive   Definite means exact or certain; definitive means conclusive or final. For example:

The incorporated area has *definite* boundaries.
The scientist's findings were *definitive*.

Demolish, destroy   Both indicate doing away with something completely, so it's not possible to partially destroy something, and it's redundant to say something was completely demolished.

Diagnosis, prognosis   A diagnosis tells us the state of something; a prognosis predicts the future developments related to that thing. For example: The doctor's *diagnosis* was cancer and her *prognosis* wasn't good.

Differ from, differ with   To differ from something is to be unlike it; to differ with someone is to disagree.

Dilemma   A dilemma is worse than a problem or a concern. A person facing a dilemma has to choose between two unattractive alternatives.

Disabled, handicapped   Disabled is preferred. However, neither should be used if the disability isn't germane to the story.

Disinterested, uninterested   Disinterested means impartial; uninterested means having no interest in something. You can't be disinterested in a movie.

Dispute   See **rebut**.

Dissociate   Dissociate means to end a connection or association with. Note that the word does not contain an "a". It's not disassociate.

Dived, dove   Dived is the past tense of dive. Dove is often used in this way (as in the boys dove into the water), but dived is more precise. Dove presents the additional problem that it might be pronounced as dove (a bird).

Down Syndrome   Not Down's Syndrome.

Downward   See **afterward**.

Due to, thanks to, because of   Because of is better. You certainly don't want to write a sentence like this, which we heard during one of the worst winter storms on record: "Power lines are down all across the area *thanks to* a severe ice storm." Why would anyone be thankful to be without electricity in subzero weather? The power lines were down *because of* the ice storm.

Each, either, neither Use either when referring to one or the other of two objects or people; use each when referring to both or all of two or more things or persons. However, *each* word takes singular verbs, unless either or neither is followed by both a singular and a plural noun or pronoun. Then the verb takes the form of the noun or pronoun closest to it. For example:

Each of us *needs* to make an effort to succeed.
Either of the two options *is* acceptable.
Either he or they *have* to show up.
Neither *is* suitable for the position.
Neither they nor he *wants* to leave the company.
Neither he nor they *want* to leave the company.

Also see **both**.

Each other, one another Two people look at *each other,* but more than two people look at *one another.*

Eager See **anxious**.

Effect See **affect**.

Effective, efficient Something that's effective gets the job done. Getting it done with a minimum of time and effort means you're efficient. So, something can be effective without being very efficient. You can skateboard from Chicago to St. Louis and you'd get there eventually, but you'd expend a lot of energy and use a lot of time doing so.

Effluent See **affluent**.

Either See **each**.

Elicit See **illicit**.

Elude See **allude**.

Embargo See **boycott**.

Empathy, sympathy Both words mean to share the feelings of another, but empathy goes a bit further than sympathy and means being able to imagine yourself in someone else's situation.

Enact See **adopt**.

Enormity, enormousness Enormity refers to something outrageously heinous or offensive; enormousness refers to massive size. For example:

The *enormity* of his crime was beyond belief.
The *enormousness* of the mountain was truly impressive.

Ensure See **assure**.

Epigram, epigraph, epitaph, epithet An epigram is a witty saying. Epigraphs and epitaphs are inscriptions on monuments or tombstones. An epithet is a word or phrase used to characterize a person or thing and often carries a negative connotation.

Eternity, infinity Eternity refers to endless time; infinity refers to anything that's infinite or endless.

Everybody, every one See **anybody**.

Evidently See **apparently**.

Except See **accept**.

Excite, incite   Excite means to arouse the emotions of (normally taken to mean arousing positive emotions); incite means to influence someone to act.

Expect   See **anticipate**.

Explicit, implicit   Explicit means clearly stated; implicit means implied or suggested. Therefore, something that's implicit is open to interpretation. In broadcast writing, we should always clearly state what we mean.

Famous, infamous   Famous means widely known and popular; infamous also means widely known, but carries a negative connotation. For example, at times in his career Mohammed Ali has been famous. At one point, however, he was infamous.

Farther, further   Use farther to refer to physical distance and further for all other uses. For example:

Los Angeles is *farther* from New York than from Denver.
The board members voted to study the proposal *further*.
We have much *further* to go to come to an agreement.

Fathers-in-law   As written.

Fewer   See **less**.

Figurative, literal   Figurative means symbolic, not literal. Literal means exact.

Firm   A firm is a partnership, such as a law firm. The term shouldn't be used to refer to companies or corporations, both of which are incorporated business entities. Firms aren't incorporated.

Flagrant   See **blatant**.

Flail   The word means to whip or beat. Some dictionaries include "a wild waving of the arms" among the definitions.

Flammable   See **inflammable**.

Flaunt, flout   Flout means to show disdain for; flaunt means to make a showy display of something to draw attention.

Flounder, founder   As verbs, flounder means to struggle helplessly and founder most commonly refers to ships and means to sink or run aground. Ships don't flounder because inanimate objects can't struggle.

Forward   See **afterward**.

Further   See **farther**.

Gender, sex   Use gender when you're referring to the way a group of people is viewed by society; use sex when you're talking about the biological differences between men and women.

Gentleman   See **boy**.

Gibe, jibe, jive   Gibe means to taunt or sneer, jibe means to agree (or, in sailing, to shift direction) and jive means either swing music or talk meant to deceive or confuse. For example:

They *gibed* him about his lack of athletic ability.
The two suspects told stories that didn't *jibe*.
The senator's speech was nothing but *jive*.

Girl   See **boy**.

Good   See **bad**.

Got   This is one of the most overused words in the English language. Got is the past tense of get. For example: I got an "A" on the test. Got shouldn't be used to add emphasis to the words "has" or "have." For example, it's unnecessary to say: "You have got to see Joe's new car" or "The city council has got to make a decision soon." "You've got" means the same thing as "you have got" and shouldn't be used, nor should she's got, he's got, we've got and so forth. A television station in central Florida uses the slogan: "We've got you covered." Perhaps the promotions people think that's catchy, but the news people should never put up with the use of such as that in the station's PR campaign. The line "I've got you babe" might be acceptable in a song by Sonny and Cher (we just admitted to having been around for a long time), but it's not acceptable when you're trying to write with precision.

Government, junta, regime, administration   Governments and juntas are ruling groups. The only difference is that juntas are in power after a coup (an overthrow of the existing government). A regime is a political system, and an administration is the people who make up the executive branch of a government.

Handicapped   See **disabled**.

Hanged, hung   People are hanged (though not often anymore), and objects are hung. For example:

They *hanged* the horse thief at noon.
The stockings were *hung* by the chimney with care.

He, him, I, me, she, her   There's often a lot of confusion about which one of these pronouns to use when they're used in conjunction with a noun or another pronoun. The key is to remove the noun or the second pronoun and the word "and." In other words, consider the pronoun by itself. For example, look at this sentence: "Barbara went to the store with Veronica and I." It should be "with Veronica and me." Take the words "Veronica" and "and" out of the sentence. You wouldn't say Barbara went to the store with I; you'd say she went to the store with me. So, decide on the pronoun and then add the other words back into the sentence. Some other examples:

I watched the movie with Bob and *her*.
He and I are on the football team. (Here you have to use the singular verb with the singular pronoun "I" when you take "he and" out of the sentence. Considering the pronoun by itself the sentence would read: "I am on the football team." Don't be confused by the need to change from plural to singular verbs at times. The concept is the same.)
Lou's not as smart as *she*. (This type can be a little tricky. There are a couple of implied words at the end of this sentence. What we're really saying is "Lou's not as smart as she is smart." Turn the sentence around, and you'll see why it should be "she." If Lou isn't as smart as she, that means that she is smarter than Lou. You wouldn't say her is smarter than Lou.)

He, she   There's no gender-neutral singular pronoun in English. In the past, writers have used "he" when the sex of the subject was unknown, but this is now considered sexist. To say "he or she" sounds stiff, so in broadcast it's best to restate the sentence and use the plural pronoun "they." For example:

A student should do the best *he* can. (sexist—not all students are male)
A student should do the best *he or she* can. (grammatically correct, but

sounds a bit awkward and nonconversational)
Students should do the best *they* can. (best choice)

Historic, historical   Something is historic if it makes history or is significant in history. Anything that's part of history is historical. However, this distinction has virtually disappeared.

Hopeful, hopefully   Use hopeful and hopefully to describe someone's feelings, not as a substitute for "I hope." For example:

I hope the professor will change my grade. (If you said "hopefully, she will change my grade," you're saying she will change it and will be hopeful about something while she's doing it.)
Hopefully, I made my request for a grade change. (In other words, I was hopeful that my request would be honored.)
"Most Americans *hope* the tensions in the Middle East will end soon." (Rather than "hopefully, the tensions will end soon." Tensions can't be hopeful.)

Hung   See **hanged**.

I   See **he**.

Illicit, elicit   Illicit means unlawful; elicit means to bring to mind. For example:

She was convicted of *illicit* use of campaign funds.
Seeing him at the reunion *elicited* memories of high school.
Note: These words are used frequently by reporters and writers trying to sound knowledgeable. Both sound somewhat nonconversational, don't they? In the first sentence "illegal" would work better, as would "brought back" in the second sentence.

Immoral   See **amoral**.

Impeach   Impeach means to accuse a public official of wrongdoing. It doesn't mean "to remove from office." Bill Clinton was impeached but not removed from office.

Implicit   See **explicit**.

Imply, infer   Imply means to suggest or indicate something without saying it directly; infer means to draw a conclusion from. For example:

The speaker *implied* that a new university president would be appointed.
I *inferred* that there had been problems with the current university administration.

Impromptu   Impromptu means without planning. Anything that involves an invitation or notice to attend can't be impromptu.

Incite   See **excite**.

Incredible, incredulous   Incredible means unbelievable; incredulous means skeptical. For example: When he described the ride as *incredible,* she gave him an *incredulous* look.

Indict   Indict means to bring legal charges against. Don't write that someone was indicted for murder because that sounds as though you think the person did it. Say the person was indicted on a charge of murder (or bribery, arson and so on).

Inexpensive   See **cheap**.

Infamous   See **famous**.

Infectious   See **contagious**.

Infer   See **imply**.

Infinity   See **eternity**.

Inflammable, flammable   Both mean capable of burning, but inflammable sounds as though it means exactly the opposite. Use flammable it you mean capable of burning, and describe something that won't burn as nonflammable. (Hyphenate words like this to make them easier to read.)

Insure   See **assure**.

Inter, intra   The prefix inter means between two or more items in the same category; intra means within or between two parts of the same thing. For example:
interstate—goes from one state to others
intercollegiate athletics—contests between teams from different colleges or universities
intramural sports—students on teams within the same school play against each other

invaluable, valuable, valueless   Invaluable means of immeasurably great value, and often carries the added connotation of irreplaceable. Valuable means of great value or price, but isn't as strong as invaluable. Valueless means without value.

Irritate   See **aggravate**.

Issue   An issue is a point in question or dispute. Therefore, all issues involve controversy; so there's no need to refer to a controversial issue, and there's no such thing as a noncontroversial issue.

Itch, scratch   Itch is a noun, and scratch is a verb. To relieve the discomfort caused by an itch, you scratch. You can't itch something.

Jail   See **prison**.

Jerry-built, jury-rigged   Jerry-built means put together hastily and with flimsy materials. Jury-rigged means assembled quickly with materials on hand. So, something might have been jury-rigged without being jerry-built. Broadcast engineers have been known to jury-rig entire remote systems that are very sturdy and work beautifully.

Jibe, jive   See **gibe**.

Junta   See **government**.

Jurist, juror   A jurist is an expert at law; a juror is a member of a jury. A jurist might or might not be a judge.

Ketchup   Other spellings aren't correct and could lead to pronunciation problems (such as catsup or catchup).

Killer   See **assassin**.

Kudos   The word means credit or praise for an achievement and takes singular verbs. For example: Kudos *is* in order for your graduation with honors.

Lady   See **boy**.

Last, latest, past   When one says last night, there's not much room for confusion about what's meant. Everyone knows the speaker is talking about the most recent period of darkness. The same is true of last week. But when you write "the last week," there *is* room for confusion, as in: "John wrecked his car twice in the last week." The question that arises is, In the last week of what? John's life on earth? Don't use "the last" unless there will be no more of whatever we're talking about. Therefore, the sentence we wrote earlier should read: "John wrecked his car twice in the *past* week." So, don't write something happened in the last month, or in last year, or in the last decade, or in the last millennium unless the world is about to end. Also, if you write something about John's last trip to the store, the implication is that John will never again go to the store. Write John's latest or most recent trip.

Lay   See **lie**.

Leave alone, let alone   Leave alone means to depart from or cause to be in solitude. Let alone means to allow to be undisturbed. If you ask someone to leave you alone, that means you want to be by yourself. If you want the person not to harass you, you would ask to be let alone.

Lend, loan   Lend is a verb; loan is a noun. You lend something, such as your car or money. What you lend is a loan.

Less, fewer   Use less when something can't be numbered and fewer when numbering is possible. For example:

There are *fewer* oranges on the trees this season.
There is *less* fruit on the trees this season.

You can number *pieces* of fruit or specific types of fruit, but you can't number fruit. Likewise, you can number hours or minutes, but you can't number time.

Note: Although it would be very time-consuming to count grains of sand, it is possible. However, although it's possible to number grains of sand, it's not possible to number sand itself. Think about it this way, using sand as an example: Can I say, "There's one grain of sand, and there's another"? Can I say, "There's one sand and there's another"? If the answer is yes, then use fewer (as in grains of sand, pieces of fruit, lumps of coal); if the answer is no, then use less (as in sand, fruit, or coal).

Less than   See **over**.

Libel, slander   Libel is defamation in writing or printing; slander is defamation by the spoken word. In the vast majority of modern legal cases, courts haven't distinguished between whether material was broadcast or printed, and most suits brought against media outlets are libel suits. Because of the reach and permanence of broadcast, material that defames is considered to have been "published."

Lie, lay   Lie means to tell an untruth or to recline. Lay means to place something on something else. You *lie* down, but you *lay* something down. The problem comes with lie (recline) in the past tense, which is lay. For example:

He felt so bad he wanted to *lie* down and die.
He *lay* down and died.

Here's how to conjugate the verbs: *Lie (tell an untruth): lie, lied, lied*

I cannot tell a *lie*.
I *lied* to my mother.
I've *lied* in similar situations.

Lie (recline): lie, lay, lain

I will *lie* on the bed.
Yesterday, I *lay* on the couch until noon.
I've *lain* in bed all day when I've been sick.

Lay (place something) lay, laid, laid

I will *lay* my books on the table.
I *laid* my books on the table when I got home.
I've *laid* my books there before.

You can see that the two ways to use "lay" can create some problems. But you wouldn't want to say he lied down, because that leads to confusion. Initially, it sounds as though you're saying he told an untruth.

Like, such as   Like means similar to. Use "like" when you're comparing two things and "such as" when mentioning something as an example of a broader category. For instance:

Joe is *like* Pete in many ways. (The two are similar.)
Mothers *such as* Betty Jones are in favor of the new grant for child-care facilities.

Betty Jones is among those mothers who favor the grant. If you write mothers *like* Betty Jones are in favor, what you're saying is that mothers similar to her are, but perhaps she herself isn't. Also, don't substitute like for "as" or "as if."

He studies, *as* he should. (He should study and he does.)

If you write he studies *like* he should, you're making a judgment about his particular study habits. Perhaps he studies with the CD player at full volume. Are you saying he should study in that way?

Lion's share   This phrase means more than "the majority of." It means all or nearly all.

Literal   See **figurative**.

Loan   See **lend**.

Majority, plurality   The majority is more than half of the total, often referred to as 50 percent plus one. When there are more than two candidates for office, the candidate receiving more votes than any other has received the plurality of votes, but not 50 percent. This often means there must be a runoff between the top two vote-getters.

Man, mankind   Other words are preferable, such as humans, people or humanity for mankind, and a person or an individual for man. Also see **boy**.

Masochism, sadism   Masochism means enjoying inflicting pain on yourself; sadism means enjoying inflicting pain on others. The pain doesn't necessarily have to be physical. People who fall into these categories are masochists or sadists.

Mass   Priests don't say Mass; Catholics celebrate Mass.

May, might, can, could   These are often used interchangeably. They shouldn't be. The key question, as with all words used in broadcast, is, Might the viewers take what you've written in a way that's different from how you intended it? For example, the following sentence could be interpreted two different ways.

Jane *may* go to the park.

Do you mean Jane might decide to go to the park, or that Jane has permission to go to the park? In instances when you mean that something might happen, use might and there will be less room for confusion. The same is true for "can." Use "can" when you mean "is able." For example:

Can Jane go to the park?

We don't know if you're asking if she has permission to (if you are, use may) or if she's physically able to. In that case, use "can." The word "could" should be used when there's a condition attached.

Jane *could* have ridden to the park if her bike wasn't broken.

Me   See **he**.

Media   The word media is plural and takes plural verbs. It means all forms of mass communication considered together. A single form of mass communication, such as television, is a medium. Mediums are palm readers.

Mediate   See **arbitrate**.

Might   See **may**.

Misuse   See **abuse**.

Modern   See **contemporary**.

Moral, morale   Moral deals with right and wrong; morale refers to one's confidence, self-esteem and the like.

More than   See **over**.

Mothers-in-law   As written.

Mr., Mrs., Miss, Ms.   All are courtesy titles. See Chapter 1.

Murderer   See **assassin**.

Neither   See **each**.

Next of kin   This is brutally nonconversational. When's the last time you used that phrase in a chat with a friend? Use family or relatives, either of which would be used in a conversation rather than next of kin, which wouldn't.

Nobody, no one   See **anybody**.

None   None means not one in most uses, and takes singular verbs. There are times when saying not one of something doesn't make sense, such as "not one clothes" or if you're referring to no amount of something. Read the sentence and substitute not one for none and see if it makes sense. If it does, use a singular verb. If it doesn't make sense, use a plural verb. For example:

None of the children *was* injured in the fire.
None of his clothes *are* worth much.

However, even if you know something is grammatically correct, it might sound wrong to you, and if it sounds wrong to you, it will probably sound wrong to some of the viewers or listeners. So in the first example, you wouldn't change the sentence to make it grammatically incorrect and you might not want to write it the way it's written because the word "none" is used incorrectly so often it sounds wrong when you use it the right way. So rewrite the sentence: "All of the children escaped injury in the fire."

Notorious, notable   Notorious means widely but unfavorably known. Notable is a synonym for prominent or noteworthy. When one gains notoriety, he or she is *unfavorably* thought of.

Number, total   "The number" or "the total" takes singular verbs; "a number" or "a total" takes plural verbs. See **average**.

Obscene, pornographic   Anything that's highly offensive is obscene. Pornographic material is designed to stimulate sexual thoughts. Obscene material might or might not be pornographic.

Observance, observation   An observance is the act of complying with a law or custom or of taking part in a ceremony. Observation is the act of noticing. So, to say that the couple celebrated the *observation* of their 50th anniversary would be incorrect.

Occur, take place   Things that occur happen with no planning. Things that take place are planned.

Olympics   This is a plural noun: "The Summer Olympics *are* held every four years." They are considered a collection of different sports events, not a single entity.

One   The question of which possessive pronoun to use with "one" or "a person" creates some problems. To say, "one's home is one's castle" sounds very stiff, but so does "one's home is his or her castle." Also, you wouldn't want to use "is his castle" or "is her castle," nor would you say "is their castle," because you're talking about a single individual and "their" is plural. Try: "People's homes are their castles."

One another   See **each other**.

Opponent   See **adversary**.

Oral, verbal   Oral means of the mouth; verbal means using words, which can be written or spoken. You could say "she verbalized her feelings" or "they made verbal arguments" if you mean that someone spoke; but there's some room for confusion unless you explain that you specifically mean words were uttered. Of course, you wouldn't say "she oralized her feelings." Write: "She spoke about her feelings."

Over, more than, under, less than   Over and under are frequently misused. Use under and over when something is physically under or over something else. However, when you mean a greater or lesser amount or number of something, use more than or less than. For example:

The plane flew *over* the field.
The car cost *more than* 30-thousand dollars.
The car was *under* water.
The house sold for *less than* 100-thousand dollars.

Also, people don't argue *over* something; they argue *about* it. And "through the years" is preferable to "over the years."

Overlook, oversee   Overlook means to ignore or to fail to see. It also means to have a view of. Oversee means to supervise. For example:

I *overlooked* the small print in this contract.
I've decided to *overlook* your latest temper tantrum.

The house *overlooks* the canyon.
I'll *oversee* the construction project.

Pardon, parole, probation   A pardon results in the forgiveness of the charges against a person; he or she faces no further punishment. A pardon is granted by a chief of state. Parole means the person was let out of prison before the end of the sentence. It's granted by a parole board. A person on probation is convicted but doesn't actually serve time, if the person doesn't mess up again. A suspended sentence is the same as probation.

Pass   See **adopt**.

Past   See **last**.

Persecute, prosecute   Persecute means to harass; prosecute means to bring legal proceedings against. Members of the legal profession aren't supposed to persecute people, but some are supposed to prosecute those accused of wrongdoing.

Person, people   Use person when speaking about an individual and people when the reference is to more than one person. Avoid persons.

Personal, personnel   Personal means private or pertaining to an individual. Personnel means workforce or employees. There's a big difference between a manager making personal decisions and making personnel decisions.

Persuade   See **convince**.

Phenomenon, phenomena   Phenomenon is singular; phenomena is plural. You wouldn't write about *a* phenomena.

Plurality   See **majority**.

Pornographic   See **obscene**.

Possible, probable   Something that's possible might happen; if it's probable, it's *likely* to happen.

Precede, proceed   Precede means to come before; proceed means to move forward. For example:

Ninth grade *precedes* tenth grade.
Let's *proceed* to the next item on the agenda.

Prescribe, proscribe   To prescribe is to suggest the use of something. To proscribe is to forbid or prohibit something. For example:

The doctor *prescribed* a powerful pain killer.
The judge *proscribed* him from having further contact with his ex-wife.

Presently   See **currently**.

Prison, jail   Generally, people serve time in prison for committing felonies. Jails are for minor offenders or those awaiting trial or sentencing on any charge. Penitentiaries and correctional facilities are prisons.

Probable   See **possible**.

Probation   See **pardon**.

Proceed   See **precede**.

Prognosis   See **diagnosis**.

Proscribe   See **prescribe**.

Prosecute   See **persecute**.

Prostate, prostrate   The prostate is a gland; prostrate means lying down, in a prone position. Hence, no one suffers from *prostrate* cancer.

Proved, proven   Proved is the past tense of prove; proven is an adjective describing something tested and shown to be effective. For example:

The lawyer had *proved* her case.
The program is a *proven* ratings winner.

Ravage, ravish   Ravage means to inflict great damage or destroy; ravish means to rape or abduct and carry away. For example:

The storm *ravaged* the town.
The attacker *ravished* the sisters.

Rebut, refute, dispute   To rebut or dispute is to argue to the contrary, to debate or quarrel; to refute is to prove something wrong or false. A television station in south Florida once ran a promotional spot that said its anchor was correct about something although other media in the area *refuted* him. If he was proved wrong, how could he have been right?

Recur   Not reoccur.

Regime   See **government**.

Reluctant, reticent   Reluctant means unwilling to act; reticent means unwilling to speak.

Reputation   See **character**.

Resident   See **citizen**.

Revert   Revert means to go back to a former place, position or state of being. Revert back is redundant.

Rifle, riffle   Rifle is to plunder or steal; riffle is to rapidly leaf through a book or paper. You can't rifle through someone's papers, but riffle is rarely used and might sound strange to some viewers. Use snooped or some other similar verb.

Rob, burglarize, steal   Rob means to strip or deprive someone of something *by force*. Burglary is a crime of stealth usually involving breaking and entering. Therefore, people are robbed and places are burglarized. Anyone who takes something dishonestly has stolen.

Runners-up   Not runner-ups.

Sadism   See **masochism**.

Sanction   This word has two different meanings. It can mean to approve or to punish. If you use this word, be sure your meaning is clear.

Schizophrenia, split personality   These aren't the same. Schizophrenics can't distinguish fantasy from reality. Someone with a split personality has two or more distinct personalities, each with its own character traits.

Scratch   See **itch**.

Semiannual   See **biennial**. Semiannual is the correct spelling, but you might want to spell it semi-annual to make it easier to read.

Sensual, sensuous   Both mean affecting the senses, but are often used with a sexual connotation. People are sensual and things are sensuous.

Sex   See **gender**.

She   See **he**.

Shell, bullet   Shotguns and some military weapons fire shells. Handguns and rifles fire bullets. The pellets from a shotgun shell are called shot.

Since, because   In some instances, "since" can be used to indicate a causal relationship, but that's not the primary use of the word. It should be used to mean "from then until now." Sometimes since can mean "because," but because always means because. Why take a chance of using since incorrectly? Use because. For example:

Since she came to live here, she's been disagreeable.

Do you mean that she's been disagreeable because she came to live here, or that she's been disagreeable from the time she came to live here until now? "Since" leaves room for confusion as to your meaning. "Because" does away with the confusion.

Sisters-in-law   As written.

Skeptical   See **cynical**.

Slander   See **libel**.

Somebody, someone   See **anybody**.

Sons-in-law   As written.

Split personality   See **schizophrenia**.

Steal   See **rob**.

Such as   See **like**.

Sympathy   See **empathy**.

Take   See **bring**.

Take place   See **occur**.

Tamper, tinker   Tamper means to meddle harmfully; tinker means to fuss clumsily or to idly examine.

Tap   See **bug**.

Than, then   Than is used to introduce the second item of a comparison. Then means at that time or next in order. For example:

John is taller *than* Bill.
Then the board voted to give the mayor a raise.

Thanks to   See **due to**.

That, who, which   Use "that" when you're referring to anything other than people or animals with names. In those cases, use "who." "Which" should only be used to introduce a nonessential clause or when "that" has already been used in the sentence. For example:

How to use "that" is the rule *that* is broken most often.
John is the student *who* breaks the rule most often.
Spike is the dog *who* accompanies John everywhere.
The rule, *which* is broken often, is the subject of much debate.
The professor said *that* it's the rule *which* is broken most often.

The See "**a.**"

Tinker See **tamper**.

Total See **number**.

Toward See **afterward**.

Under See **over**.

Uninterested See **disinterested**.

Unique If something is unique, it's one of a kind. Things or people can't be quite unique or very unique or one of the most unique. They're either unique or they're not.

Unknown, unnamed Everyone has a name. Assailants, robbers and the like are unknown, not unnamed. If the police know who the bad guy is but aren't saying, he still has a name. He's just unidentified.

Upward See **afterward**.

Valuable, valueless See **invaluable**.

Verbal See **oral**.

Watch, warning In weather, a watch means that a hurricane might pose a threat to a specific area. A warning means that the hurricane is expected to hit a certain area within 24 hours. With tornadoes, a watch means that a tornado is possible; a warning means that a tornado exists or is suspected to have formed.

Well See **bad**.

Well-known, widely known People who are famous are widely known. A fact that is known by many people is well-known. For example:

Sylvester Stallone is *widely known.*
It's *well-known* that the sky is blue.

What, which What should be used when the category is unknown, but which should be used when referring to a specific item in a category. For example: *What* do you want to do this weekend? I want to go to a movie. *Which* movie do you want to see? It would be incorrect to say, *What* movie do you want to see?

Whereabouts Takes singular verbs. For example: The whereabouts of the robber *is* unknown. However, whereabouts isn't very conversational. Use location or something similar.

While See **although**.

Who, which See **that**.

Woman See **boy**.

Wreck, wreak Wreck means to destroy; wreak means to inflict.

INDEX